KIDS

Pennsylvania

A PARENT'S GUIDE TO EXPLORING FUN PLACES IN PENNSYLVANIA WITH CHILDREN. . .YEAR ROUND!

Kids Love Publications
1985 Dina Court
Powell, OH 43065

Dedicated to the Families
of Pennsylvania

TABLE OF CONTENTS

State Map
With Major Routes & Cities Marked

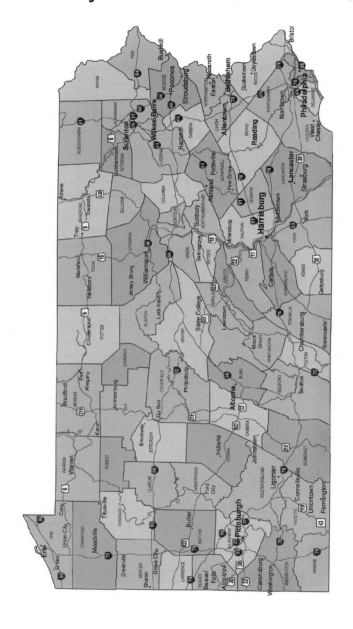

Chapter Area Map

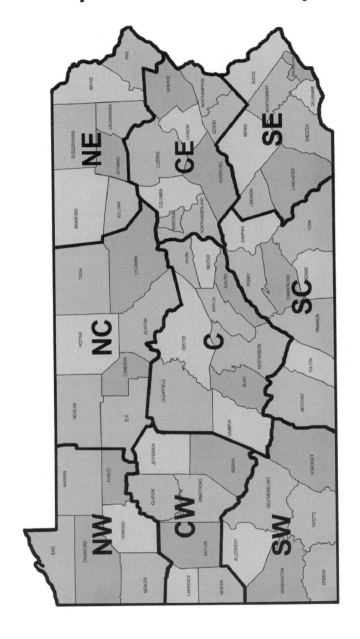

CITY INDEX (Listed by City & Area)

CITY INDEX (Listed by City & Area)

Acknowledgements

Special feelings while researching and writing this book are dedicated to my Dad, Edwin Darrall. Being raised in Pittsburgh and loving to visit and travel his home state, I feel his heart in this project all the time. Parents...you do leave priceless memories with your kids when you take the <u>time</u> *to plan trips and are passionate about family time! – Michele*

We are most thankful to be blessed with our parents, Barbara (Darrall) Callahan and George & Catherine Zavatsky who helped us every way they could – researching, typesetting, proofing and babysitting. Several Pennsylvania relatives *(Grandma Hanzel & The Baumgardner Family)* welcomed us into their homes, provided great ideas, and even gave us personal tours of their communities. Our own young kids, Jenny and Daniel, were delightful and fun children during all of our trips across the state.

We both sincerely thank each other – our partnership has created a great "marriage of minds" with lots of exciting moments and laughs woven throughout. Above all, we praise the Lord for His many answered prayers and special blessings throughout the completion of this project.

We think Pennsylvania is a wonderful, friendly area of the country with more activities than you could imagine! Our sincere wish is that this book will help everyone "fall in love" with Pennsylvania!

In a Hundred Years...

It will not matter, The size of my bank account...
The kind of house that I lived in, the kind of car
that I drove... But what will matter is...
That the world may be different
Because I was important in the life of a child.

- *author unknown*

HOW TO USE THIS BOOK

If you are excited about discovering Pennsylvania, this is the book for you and your family! We've spent over a thousand hours doing all the scouting, collecting and compiling (*and most often visiting!*) so that you could spend less time searching and more time having fun.

Here are a few hints to make your adventures run smoothly:

- ❑ Consider the **child's age** before deciding to take a visit.
- ❑ Know **directions** and parking. Call ahead (or visit the company's website) if you have questions *and* bring this book. Also, don't forget your camera! *(please honor rules regarding use)*.
- ❑ **Estimate the duration** of the trip. Bring small surprises (favorite juice boxes) travel books, and toys.
- ❑ Call ahead for **reservations** or details, if necessary.
- ❑ Most listings are **closed major holidays** unless noted.
- ❑ Make a **family "treasure chest"**. Decorate a big box or use an old popcorn tin. Store memorabilia from a fun outing, journals, pictures, brochures and souvenirs. Once a year, look through the "treasure chest" and reminisce. "Kids Love Travel Memories!" is an excellent travel journal & scrapbook that your family can create. *(See the order form in back of this book)*.
- ❑ Plan **picnics** along the way. Many Historical Society sites and state parks are scattered throughout Pennsylvania. Allow time for a rural/scenic route to take advantage of these free picnic facilities.
- ❑ Some activities, especially tours, require **groups** of 10 or more. To participate, you may either ask to be part of another tour group or get a group together yourself (neighbors, friends, organizations). If you arrange a group outing, most places offer discounts.
- ❑ For the latest **updates** corresponding to the pages in this book, visit our website: **www.kidslovepublications.com**.
- ❑ Each chapter represents an area of the state. Each listing is further identified by city, zip code, and place/event name. Our popular **Activity Index** in the back of the book **lists places by Activity Heading** (i.e. State History, Tours, Outdoors, Museums, etc.).

MISSION STATEMENT

At first glance, you may think that this is a book that just lists hundreds of places to travel. While it is true that we've invested thousands of hours of exhaustive research (*and drove nearly 4000 miles in Pennsylvania*) to prepare this travel resource...just listing places to travel is not the mission statement of these projects.

As children, Michele and I were able to travel extensively throughout the United States. We consider these family times some of the greatest memories we cherish today. We, quite frankly, felt that most children had this opportunity to travel with their family as we did. However, as we became adults and started our own family, we found that this wasn't necessarily the case. We continually heard friends express several concerns when deciding how to spend "quality" and "quantity" family time. 1) What to do? 2) Where to do it? 3) How much will it cost? 4) How do I know that my kids will enjoy it?

Interestingly enough, as we compare our experiences with our families when we were kids, many of our fondest memories were not made at an expensive attraction, but rather when it was least expected.

It is our belief and mission statement that if you as a family will study and use the contained information to create family memories, these memories will grow a stronger, tighter family. Our ultimate mission statement is, that your children will develop a love and a passion for quality family experiences that they can pass to another generation of family travelers.

We thank you for purchasing this book, and we hope to see you on the road (*and hearing your travel stories!*) God bless your journeys and happy exploring!

George, Michele, Jenny and Daniel

GENERAL INFORMATION

Call *(or visit the websites)* for the services of interest.

- ❏ Biking Directory of PA. (717) 787-6746. Free through Penn Dot.
- ❏ PA State Association of County Fairs. (717) 365-3922 or **www.pafairs.org/FairsAlpha.htm**
- ❏ PA Tourism. (800) VISIT-PA or **www.experiencepa.com**
- ❏ PCOA. PA Campground Owners Association Directory. (888) 660-7262. **www.pacamping.com**
- ❏ PA Fish and Boat Commission. **www.fish.state.pa.us** or (717) 657-4518. Information on FISH FARMS/HATCHERIES is here. Fun place to tour.
- ❏ PA Snowmobile Hotline. (717) 787-5651.
- ❏ PA State Forests. **www.dcnr. state.pa.us/forestry/stateforests/** or (717) 783-7941.
- ❏ PA State Parks. (888) PA-PARKS or **www.dcnr.state.pa.us/stateparks/ index.htm.** Junior Naturalist Program & Cabin/Camping Rentals.
- ❏ Statewide Fall Foliage Hotline. (800) FALL-IN PA or **www.fallinpa.com**
- ❏ **C** - Cambria County Conservation (814) 472-2120 or **cccd@twd.net**
- ❏ **C** - Centre County Region Parks and Recreation. (814) 281-3071.
- ❏ **C** - Penn State Athletics, State College. Nittany Lions. (800) 833-5533 or (800) 863-1000 tickets or **www.gopsusports.com.** Baseball, basketball, fencing, field hockey, football, golf, gymnastics, soccer,

softball, swimming, tennis, track, volleyball and wrestling.

- ❏ **CE** - Dam Releases. LeHigh River Area. (717) 424-6050. Releases create whitewater and rapids. Call for rafting outfitters. Late Spring and Early Fall.
- ❏ **NC** - PA Canyon Country. Wellsboro. (717) 724-1926.
- ❏ **NE** – POCONO's Tourist Information. (800)-POCONOS or **www.800poconos.com**. Ask about selection of whitewater rafting, canoeing and riding stables.
- ❏ **NW** - Venango County Parks. (814) 676-6116.
- ❏ **SC** - York County Parks. York. (717) 840-7440. **www.york-county.org**
- ❏ **SE** - Berk's County Parks and Recreation Department. Wyomissing. (610) 372-8939 or **www.berksparkandrec.org**
- ❏ **SW** - Allegheny County Parks Department. (412) 350-PARK.
- ❏ **SW** - Laurel Highlands River Tours. **www.laurelhighlands.com**.
- ❏ **SW** - Pittsburgh CVB. (888) 849-4753 or **www.visitpittsburgh.com**.
- ❏ **SW** - University of Pittsburgh Athletics. (412) 648-PITT, (800) 643-PITT or **www.pittsburghpanthers.com**.
- ❏ **SW** - Washington County Department of Parks and Recreation. (724) 228-6867.

Check out these businesses / services in your area for tour ideas:

AIRPORTS

All children love to visit the airport! Why not take a tour and understand all the jobs it takes to run an airport. Tour the terminal, baggage claim, gates and security / currency exchange. Maybe you'll even get to board a plane.

ANIMAL SHELTERS

Great for the would-be pet owner. Not only will you see many cats and dogs available for adoption, but a guide will show you the clinic and explain the needs of a pet. Be prepared to have the children "fall in love" with one of the animals while they are there!

BANKS

Take a "behind the scenes" look at automated teller machines, bank vaults and drive-thru window chutes. You may want to take this tour and then open a savings account for your child.

CITY HALLS

Halls of Fame, City Council Chambers & Meeting Room, Mayor's Office and famous statues.

ELECTRIC COMPANY / POWER PLANTS

Modern science has created many ways to generate electricity today, but what really goes on with the "flip of a switch". Because coal can be dirty, wear old, comfortable clothes. Coal furnaces heat water, which produces steam, that propels turbines, that drive generators, that make electricity.

FIRE STATIONS

Many Open Houses in October, Fire Prevention Month. Take a look into the life of the firefighters servicing your area and try on their gear. See where they hang out, sleep and eat. Hop aboard a real-life fire enine truck and learn fire safety too.

HOSPITALS

Some Children's Hospitals offer pre-surgery and general tours.

NEWSPAPERS

You'll be amazed at all the new technology. See monster printers and robotics. See samples in the layout department and maybe try to put together your own page. After seeing a newspaper made, most companies give you a free copy (dated that day) as your souvenir. National Newspaper Week is in October.

RESTAURANTS

PIZZA HUT & PAPA JOHNS

❑ Participating locations

Telephone the store manager. Best days are Monday, Tuesday and Wednesday mid-afternoon. Minimum of 10 people. Small charge per person. All children love pizza – especially when they can create their own! As the children tour the kitchen, they learn how to make a pizza, bake it, and then eat it. The admission charge generally includes lots of creatively made pizzas, beverage and coloring book.

KRISPY KREME DONUTS

❑ Participating locations

Get an "inside look" and learn the techniques that make these donuts some of our favorites! Watch the dough being made in "giant" mixers, being formed into donuts and taking a "trip" through the fryer. Seeing them being iced and topped with colorful sprinkles is always a favorite of the kids. Contact your local store manager. They prefer Monday or Tuesday. Free.

SUPERMARKETS

Kids are fascinated to go behind the scenes of the same store where Mom and Dad shop. Usually you will see them grind meat, walk into large freezer rooms, watch cakes and bread bake and receive free samples along the way. Maybe you'll even get to pet a live lobster!

TV / RADIO STATIONS

Studios, newsrooms, Fox kids clubs. Why do weathermen never wear blue clothes on TV? What makes a "DJ's" voice sound so deep and smooth?

WATER TREATMENT PLANTS

A giant science experiment! You can watch seven stages of water treatment. The favorite is usually the wall of bright buttons flashing as workers monitor the different processes.

U.S. MAIN POST OFFICES

Did you know Ben Franklin was the first Postmaster General (over 200 years ago)? Most interesting is the high-speed automated mail processing equipment. Learn how to address envelopes so they will be sent quicker (there are secrets). To make your tour more interesting, have your children write a letter to themselves and address it with colorful markers. Mail it earlier that day and they will stay interested trying to locate their letter in all the high-speed machinery.

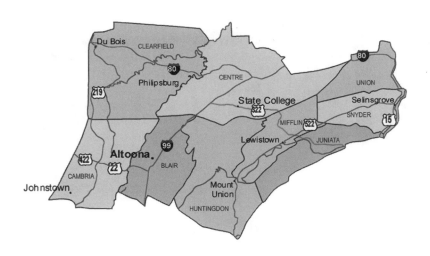

Chapter 1
Central Area

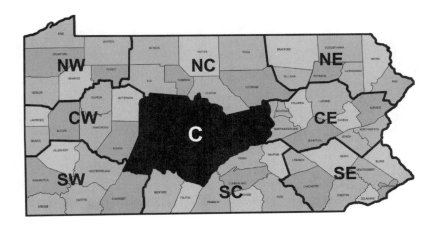

2

Our Favorites...

Allegheny Portage Railroad

Boal Mansion / Columbus Chapel

Horseshoe Curve

Johnstown Inclined Plane & Flood Museum

Railroader's Memorial

Inside The Columbus Chapel

FORT ROBERDEAU HISTORIC SITE

Altoona - *RD #3 Box 391 (I-99, Bellwood Exit), 16601.* **Web:** *www.sru.edu/Depts/pcee/FacilityDir/FortRoberdeauHistoricSite21.htm* *Phone: (814) 946-0048. Hours: Tuesday-Saturday 11:00am-5:00pm, Sunday 1:00-5:00pm (May-October). Admission: $1.00-$3.00.* A reconstructed 1778 fort with exhibits. Original site of a Revolutionary War fort established to mine lead for the army. Includes miners quarters, officers quarters, barracks and blacksmith. Includes 47 acres with 3 nature trails and various habitats. Environmental education programs are available to groups from schools, community organizations, etc. Topics include "Discovery Trail Walk", birds, trees, wild edible plants, reading the landscape, and stream study. Living history re-reenactments. (Summer)

QUAINT CORNER CHILDREN'S MUSEUM

Altoona - *2000 Union Avenue (Downtown SR36), 16601. Phone: (814) 944-6830. Hours: Thursday-Saturday 1:00-5:00pm. Admission: $3.00 general.* This is a real Victorian home that kids are allowed to explore - in fact, they're encouraged to snoop around. Probably the cutest and most popular areas are the closets and climbing the ladder into Grandma's Attic at the very top of the house. The kitchen is set up as the craft center of the house and the Dinosaur Room (complete with sandbox) is in the basement.

ALTOONA CURVE BASEBALL CLUB

Altoona - *1000 Park Avenue (games played at Blair County Ballpark), 16602.* **Web:** *www.altoonacurve.com* *Phone: (814) 943-5400 or (877) 99-CURVE.* Enjoy AA Baseball in a beautiful ballpark. A Pittsburgh Pirate's Affiliate.

HORSESHOE CURVE NATIONAL HISTORIC LANDMARK

Horseshoe Curve Road (6 miles West of Altoona)

Altoona 16602

- ❑ Phone: (888) 4-ALTOONA **Web: www.railroadcity.com**
- ❑ Hours: Daily 10:00am-7:00pm (April-October). Tuesday-Sunday 10:00am-4:00pm (November-December)
- ❑ Admission: $3.50 adult, $3.00 senior, $1.75 child (5-18). Discount combo pricing with Railroader's Museum.
- ❑ Miscellaneous: Large Gift shop.

Developed in 1854, the Penn Railroad needed to expand west, but through the mountainous terrain. This curve was developed because, even if a bridge could be built, no locomotive could climb the steep grade. To solve this crossing problem, they built a track around the inside curves of the large mountain range. Inside the Interpretive Center, you can view a video of the curve's history and see a model of what the land looked like before the railroad changed the landscape. Kids like the push button display of train sounds as they make the turn (gaining speed, upgrade and downgrade). The highlight is the funicular ride up to the elevation area (or you can walk up - 200 steps) where you can look out onto the horseshoe track. There's a good chance a train (the railroad still uses this curve) will pass through while you are visiting.

LAKEMONT PARK

Altoona - *700 Park Avenue (I-99 to Frankstown Road), 16602.* **Web: www.lakemontparkfun.com** *Phone: (814) 949-PARK or (800) 434-8006. Hours: Daily 11:00am-dark (Summers). Weekends only in late May and early September, Noon-8:00pm. Admission: Buy individual or package tickets. Over 30 rides and attractions. Island Waterpark. Go-Kart tracks, mini-golf, picnic areas and arcade. Kids Mini-Indy and Kiddie Lane.*

RAILROADER'S MEMORIAL MUSEUM

1300 Ninth Avenue (off 17th Street on I-99)

Altoona 16602

- ❏ Phone: (814) 946-0834 **Web: www.railroadcity.com**
- ❏ Hours: Daily 9:00am-5:00pm (April-October). Closed Mondays (November-March).
- ❏ Admission: $8.50 adult, $7.75 senior (62+), $5.00 child (5-18). Discount Combo Prices w/ Horseshoe Curve.
- ❏ Miscellaneous: Museum store.

"Here in Altoona an army of railroaders designed, built, maintained, and moved the Pennsylvania Railroad, the largest railroad in the world...in so doing, they changed the face of America...this is their story!" Why was Altoona chosen to be the heart of construction? (watch a 27 minute film to find out). Listen to the folks talk about their life at local scenes depicting a home, church, newsstand, and clubs. The "News Boy" is funny to listen to. Learn how railroad workers laid the tracks, worked in shops (the test lab is pretty eye opening) and designed and built locomotives. This museum has less focus on displays of trains and more on the lives and work habits of people involved. Nice change.

ALTOONA SYMPHONY ORCHESTRA

Altoona - *1331 - 12th Avenue (Office) #107, 16603. Phone: (814) 943-2500. Web: www.altoonasymphony.org* Features classical, pops and children's concerts.

BLAIR COUNTY MUSEUM

Altoona - *Oak Lane off Logan Blvd. - P O Box 1083 (US20 to Logan Blvd), 16603. Phone: (814) 942-3916. Hours: Tuesday-Sunday 1:00-4:30pm (June-Labor Day). Weekends only (April, May, September, October). Admission: $2.00-$4.00 (age 5+). Tours: 1 hour long. Web: www.blaircohistoricalsociety.homestead.com/home.html* Historic Baker Mansion. Interprets local transportation and industrial history (iron, railroads). Civil War, elaborate home furnishings. Check out the tubes used to send orders to servants.

CENTRE COUNTY MUSEUM

Bellefonte - *203 North Allegheny Street, 16823. Phone: (814) 355-1516. Web: http://centrecountyhistory.org/mansion.html Hours: Monday-Friday 9:00am-5:00pm, Saturday 9:00am-Noon and 1:00-5:00pm.* Housed in the historic Miles-Humes Home. Centre Furnace Mansion in State College began the charcoal iron-making industry in this region. Mansion open Sunday, Monday, Wednesday, Friday 1:00-4:00pm.

BOAL MANSION MUSEUM / COLUMBUS CHAPEL

300 Old Boalsburg Road (US322 - Business Route)

Boalsburg 16827

❑   Phone: (814) 466-6210 **Web: www.boalmuseum.com**

❑   Hours: Tuesday-Saturday 10:00am-5:00pm, Sunday Noon-5:00pm (Summer). Tuesday-Sunday 1:30-5:00pm (May, September, October).

❑   Admission: $10.00 adult, $8.00 senior (59+), $6.00 child (7-16).

❑   Miscellaneous: Still privately owned. Tour takes about 1½ hours.

Want to see a real part of Christopher Columbus? On the grounds of the originally furnished mansion is the Columbus Chapel that was brought here from Spain in 1909. They actually have a sea desk once owned by Columbus and many Columbus family heirlooms dating back to the 1400's. The highlight of this place begins with your first step inside the chapel. If you're like us...your mouth will drop wide open in disbelief as you begin to notice the centuries-old heirloom pieces. Many of the artifacts look like movie props (the natural way they have aged makes it hard to believe they are real!) Actual parchment family documents, the family cross, a copy of the family tree and 2 actual pieces of the "true" cross are awesome to see up close. It's just incredible that all of this history is in a small town museum! Also on the grounds are the mansion and several exhibit rooms. The first exhibit room contains medieval armor, a scale model of the Santa Maria and other family memorabilia. The "Country Life" room contains a beautifully restored 1850's stage coach, a buckboard buggy, farm tools, the 1816 accounts book from David Boal's tavern and many more farm and kitchen implements. The Weapons Room contains a large collection of swords, rifles and pistols from the Revolutionary War through World War I, including David Boal's Pennsylvania long rifle from the 1790's and Captain John Boal's officer's sword from the Civil War. Hearing stories about the Boal family and their home can be interesting, too.

PENNSYLVANIA MILITARY MUSEUM

Boalsburg - *PO Box 160A (US322), 16827. Phone: (814) 466-6263. Web: www.psu.edu/dept/aerospace/museum Miscellaneous: NOTE: The museum was closed for extensive renovations and the addition of a visitor center on October 6, 2002, with a planned Grand Reopening sometime in 2005.* Honoring Pennsylvania's soldiers from Benjamin Franklin's first volunteer unit to Operation Desert Storm. Younger children enjoy climbing on tanks and cannons outside in the park, but it takes older kids to enjoy the museum. As they study American History, this place brings it to life, especially the World War I trench scene, complete with sound and light effects. The museum only focuses on citizen soldiers – "the men and women of Pennsylvania who served their country in time of war."

TUSSEY MOUNTAIN SKI AREA

Boalsburg - *301Bear Meadow Road - Route 322, 16827. Phone: (814) 466-6266 or (800) 733-2754. Web: www.tusseymountain.com* Longest Run: 2700 ft.; 8 Slopes & Trails plus snowboarding.

PENN'S CAVES

222 Penns Cave Road (SR 192 East, Near I-80, Exit 14)

Centre Hall 16828

❏   Phone: (814) 364-1664, **Web: www.pennscave.com**
❏   Hours: Daily 9:00am-5:00pm (February 15 - May 31). Daily 9:00am-7:00pm (June 1 - August 31). Daily 9:00am-5:00pm (September 1 - November 30). Weekends Only 11:00am-5:00pm (December). Closed Thanksgiving and Christmas Day.

❑   Admission: $10.75 adult, $9.75 senior, $5.00 child (2-12).

❑   Tours: Cave - 1 mile guided tour by motorboat - approximately 1 hour long.

America's only all-water cavern and wildlife (1000 acre) sanctuary. Colored lights enhance "The Statue of Liberty", "The Garden of Gods" and "Niagara Falls". The farm and wildlife tour is a guided 90-minute motorized tour over the thousand acres of Penn's Cave forests and fields and a natural habitat for birds, plants, and animals. North American animals, such as deer, elk, wolves, bears, bison, and mustangs are seen, as well as longhorn cattle. Come to Penn's Cave and enjoy both tours. You will be educated about the geology, biology, and geography of Central Pennsylvania.

BLUE KNOB ALL SEASONS RESORT / SKI AREA

Claysburg - *PO Box 247 (between Altoona & Johnstown, in north corner of Bedford County), 16625. Phone: (814) 239-5111.* **Web:** ***www.blueknob.com*** Activities include skiing/snowboarding, a tubing park, and cross country skiing. In the warmer months, golfing, hiking and trail biking are big attractions. All condos are furnished with fully equipped kitchens and fireplaces. Longest Run: 2 miles; 34 Slopes & Trails.

LAKE RAYSTOWN RESORT

100 Chipmunk Crossing (Route 994), **Entriken** 16638

❑   Phone: (814) 658-3500 **Web: www.raystownresort.com**

The Resort is located between Harrisburg and Pittsburgh in Entriken on Pennsylvania's largest inland lake with 118 miles of scenic shoreline and thousands of acres of pristine woodlands and streams. Lodge rooms, boating and boat rentals, Hiking, Biking and Fitness Trails, Camping and Cottages, Swimming and Beach Areas. Other attractions:

❑   PROUD MARY TOURBOAT: Sightseeing cruises. Food available. Scheduled departures by season (April - October). Admission: Adults $7.50+, Children 50% off Adult pricing (under 12), *(for most cruises).*

❑   WILDRIVER WATER PARK: Speed slides, twisting slides, whitewater tubing slides, Children's splash pool and mini-golf. $4.00-$14.00 depending on activity.

ALLEGHENY PORTAGE RAILROAD & NATIONAL HISTORIC SITE

110 Federal Park Road (US22, Gallitzin exit - follow signs)

Gallitzin 16641

❑   Phone: (814) 886-6150 **Web: www.nps.gov/alpo/welpo.htm**
❑   Hours: Daily 9:00am-5:00pm (with extended hours possible in the summer). Closed on some federal holidays.
❑   Admission: $3.00 adult (age 17+). FREE for children and park pass holders.
❑   Miscellaneous: Visitor Center with 20 minute film. Costumed presentations during the summer. Lemon House - restored tavern and business office on premises along with the Engine House and walking trails to the incline site.

You'll be amazed at the ingenuity of railroad engineers back then! The problem was the Allegheny Mountains. No trains or canals could get through them before the idea of the "incline" was introduced. Called "an engineering marvel" at its opening, travel that took three weeks by wagon took only four days by railroad and canal. It used a combination of 10 inclines and horses on steam locomotives pulling cars on levels in between. It's difficult to visualize until you see the working small-scale model in the center of the museum - then it all makes sense (still in amazement of course!). With a hands-on demonstration, you can personally try turning a wheel hooked to balanced and unbalanced weights. This clearly demonstrates the need for balanced (one car up - one car down at the same time) inclines.

TUNNELS PARK

Gallitzin - *702 Jackson Street (off Route 22 - Follow signs), 16641.* **Web: www.visitjohnstownpa.com/attractions.html** *Phone: (814) 886-8871. Hours: Daily, daylight hours. Admission: FREE.* See and feel the awesome power of the trains passing through the Allegheny Tunnel (modified 1854). Also on site is a PRR walkway and railroad signal and a restored PRR caboose - climb aboard to see the sleeping quarters and pot-bellied stove. Three tunnels to view that were built with picks and shovels using over 300 immigrants to complete it. This is a cute side trip between visits to the Allegheny Portage Railroad and Horseshoe Curve.

SEVEN POINTS CRUISES

Hesston - *RD #1, Route 26 (Seven Points Marina), 16647. Phone: (814) 658-3074.* **Web: www.7pointsmarina.com/cruises1.htm** *Hours: May - mid-October. Summers usually have 3 cruises. Admission: $10.00 adult, $9.00 senior, $3.00 child (2-8). (15 passenger minimum on all cruises). Tours: 90 minutes, 23 miles. Heated and air-conditioned.* Public sightseeing boat cruises where you can view wooded shoreline (esp. cedar trees), wild turkey, deer, beaver, bald eagles, and ravens. Close to Lake Raystown Resort (waterpark and activities). Ask for the "Kids Kruz" that includes tour, box lunch, fish feeding, and demonstration of "rack storage" of 200+ boats in a warehouse (real neat if you're not a boater and already familiar with this).

CANOE CREEK STATE PARK

Hollidaysburg - *RR 2, Box 560 (US 22), 16648. Phone: (814) 695-6807.* **Web: www.dcnr.state.pa.us/stateparks/parks/canoe.htm** The park boasts one of the largest bat colonies in the Eastern US. The visitor center has natural and historical exhibits and information. Beach, Boat Rentals, Horseback Riding, Sledding, Limestone kilns, Modern Cabins, Trails, and Cross-Country Skiing.

BALD EAGLE STATE PARK

Howard - *149 Main Park Road (off PA Route 150, midway between Milesburg and Lock Haven, it is accessible by I- 80), 16841.* **Web: www.dcnr.state.pa.us/stateparks/parks/bald.htm** *Phone: (814) 625-2775.* The rugged Bald Eagle Mountain and Allegheny Plateau of the 1,730-acre lake features unlimited horsepower boating, hiking and butterfly trails. Swimming is available at the sand beach. Boat Rentals, Year-round Education & Interpretation Center, Sledding, Campsites, Hiking, and Fishing.

GREENWOOD FURNACE STATE PARK

Huntingdon - *RR 2, Box 118 (SR 305 North), 16652. Phone: (814) 667-1800. Web: www.dcnr.state.pa.us/stateparks/parks/g-wood.htm* Relive the 1800s by visiting this 423-acre park, site of an active iron furnace community. Greenwood Furnace was the site of an active iron furnace community from 1834 to 1904. The visitor center is a restored blacksmith shop and provides historical programming. Along the Mid-State Trail to the Greenwood Forest Fire Lookout Tower, you can view charcoal hearths where wood was made into charcoal. Beach and Campsites.

LINCOLN CAVERNS & WHISPER ROCKS

Huntingdon - *RR #1 Box 280 (I-76 to US 522 north to US 22 west), 16652. Web: www.lincolncaverns.com Phone: (814) 643-0268. Hours: Daily open at 9:00am until dark. Daily 9:00 am-4:00pm (March and November, December - Weekends only). Admission: $9.50 adult, $8.50 senior (65+), $5.50 child (4-12). Miscellaneous: Gift shop, nature trails, gem panning.* Close to Raystown Lake. 2 crystal caverns - Lincoln and Whisper Rock. Winding passages, large "rooms" with massive and delicate flowstones, pure white calcite and crystals. Ask about seasonal "Kids' Cave Crawls".

SWIGART ANTIQUE AUTO MUSEUM

Huntingdon - *PO Box 214 (US22 East), 16652. Phone: (814) 643-0885. Hours: Daily 9:00am-5:00pm (Memorial Day Weekend-October). Admission: $2.00-$4.00.* See over 40 cars on display and the world's largest collection of cars, toys, license plates, bicycles and clothing. There's a special focus on cars made by smaller companies like Tuckers…the amusing stories are interesting.

ROTHROCK STATE FOREST

Huntington - *Rothrock Lane - Box 403, 16652. Phone: (814) 643-2340. www.dcnr.state.pa.us/forestry/stateforests/forests/rothrock/rothrock.htm* Vistas or scenic overlooks are a major attraction for many forest visitors. The best known and most easily accessible is the well-known overlook atop Tussey Mountain along PA Route 26 at the Centre/Huntingdon County line. 93,349 acres of Fishing, Camping,

Hiking, Cross-Country Skiing, Snowmobile and Bike Trails, and Picnic Areas.

TROUGH CREEK STATE PARK

James Creek - *RR 1, Box 211 (PA Route 994), 16657. Phone: (814) 658-3847. Web: www.dcnr.state.pa.us/stateparks/parks/t-crek.htm* Located along a scenic gorge where Great Trough Creek cuts through Terrace Mountain and empties into Raystown Lake. Campsites, Modern Cabins, Fishing and Hiking.

WARRIORS PATH STATE PARK

James Creek - *RR 1, Box 211 (c/o Trough Creek), 16657. Phone: (814) 658-3847. www.dcnr.state.pa.us/stateparks/parks/warriors.htm* Natural cliffs, boating, and part of Raystown Lake area.

JOHNSTOWN CHIEFS HOCKEY

Johnstown - *326 Napoleon St (Cambria County War Memorial Arena), 15901. Web: www.johnstownchiefs.com Phone: (800) 243-8499. Admission: ~$10.00.* ECHL Hockey (October-April)

JOHNSTOWN SYMPHONY ORCHESTRA

Johnstown - *227 Franklin Street, Suite 302 (University of Pittsburgh at Johnstown's Pasquerilla Performing Arts Center), 15901. Web: www.johnstownsymphony.org Phone: (814) 535-6738.* Young Peoples Concerts for grade school students and a Christmas concert.

JOHNSTOWN INCLINED PLANE

711 Edgehill Drive (off SR56, 403 or 271 & Johns St.)

Johnstown 15905

- ❏ Phone: (814) 536-1816 **Web: www.inclinedplane.com**
- ❏ Hours: Weekdays 7:00am-10:00pm, Saturday 7:00am-Midnight, Sunday 9:00am-10:00pm (Summer). Daily Noon-6:00pm (rest of year). Extended hours from Thanksgiving-New Years. Closed Christmas and New Years.
- ❏ Admission: $4.00 adult, FREE senior (65+), $2.50 child (2-12). Round Trip.

❑   Miscellaneous: Gift shop. Visitor's center. Laser light sculptures lit on weekend nights. Observation deck on top.

Brightly lit, it is the world's steepest vehicular inclined plane (71 % grade) with a panoramic view of the city through viewing windows. After the flood, many residents wanted to live up on the hill...but they needed a way to commute. It was also used as an escape route during subsequent floods. A viewing window looking into the motor room explains the "physics" behind the scenes. Hang on tight to those little ones! Ride on the incline and then dine at the top. Spectacular views of the valley and see the largest American flag in the county (814-536-1816). The JAMES WOLFE SCULPTURE TRAIL is the first nature trail with sculptures made from steel. It honors the city's steel heritage with ten pieces, eight on the trail. Most photographed and visible is "Steel Floats" (Bottom of the incline)

JOHNSTOWN FLOOD MUSEUM
304 Washington Street (off SR56 West to Walnut Street Exit)
Johnstown 15907

❑   Phone: (814) 539-1889 **Web: www.jaha.org/flood/index.htm**
❑   Hours: Daily 10:00am-5:00pm.
❑   Admission: $4.00-$6.00 (age 6+). Includes Heritage Discovery.
❑   Miscellaneous: Museum store. Film shown hourly (25 minutes long). Film has some screaming that may frighten young children.

Hear and see the story of the infamous disaster of 1889 focusing on both the tragedy and triumph of the human spirit. View the Academy Award Winning "The Johnstown Flood" documentary film (shown hourly) with multi-media exhibits including an animated map with sound and light effects showing water movement. On May 31, 1889, a phenomenal storm and a neglected dam led to the natural disaster in which 2209 people died. It turned a thriving town into a wasteland..."it was a roar and a crash and a smash...". Other exhibits include: A Quilt - used as a rescue rope, A Wall of Wreckage in 3-D (17 feet tall - flood wall was actually 40 feet tall). It really captures the horror of the moment, yet is subtle enough to not scare school-aged children.

JOHNSTOWN HERITAGE DISCOVERY CENTER

Johnstown - *(Route 56, at the corner of Broad Street and Seventh Ave.), 15907.* **Web:** *www.jaha.org/discenter/disc_centr.htm Phone: (814) 539-1889. Hours: Daily 10:00am-5:00pm. Closed Thanksgiving, Christmas and New Years. Admission: $4.00 - $6.00 (age 6+), includes Flood Museum.* All Johnstown's immigrants were history-makers - ordinary men, women, and children who made a contribution to the rise of industrial America. And, as they kept traditions and values alive for their families and communities, they enriched the life and culture of a changing city and nation. When you visit the museum, you will be able to assume the persona of such immigrants as Josef and Maria (as well as Prokop, Katerina, Andrej, and Stefan) as you journey through the exhibit that examines the world the immigrants made in Johnstown, Pennsylvania. The visitor will be able to see and touch the environments - you will feel the sharpness of the coal mine walls and smell the scent of incense in the church. You will hear the thoughts of a young immigrant girl as she sells eggs and butter on the street to help the family's finances. Play "History Jukeboxes" - You sit down in front of the computer and tell your story. The "jukebox" records your voice and image.

JOHNSTOWN FLOOD NATIONAL MEMORIAL

Johnstown (St. Michael) - *Lake Road, Box 355 (US219 to St. Michael Exit - SR869east), 15951. Phone: (814) 495-4643.* **Web:** *www.nps.gov/jofl Hours: Daily 9:00am-5:00pm. Closed winter holidays. Admission: $3.00 adult (17+).* The flood began here - see what little is left of South Fork Dam. A documentary - "Black Friday" - a 35 minute film, puts you in the middle of the terror - a little frightening for youngsters. Remember over 2200 people died in about 10 minutes. Other recreational activities available: bird watching, cross country skiing, hiking, interpretive programs & nature walks.

BALD EAGLE STATE FOREST

Laurelton - *PO Box 147 (mostly between I-80 and US 22), 17835. www.dcnr.state.pa.us/forestry/stateforests/forests/baldeagle/baldeagle.htm Phone: (570) 922-3344.* There are thirteen streams within the Bald Eagle District totaling 47 miles that are stocked and fishable. The

District has 340 miles of drivable roads and about the same number of miles of trails. There are five designated scenic drives. ATV Trails. (7 miles), Winter Sports, and Camping.

R.B. WINTER STATE PARK

Mifflinburg - *RR 2, Box 314 (on PA Route 192, 18 miles west of Lewisburg), 17844. www.dcnr.state.pa.us/stateparks/parks/rbw.htm Phone: (717) 966-1455.* This park is situated in a narrow valley surrounded by oak forests on steep mountain ridges. A spring-fed mountain stream flows through the valley. Beach, Visitor Center, Year-round Education & Interpretation Center, Campsites, Camping Cabins, Trails, and Winter Sports.

RAVENSBURG STATE PARK

Mifflinburg - *RD 2, Box 377 (c/o R.B. Winter State Park) (on PA Route 880, eight miles southeast of Jersey Shore or eight miles north of Carroll, Exit 28 on I-80), 17844. Phone: (717) 745-7700. Web: www.dcnr.state.pa.us/stateparks/parks/raven.htm* This pretty valley is especially beautiful when the mountain laurel blooms in late June and during the fall foliage of early October.

POE PADDY STATE PARK

Milroy - *1405 New Lancaster Valley Road (c/o Reed's Gap) (entrance at Big Poe Road), 17063. Phone: (717) 667-3622. Web: www.dcnr.state.pa.us/stateparks/parks/paddy.htm* Poe Paddy State Park is located at the confluence of Big Poe Creek and Penns Creek, a trout angler's paradise featuring the nationally recognized green drake mayfly hatch in June. Hikers also walk Mid State Trail through the 250-foot long Paddy Mountain Railroad Tunnel.

POE VALLEY STATE PARK

Milroy - *RR 1, Box 276-A (c/o Reeds Gap) (east on U.S. Route 322 for 1.5 miles to near the top of the Seven Mountains Scenic Area), 17063. Web: www.dcnr.state.pa.us/stateparks/parks/poe.htm Phone: (814) 349-8778.* Boating, Fishing, Swimming w/ beach, Hiking, and Winter Sports.

REEDS GAP STATE PARK

Milroy - *1405 New Lancaster Valley Road (U.S. Route 322 from Milroy by following park signs for seven miles), 17063. Phone: (717) 667-3622.* **www.dcnr.state.pa.us/stateparks/parks/reeds.htm** Pool, Sledding, Campsites, Fishing, and Winter Sports.

PRINCE GALLITZIN STATE PARK

Patton - *966 Marina Road (SR 1021) (reached by PA Routes 36 and 53 and U.S. Route 219), 16668. Phone: (814) 674-1000.* **Web: www.dcnr.state.pa.us/stateparks/parks/p-gall.htm** The major attractions to the park are the 1,600-acre Lake Glendale and the large campground. Beach, Visitor Center, Boat Rentals, Horseback Riding, Sledding, Campsites, Modern Cabins, Fishing, Trails, and Cross-Country Skiing.

SELDOM SEEN TOURIST COAL MINE

PO Box 83 (I-76 to US219 to US22 East to Patton - Route 36)

Patton 16668

❑   Phone: (814) 247-6305   **Web: www.seldomseenmine.com**
❑   Hours: Thursday-Sunday 11:00am-6:00pm (Memorial Day Weekend -Labor Day weekend), Weekends only (June).
❑   Admission: $6.00 adult, $3.50 child (3-12).
❑   Tours: The visitor Center opens at 11:00am with the first tour entering mine at Noon. The last tour enters mine @ 5:00pm.

Go underground to learn first hand the lives and working conditions of coal miners from the past to the present. Family run operations, so tours are given by miners or descendants. You'll learn that coal was dug by hand, loaded on cars and hauled from the mine by mules - for as little as 25 cents per ton!

MOSHANNON STATE FOREST

Penfield - *RR #1, Box 184, 15849. Phone: (814) 765-0821.* **Web: www.dcnr.state.pa.us/forestry/stateforests/forests/moshannon/moshan non.htm** 188,885 acres of Fishing, Rugged Camping, Hiking, Bike and Horse Trails, and Winter Sports.

PARKER DAM STATE PARK

Penfield - *RD 1, Box 165 (I- 80, take Exit 18 onto Route 153 North, Turn right onto Mud Run Road), 15849. Phone: (814) 765-0630. Web: www.dcnr.state.pa.us/stateparks/parks/p-dam.htm* The CCC Interpretive Center interprets the Civilian Conservation Corps. Parker Dam is a good base to explore the surrounding state forest. Beach, Visitor Center, Boat Rentals, Sledding, Campsites, Rustic Cabins, Hiking Trails, and Cross-Country Skiing.

S. B. ELLIOTT STATE PARK

Penfield - *RD 1, Box 165 (c/o Parker Dam) (off of PA Route 153 just north of Exit 18 of I- 80), 15849. Phone: (814) 765-7271. Web: www.dcnr.state.pa.us/stateparks/parks/sblliott.htm* S.B. Elliott is a quiet, rustic, mountaintop recreational area just off of I-80 near the mid-point of the state. This 318-acre park, in the heart of the Moshannon State Forest, is entirely wooded and offers picturesque areas of forest and swamp meadows and typical second growth mixed hardwood and oak timber. Camping, Rustic Cabins and Winter Sports.

BLACK MOSHANNON STATE PARK

Philipsburg - *RR 1, Box 185 (PA Route 504), 16866. Phone: (814) 342-5960. Web: www.dcnr.state.pa.us/stateparks/parks/b-mo.htm* Black Moshannon State Park features the Black Moshannon Bog Natural Area. Trails and a boardwalk help people explore the birds and plants of the bog and surrounding forests. According to local tradition, American Indians called this watershed "Moss-Hanne," meaning "moose stream," thus the origin of the park's name. Appropriately, the "black" in the park name describes the tea-colored waters. Beach, Mountain Biking, Boat Rentals, Campsites, Modern Cabins, Trails, and Cross-Country Skiing.

EAST BROAD TOP RAILROAD

Rockhill Furnace - *PO Box 158 (I-76, exit 13 to US522 North, Orbsonia Station), 17249. Phone: (814) 447-3011.* **Web: www.spikesys.com/EBT/visiting.html** *Hours: Weekends at 11:00 am, 1:00 & 3:00pm. (June-October). Admission: $9.00 adult, $6.00 child (2-12). Tours: 50 minutes, 10 mile trip.* Ride an authentic steam powered train through a valley as you learn railroad history. Station gift shop.

ROCKHILL TROLLEY MUSEUM

PO Box 203 (PA Turnpike, exit 13 to US522 North to Route 994 - Meadow Street), **Rockhill Furnace** 17249

- ❑ Phone: (814) 447-9576 (weekends only) (610) 437-0448
  Web: www.rockhilltrolley.org/home.htm
- ❑ Hours: Weekends and Holidays 11:00am-4:00pm (Memorial Day-October).
- ❑ Admission: $4.95 adult, $1.95 child (2-12).
- ❑ Tours: Every 1/2 hour service.
- ❑ Miscellaneous: Pennsylvania Transportation Museum and restoration shop where volunteers are always working on new projects. Ice Cream night trolleys - $3.00.

Take the 2 1/2 mile trolley rides along with a motorman on an antique streetcar - unlimited rides on many different varieties of streetcars. Even though they run on a standard railroad track, streetcars or interurbans (city to city) are powered by electricity. Wires running along the length of main streets were connected to rods moving along a set track. The grandparents will remember this form of transport and have fun memories to share of the friendships that freely developed on the way to work or to the movies.

INDIAN CAVERNS

Spruce Creek - *(take Rt. 22 west to Waterstreet then Rt. 45), 16683. Phone: (814) 632-7578.* **Web: www.indiancaverns.com** *Hours: Daily 10:00am-6:00pm (Summers). Daily 10:00am-4:00pm (May, September, October). Admission: $4.50 (6-12) - $9.00 adult.* Known for their massive formations. Authentic Indian history - 400 relics and tablet of picture writing found in cave. A mile of lighted walkways - includes a one-of-a-kind "Star Room" grotto and "Frozen Niagara".

PENN STATE UNIVERSITY PARK CAMPUS

(Hetzel Union Building) (off US322), **State College** 16801

- ❏ Phone: (800) PSU-TODAY
  www.alumni.psu.edu/VRPennState/VirtualAmbassador/links.html
- ❏ Hours: Mostly weekdays. Some museums also open Saturday & Sundays - Call first.
- ❏ Tours: Call for reservations.

Things you can see:

- ❏ NITTANY LION SHRINE - The 13 ton block of Indiana limestone shaped like the mascot, Nittany Lion.
- ❏ FOOTBALL HALL OF FAME - Greensburg Sports Complex, (814) 865-0411. Nittany Lion football greats.
- ❏ MUSEUM OF ANTHROPOLOGY - (814) 865-3853. Ethnographic and archeological collection.
- ❏ FROST ENTOMOLOGICAL MUSEUM - (814) 865-2865. 250,000 insects!
- ❏ EARTH & MINERAL SCIENCES MUSEUM - (814) 865-6427. Minerals and paintings depicting Pennsylvania's mineral industries.
- ❏ PALSNER MUSEUM OF ART - (814) 865-7672.
- ❏ PENN STATE BOOKSTORE - (814) 863-0205.
- ❏ COLLEGE OF AGRICULTURAL SCIENCES - Dairy, beef and sheep research center, deer pens. Look for Coaly the mule.
- ❏ THE CREAMERY - west on Bigler Road (865-7535). Approximately 500,000 cones of ice cream are sold here each year. These dairy products are produced in Borland Lab, located directly behind the Creamery. These products are used throughout the campus. Ben and Jerry actually took a correspondence course through Penn State to learn about ice cream production.

STONE VALLEY RECREATION AREA

State College - *(CR1029 - off SR26 South), 16801. Phone: (814) 863-1164. Center - (814) 863-2000. Hours: Dawn – Dusk. Admission: FREE. Web: www.psu.edu/Stone_Valley/* Boating, fishing, hayrides, ice skating, sledding, cross-country skiing, hiking and equipment rental. Cabins, Shauer's Creek Environmental Center - Raptor Center (rehabilitate injured large birds) and Day Camps. FREE Admission. Fees for rentals.

SHIKELLAMY STATE PARK

Sunbury - *Bridge Avenue (Blue Hill is reached from the town of Shamokin Dam on US 11north. Marina off of PA 147), 17801. Web: www.dcnr.state.pa.us/stateparks/parks/shilk.htm Phone: (717) 988-5557.* The marina provides access to unlimited horsepower boating on Lake Augusta that is formed by an inflatable dam on the Susquehanna River. The Blue Hill area is across the river from the Marina and provides panoramic views of the confluence of two branches of the Susquehanna River. Boat Rentals.

DELGROSSO'S AMUSEMENT PARK

Old Route 220 (I-99 North, Exit Grazierville or Bellwood)

Tipton 16684

❑   Phone: (814) 684-3538 **Web: www.delgrossos.com/dap.html**
❑   Hours: Tuesday-Sunday (Summer). Open Holiday Mondays only. Weekends in May and September. Open at 11:00am.
❑   Admission: FREE. (All-day passes, ~$9.00 and individual ride prices, ~50c each available).

30 rides and attractions. Most of the rides are old-fashioned spinning rides and roller coaster. Mini-golf - (18 holes with lakes and waterfalls), Go-Karts, mini-train rides and an Interactive water park. Free concert series during the summer.

CANDYLAND

Tyrone - *30 West 10th Street (I-99 to SR453 or SR220), 16686. Phone: (814) 684-0857. Web: www.gardnerscandies.com Hours: Monday-Saturday 9:30am-9:00pm, Sunday 1:00-9:00pm. Admission: FREE.* Nostalgic walk through a penny candy store.

For updates visit our website: www.kidslovepublications.com

Big candy counters with large jars of candy. Also stop in the Candy Kitchen where old-time (mostly brass) equipment is displayed. Take a look at their giant Taffy Hook. Mr. Gardner started "the sweetest place in town" in 1897 and still has licorice whips and candy buttons for sale.

WINDBER COAL HERITAGE CENTER

Windber - *501 15th Street (off SR56), 15963. Phone: (877) 826-3933. Web: www.allegheny.org/windber/center.htm Hours: Tuesday-Saturday 10:00am-5:00pm (May-October). Admission: $1.50-$3.50.* Mine #40 Scenic Overlook has 3 floors of exhibits, videos, and interactive maps. A working mine seam exhibit is interesting and other exhibits help you to experience the life of a miner and his family. See working and living conditions - "The Underground Farmer" as they were called. Cities were created overnight by mining companies - Windber being a model town. Unique coal gift shop.

WOODWARD CAVE

Woodward - *SR 45 (US 22 east to Water Street, then SR 45 east), 16882. Phone: (814) 349-9800. Web: www.woodwardcave.com Hours: Daily 9:00am-7:00pm (Summer). Friday-Sunday 10:00am-4:00pm (Spring, Fall). Admission: $5.00-$10.50 (age 2+). Tours: 50 - 60 minutes, guided.* Five big, well-lit rooms include the "Ball Room", "Square Room". "Hanging Forest" , "Hall of Statues" , "Tower of Babel" (largest stalagmites in U.S.) and "Upper Room" (cathedral ceiling). Indian burial room and the passageways are wide and flat.

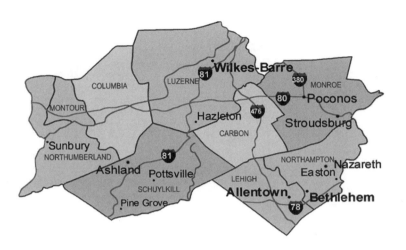

Chapter 2
Central East Area

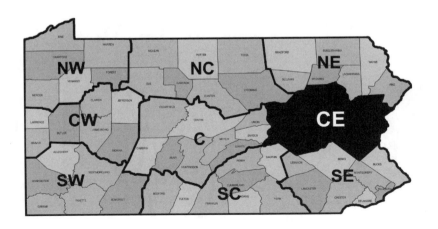

Our Favorites...

Crayola Factory

Eckley Miner's Village

Martin Guitar Company

Mrs. T's Pierogies Tour

National Canal Museum & Canal Ride

Pioneer Tunnel Coal Mine

Water Gap Trolley

Freshly Made Crayons !

ALLENTOWN ART MUSEUM

Allentown - *31 North Fifth Street (5th & Court Streets), 18101.
Phone: (610) 432-4333.* **Web: *www.allentownartmuseum.org***
*Hours: Tuesday-Saturday 11:00am-5:00pm, Sunday Noon-
5:00pm. Admission: $2.00-$5.00 (over 12).* European to
architecture of Frank Lloyd Wright to American art. Gem
Collection, photography, textiles, museum shop. Art Ways with
hands-on and touchable art & Family Fun Days or ArtVentures.

LEHIGH COUNTY MUSEUM

501 Hamilton Street - PO Box 1548 (Old Courthouse)

Allentown 18101

❑   Phone: (610) 435-1074
     Web: www.users.voicenet.com/~lchs/museum/lchsmus.html
❑   Hours: Monday-Saturday 10:00am-4:00pm, Sunday 1:00-4:00 pm.
❑   Admission: $2.00 (age 14+). Otherwise FREE.
❑   Miscellaneous: Original Indian inhabitants, Pennsylvania German
     and local historians. Geology Garden adjacent.

Other properties worth a look in this county are:

❑   CLARISVILLE ONE-ROOM SCHOOLHOUSE- 2917 Rte.
     100. (May - September weekends)
❑   SAYLOR CEMENT INDUSTRY MUSEUM - 245 N. 2nd. On
     site, 9 cement kilns from beginnings of cement industry (May -
     September weekends)
❑   HAINES MILL MUSEUM - 3600 Dornay Park Road. Operating
     gristmill built in 1760 shows milling techniques (May -
     September weekends)
❑   LOCH RIDGE FURNACE MUSEUM (Alburtis) - 525
     Franklin. Iron furnaces, industry park (May - September)

MUSEUM OF INDIAN CULTURE & LENNI LENAPE

Allentown - *2825 Fish Hatchery Road, 18103. Phone: (610) 797-
2121.* **Web: *www.lenape.org*** *Hours: Saturday-Sunday Noon-
3:00pm (by appointment only while they reorganize the museum
management). Check their website frequently for updates.
Admission: $2.00-$3.00.* Hands-on exhibits enhance the learning of

the Native American culture. Pretend you're walking in an Indian's moccasins and head dress as you look at exhibits of their crafts and tools. Special events include corn planting in May and Time of Thanksgiving in October.

DORNEY PARK AND WILDWATER KINGDOM

3830 Dorney Park Road (I-78 West to Exit 16 B)

Allentown 18104

- ❑ Phone: (610) 395-3724 **Web: www.dorneypark.com**
- ❑ Hours: Daily (Memorial Day-Labor Day), Weekends (May and September).
- ❑ Admission: $10.50 (twilight)-$37.00 (ages 4+) (includes wet and dry park rides). Parking $7.00.

Over 100 rides and attractions. Includes 11 water slides, dozens of rides, a giant wavepool and Lollipop Lagoon for little kids. Steel Force is the longest, tallest, fastest coaster in the East. Hang Time - "hang out" thrill ride and Water Works interactive aquatic play ride. Also, high energy live shows. Aquablast is the longest elevated water slide (701ft.) in the world. Camp Snoopy and Tot Spot rides for younger set.

GAME PRESERVE

Allentown (Schnecksville) - *5150 Game Preserve Road (off SR309), 18078.* **Web: www.gamepreserve.org** *Phone: (610) 799-4171. Hours: Daily 10:00am-5:00pm (Late April - October). Admission: $4.00-$6.00 (age 2+).* Native, exotic birds, and petting zoo inhabit a 25 acre zoo. Investigation Station: Become an Investigative Agent and solve eco-crimes or solve the earth's dilemmas. Catch live animal presentations daily (look on the announcement board). Conserving species of endangered animals is a specialty. Look for their mascot bison, Wooly Bully.

REPTILAND, CLYDE PEELING'S

Allenwood (Williamsport Area) - *RR 1, Box 388, US 15 (I-80 exit 30B), 17810.* **Web: www.reptiland.com** *Phone: (570) 538-1869 or (800) REPTILAND. Hours: Daily 9:00am-7:00pm*

(Summer). Daily 10:00am-5:00pm or 6:00pm (September-May). Admission: $9.00 adult, $7.00 child (4-11). Shows: Every 90 minutes beginning at 10:30am. Cobras, alligators, pythons, vipers, are all slithering around in a tropical garden setting. You even get to touch a real snake! Meet "Big Boy" the alligator or poison dart frogs. A multi-media show reveals the close-up world of reptiles and there's often live lecture demonstrations or viewing daily feedings.

ALPINE MOUNTAIN

Analomink - *Route 447, 18320. Phone: (570) 595-2150. (800) 233-8240 (Lodging). Snow Report: (800) 233-8100.* **Web: www.alpinemountain.com** Alpine's Snowtubing Park has been expanded and now includes a new "Kiddie Park" area. Longest Run: 2640 ft.; 20 Slopes & Trails.

MUSEUM OF ANTHRACITE MINING

Ashland - *17th and Pine Streets (I-81 exit 36B, off SR61 north to Ashland, take 20th Street), 17921. Phone: (570) 875-4708.* **Web: www.phmc.state.pa.us/bhsm/toh/anthmining/anthracite.asp?secid=14** *Hours: Monday-Sunday 10:00am-6:00pm (April-November). Winters by appointment. Admission: $2.00-$3.50 (age 6+).* The focus is on tools and machinery used to mine hard coal by hand up to the surface mining operations of today. A good place to quick stop for background information on underground and strip mining. Then, to see it in person, go next door to the Pioneer Tunnel Coal Mine Tour. (Kids seem to get more out of actual mining site than pictures and displays).

PIONEER TUNNEL COAL MINE

19 th & Oak Streets (SR61 North to Downtown Area - Follow signs off Center Street SR61), **Ashland** 17921

❑   Phone: (570) 875-3850 **Web: www.pioneertunnel.com**
❑   Hours: Daily 10:00am-6:00pm (Summer). Weekdays 11:00am, 12:30pm, 2:00pm and Weekends 10:00am-6:00pm (May, September, October). Weekdays only in April. Some reserved group tours in November.

- ❑   Admission: $5.50-$7.50 adult, $4.00-$5.00 child (each activity).
- ❑   Tours: Approximately 35 minutes, given by real coal miner guides.
- ❑   Miscellaneous: Snack bar, Gift shop where most novelties are made from coal. Wooden "train" playground.

Two tour options are available and we highly recommend both. (Pre-schoolers may find the mine tour frightening due to darkness, dampness, and confined areas...but will love the lokie train tour).

- ❑   <u>COAL MINE TOUR</u> - Watch you children's eyes light up with fascination as you enter and travel 400' deep into a real working coal mine! Though closed in 1931 (because of the Great Depression), you will see and have explained all the features of a real mine. Learn how and why tunnels were built to access the coal. See the Mammoth Vein (the largest in Pennsylvania) and learn why all miners carried a safety lamp (not for light, but for safety from dangerous gases). Our guide was a real miner who carefully explained what we were seeing. He even turned out all of the lights to show how dark a real mine is! If you're concerned, the mine is inspected regularly by the state to insure its safety. If your parents or grandparents were miners, this will surely bring their stories to life. A top 10 Pennsylvania tour and we definitely agree!
- ❑   <u>TRAIN RIDE - OPEN COAL FIELD TOUR</u> - A "lokie" (steam locomotive) called the "Henry Clay" takes real mine cars to show you strip mining - where a "vein" of coal is discovered and dug out of the side of a mountain. Also stop by a relic "bootleg" coal mine where men risked life and the law during the Great Depression. They used these small illegal mines to get bags of coal to sell and heat their homes.

TUSCARORA & LOCUST LAKE STATE PARK

Barnesville - *RD 1, Box 1051 (Off I-81, exit 37), 18214. Phone: (717) 467-2404. **Web: www.dcnr.state.pa.us/stateparks/parks/l-lake.htm** This popular camping spot is heavily forested and the only cleared area is the 52-acre lake. Nestled against Locust Mountain, visitors will find many year-round recreational opportunities like boating and fishing, and opportunities to see wildlife. Beach, Boat Rentals, and Trails.

RICKETTS GLEN STATE PARK

Benton - *RR 2, Box 130 (PA Route 487), 17814. Phone: (717) 477-5675.   Web: www.dcnr.state.pa.us/stateparks/parks/ricketts.htm* Take the Falls Trail and explore the Glens which boasts a series of wild, free-flowing waterfalls, each cascading through rock-strewn clefts in this ancient hillside. The 94-foot Ganoga Falls is the highest of 22 named waterfalls. Beach/Swimming, Boat Rentals, Horseback Riding, Campsites, Modern Cabins.

DISCOVERY CENTER OF SCIENCE AND TECHNOLOGY

511 East Third Street, **Bethlehem** 18015

- ❑ Phone: (610) 865-5010 **Web: www.discovery-center.org**
- ❑ Hours: The Center is open to the public on Saturdays only 9:30am-4:30pm during the school year. Also open to the public: Thanksgiving Thursday & Friday, December 26-31, Martin Luther King Day, Presidents' Day and Easter Thursday, Friday & Monday. SUMMER HOURS (Begin the second Monday in June through Saturday after Labor Day): The Center is OPEN 6 days a week Monday-Saturday 9:30am-4:30pm. Closed July 4 and Labor Day.
- ❑ Admission: $5.00 general (4+), $4.50 senior (62+).

Family favorites include the Dark Tunnel, Kitchen Chemistry and the Laser Show. Other fun spots you'll find:

- ❑ WATERWORKS - fills one room with interactive models demonstrating water distribution, the water cycle, watersheds and natural water filters. Visitors are introduced to hands-on lessons on water contamination, preservation and the protection of the region's local water supply.
- ❑ SCIENCE PLAYGROUND - is learning through play. Enjoy a "playground" of science activities including the Giant Lever, math puzzles, polygons and geometric sandcastles.

Discovery Center Of Science & Technology (cont.)

❑ <u>BODY WORKS</u> - investigates how your body works. Take a ride with Dr. Bones and learn how the body's skeletal system works when you're in motion.

❑ <u>NATURE ZONE</u> - explores the world of nature and earth sciences. Discover why certain rocks "glow" and even "capture" your shadow in the Shadow Room.

❑ <u>WORKBENCH</u> - take apart, invent and build. Grab a screwdriver and explore technology from the inside out including taking apart and rebuilding a computer.

PENNSYLVANIA YOUTH THEATRE

Bethlehem - *211 Plymouth Street, 18015. Phone: (610) 332-1400. Web: www.123pyt.org* Productions for/by youth like Cinderella and Charlie and the Chocolate Factory.

BETHLEHEM HISTORIC AREA

459 Old York Road (off SR378 - Historic area)

Bethlehem 18018

❑ Phone: (800) 360-8687 **Web: www.historicbethlehem.org**
❑ Hours: Generally, Tuesday-Saturday 1:00-4:00pm.
❑ Admission: FREE (Walking self-guided tours). Pre-arranged building tours are $3.00-6.00/person.
❑ Miscellaneous: Best to visit during re-enacted history festivals around Christmas, Bach Festival in May, Celtic Festival in September or Musicfest in August.

Points of interest include:

❑ <u>VISITORS CENTER</u> - Learn about Moravian Missionaries who first developed this town using pre-Revolutionary German architecture. Watch a video before you take a self-guided walking tour.

❑ <u>MORAVIAN MUSEUM</u> - 66 West Church Street. Can you imagine a 5 story log cabin, built without nails? Once used as a church, dorm and workshop, now it's a Moravian historical museum.

❑ INDUSTRIAL QUARTER - Start at the Luchenbach Mill (HistoryWorks! Children's interactive gallery located on the first floor), stop at a 1761 tannery or 1762 waterworks - the first pumped municipal water system in the colonies.

JACK FROST MOUNTAIN & BIG BOULDER SKI AREAS

PO Box 707 (I-476 exit 95 or I-80 exit 284, head north to Jack Frost, head south to Big Boulder),

Blakeslee (Poconos area) 18610

❑ Phone: (800) 468-2442 **Web: www.big2resorts.com**
❑ Admission: per activity
❑ Miscellaneous: Baby sitting provided. Choose from Poconos resorts' townhouses, condominiums, cabins, or campsites. SnowMonsters skiing and snowboarding programs are geared towards kids to teach them basic techniques and important safety tips in a fun environment! Chairlifts and SkiCarpets (make it easier for younger skiers to move up the mountains).

BIG BOULDER SKI AREA - Longest Run: 2900 ft.; 14 Slopes & Trails. Five family and seven single tubing chutes.

JACK FROST SKI AREA - Longest Run: 2700 ft.; 21 Slopes & Trails.

RIDE ATV PARK - 4 wheeler vehicle park with curves, hill, whoop-de-doos, mud pits. Smaller course and ATV's for youngsters. Fee includes rentals.

SPLATTER - 2500 acres of paintball fields (many with special themes). Year round.

WHEELS SKATE PARK - Inline skate and board park with half pipes, quarter pipes, rail slides and pyramids. Kids area. Rentals. Daily (April - October).

CATAWISSA RAILROAD COMPANY

Catawissa - *119 Pine Street (office at 111 Main Street, 1/2 block away), 17820.* **Web: *www.caboosenut.com*** *Phone: (570) 356-2345.* Thirteen restored cabooses, two railroad bridges, and a tunnel are open and free to visitors. Or, stay overnight in one of several fully-restored cabooses.

WEISER STATE FOREST

Cressona - *Box 99, 17929. Phone: (570) 385-7800.* **Web: *www.dcnr.state.pa.us/forestry/stateforests/forests/weiser/weise r.htm*** Within the Weiser State Forest are some very rugged and secluded wooded areas that can be reached by 65 miles of rough fire suppression roads. Fishing, Trails, Snow-Mobiling Trails and Cross-Country Skiing.

WATER GAP TROLLEY

Main Street, Rte. 611 (I-80, exit 310)

Delaware Water Gap 18327

- ❑ Phone: (570) 476-9766
- ❑ Hours: Daily 10:00am-4:00pm (April-November).
- ❑ Admission: $4.00-$7.00.
- ❑ Tours: All weather trolleys, narrated scenic, historical tour of area. 1 hour long. Trolley leaves every 1 1/2 hours.
- ❑ Miscellaneous: Picnic areas and miniature golf on premises.

Replica streetcars take a relaxed tour of the Water Gap - Shawnee area where you can learn about Indians, early settlers, and some history. The first half of tour may be boring to kids but the second half stops at Chief Taminy's face formed from rough edges in the mountain rocks (like a natural profile - Mt. Rushmore). Also stop at the Cold Air Cave (regardless of the outside temperature; the air rushing out of the entrance to the small cave is always 38 degrees F. – your kids will say – really cool!).

BUSHKILL PARK

Easton - *2100 Bushkill Park Drive, 18040. Phone: (610) 258-6941.* **Web: *www.bushkillpark.com*** *Hours: Weekends Noon-6:00pm (Memorial Day - Mid-June), Wednesday-Sunday Noon-6:00pm,*

Friday-Saturday until 9:00pm (Mid-June - Labor Day). Admission: FREE (weekdays). $3.00 Weekends and Holidays. Individual Ride Tickets are $0.75. Miscellaneous: Picnic. Concessions. Mini-golf. This is the same kind of park your parents went to. Most rides are 30-50 years old. A 1926 Allan Herschell Carousel with Grand Wurlitzer organ. 9 Kiddie rides and 8 large rides. Carousel Candy Factory - chocolate handmade before your eyes.

CRAYOLA FACTORY

30 Centre Square, Two Rivers Landing (Look for giant box of crayons on top), **Easton** 18042

❑ Phone: (610) 515-8000, **Web: www.crayola.com**

❑ Hours: Tuesday-Saturday 9:30am-5:00pm, Sunday Noon-5:00pm (September-June). Also open Mondays (March-June). Monday - Saturday 9:30am-6:00pm, Sunday Noon – 5:00pm. (July-Labor Day). Closed Christmastime, New Years, Easter and Thanksgiving & first two weeks of January.

❑ Admission: $9.00 general (3+), $8.50 senior (65+). Includes admission to the National Canal Museum.

❑ Miscellaneous: The Crayola Store. To get the most benefit from the full admission price, be prepared to try all of the activities (that includes you Mom & Dad - you get to be kids…again!). Best to arrive early (or make reservations). Daily admission is on first-come, first-served basis.

Each person is asked to learn and think "Outside the Lines". Learn Crayola history at the Hall of Fame. Do you know what celebrity molded the 100 billionth crayon? What was his favorite color? Next, do a dozen or so interactive exhibits. "Color on the Wall" - Go ahead, it's glass and is wiped clean easily. Hurry kids, this may be your only chance to break the rules! Everyone creates "their own souvenirs to take home". Especially great is the Factory Floor exhibit where a worker mixes melted wax and colors to help you make your own souvenir crayons to take home. The most favorite color is red and our kids got to help put the wrappers on real (just manufactured) crayons. The Wax Works area allows you to actually paint with melted crayons or re-create Folk Art in another exhibit. Older kids will like the Bright Ideas area where you experiment with color and light combinations. Parents, it does get crazy in here, but if you go with the flow and start creating yourself…you CAN survive and have FUN!

HUGH MOORE CANAL RIDE PARK

Hugh Moore Park (off I-78 or off US22 to Lehigh Drive)

Easton 18042

❑   Phone: (610) 559-6613 **Web: http://canals.org/hmpark.htm**
❑   Hours: Monday-Saturday 10:30am-5:00pm, Sunday 12:45-
     5:00pm (mid-June - Labor Day). Tuesday-Friday 9:45am-
     2:20pm, Saturday, Sunday & Holidays 1:00-4:30pm (May-mid-
     June). Weekends only (September)
❑   Admission:$6.00 adult, $4.00 child (3-15).
❑   Tours: Costumed interpreter guides you on a 50-60 minute ride.
❑   Miscellaneous: Trails, picnic, boat rentals, gift shop.

The mule-drawn canal boat Josiah White II ride is on a restored section of the LeHigh Canal. The large boat and costumed drivers are carried by a mule or two. Visit the Loctender's House Museum - lifestyle of his family and also a great view of the dam, lock, and bridge.

NATIONAL CANAL MUSEUM

30 Centre Square (I-78, Easton exit & US22 - 3rd floor - Two Rivers Landing), **Easton** 18042

❑   Phone: (610) 515-8000 or (610) 559-6613
     Web: http://canals.org/museum.htm
❑   Hours: Tuesday-Saturday 9:30am-5:00pm, Sunday Noon-5:00pm
     (Closed Mondays except school holidays).
❑   Admission: Included in the purchase price of Crayola Factory
     tickets. (not available separately)
❑   Miscellaneous: Admissions are limited based on building
     capacity. Call ahead if you're traveling from out of town.

Visit a short time in history before railroads, highways, and airplanes. Follow the story lines of immigrants and locals who built and ran the canals. Hear the boatman tell stories and sing canal songs. Walk through the middle of a full size replica boat.

Hands-on exhibits help kids understand this mode of transport. Actually operate a lock model and pilot your play boat through it. Then dress up as socialites traveling the canal in luxury with Mr. Tiffany (of Tiffany glass in 1886). The Molly Polly Chunker was a luxury liner canal boat decorated in Victorian fashion. This is the best interactive way to truly understand canals and this brief era of time.

KNOEBEL'S AMUSEMENT RESORT

PO Box 317 (I-80 West to Bloomsburg exits 232, 236, 241. Rte. 232, PA 42 South to Catawissa & SR 487), **Elysburg** 17824

- ❑   Phone: (800) ITS-4-FUN   **Web: www.knoebels.com**
- ❑   Hours: Daily 11:00am-10:00pm (Summer). Weekends only (May & September).
- ❑   Admission: FREE. Pay-One-Price Plans are available Monday-Friday during the in-season. Weekends are pay-as-you-go. $.60 - $1.60 per ride.
- ❑   Miscellaneous: Restaurants. Gift shops. Mini-golf.

41 rides including the "Phoenix" - rated one of America's 10 best roller coasters. Just as many family rides as thrill or kiddie rides. Pool and water slides. Games, entertainment. An extremely family-friendly, old-fashioned attraction!

LEHIGH VALLEY VELODROME

Emmaus - *217 Main Street (Routes 100 and 222), 18049. Phone: (610) 967-7587.* **Web: www.lvvelo.org** *Hours: Friday evenings (Memorial Day weekend - August). Tickets: $3.00-$6.00.* Cheer on cyclists from around the world as they compete in pro bike racing.

LOST RIVER CAVERNS

Hellertown - *726 Durham Street (I-78, Exit 21, Rt. 412 South), 18055. Phone: (610) 838-8767.* **Web: www.lostcave.com** *Hours: Year-round. 9:00am-6:00pm (Memorial Day-Labor Day), Rest of year closes at 5:00pm. Closed Thanksgiving, Christmas, and New Year's Day. Admission: $4.00-$8.00.* Guided walking tours through beautiful crystal formations. Limestone cavern with five chambers and underground stream. Indoor tropical garden, rock museum.

YESTERDAY'S TRAIN TODAY RAIL TOUR

Jim Thorpe - *4 Lehigh Street (I-476 exit 34 South - US209 (Depot), 18229. Phone: (888) 546-8467 or (570) 325-4606. **Web: www.railtours-inc.com** Hours: Weekends & Holidays Noon-3:00pm (Mid-May - September). Also, October Fall Foliage Tours but they are longer (2 1/2 hrs.) and about triple the price. Admission: $3.00-$6.00 (ages 2+). Tours: 40 minutes long (just the right amount of time for kids).* A similar ride to local passenger trains years ago during the glorious rail excursion era. Pass lots of "Americana" small towns.

SPLIT ROCK RESORT SKI AREA

Lake Harmony - *1 Lake Drive (I-80 East to Exit 277 or I-476 to exit 95, follow Rte.940 East, 18624. Phone: (717) 722-9111. (800) 255-ROCK (Lodge). Snow Report: (717) 722-9111. **Web: www.splitrockresort.com** Lodge with 2 indoor pools, whirlpools or sauna, 18 hole championship golf course, sail on beautiful Lake Harmony, mountain bike or hike to Hickory-Run State Park, or do some skiing. Longest Run: 1700 ft.; 7 Slopes & Trails.

BELTZVILLE STATE PARK

Lehighton - *2950 Pohopoco Drive (US 209), 18235. Phone: (215) 377-0045. **Web: www.dcnr.state.pa.us/stateparks/parks/b-ville.htm*** Beltzville Lake is seven miles long and features fishing, swimming, water sports and unlimited horsepower boating. Along the shore, you can sometimes find fossils. A hike along Wild Creek Trail leads to waterfalls and Sawmill Trail wanders through forests and by a creek. Beach, Boat Rentals, & Cross-Country Skiing.

DOE MOUNTAIN SKI AREA

Macungie - *101 Doe Mountain Lane (I-476 to Quakertown exit, turn on Rte. 663 going S, then right on Rte. 29), 18062. Phone: (610) 682-7109. Snow Report: (800) I-SKI-DOE.* Long Run: 1.5 miles; 15 Slopes & Trails.

POCONO SNAKE AND ANIMAL FARM

Marshalls Creek - *Route 209 (US209 Northeast), 18335. Phone: (570) 223-8653. Hours: Daily Noon-5:00pm, weather permitting. Admission: $4.00-$5.00 (age 2+).* Visit the "Great Little Zoo". They have over 100 animals including a Siberian Tiger, a giant Anaconda, Alligators, Emus, and Mountain Lions. The antics of the monkeys, or more engaging pot belly pigs, may make your kids "squeal". Petting and feeding areas, too.

MOUNT AIRY LODGE SKI AREA

Mt. Pocono - *42 Woodland Road (Rte. 611), 18344. Phone: (717) 839-8811. (800) 441-4410 (Lodge). Snow Report: (717) 839-8811.* **Web: www.mountairylodge.com** Longest Run: 2300 ft.; 7 Slopes & Trails. Snowboard clinics offered 3 day(s)/week, 3 time(s)/day.

MARTIN GUITAR COMPANY

510 Sycamore Street (I-80 to SR33 South to SR191 South to North Broad to Beil St - Follow Signs), **Nazareth** 18064

- ❑ Phone: (610) 759-2837 **Web: www.mguitar.com**
- ❑ Hours: Monday-Friday 8:30am-5:00pm (shop and museum). Closed Holidays and week of Christmas.
- ❑ Admission: FREE
- ❑ Tours: Monday - Friday leaving promptly at 1:00 pm. Lasts one hour. Recommended for school-aged children and above because of length of tour.
- ❑ Miscellaneous: 1833 shop memorabilia, strings, books, accessories.

Founded in 1833, Martin guitars are known as "America's guitar". Used by many legendary performers, you'll start your tour in the museum shop of vintage guitars. Children are encouraged to "gently play" several guitars in the waiting area. If any of your children play the guitar, they will be especially interested in all the posters of famous performers who use Martins. The tour shows step-by-step production and is very educational. See the types of wood (cured for 4 months prior to production) used - from the usual to the exotic. Watch how each piece is computer-routed or bent in special jigs. Martin even makes their own strings to insure that "one of a kind" Martin sound. They've even produced a

$50,000 custom order guitar with diamonds in the guitar neck! Sometimes famous performers *(or their band members)* stop by the Martin plant…maybe even on your tour!

NAZARETH SPEEDWAY

Nazareth - *Highway 191, 18064. Phone: (888) 629-RACE.* **Web:** *www.nazarethspeedway.com* "America's Finest and Fastest One Mile." NASCAR Championship, Grand National, INDY 225 and Truck Series. (April - July).

BLUE MOUNTAIN SKI AREA

Palmerton - *1600 Blue Mountain Drive, 18071. Phone: (610) 826-7700. Snow report: (800) 235- 2226* **Web:** *www.skibluemt.com* 1,082-foot vertical, plenty of trails for ALL abilities plus a half-pipe and two terrain parks. Longest Run: 6400 ft.; 29 Slopes & Trails plus snowboarding.

BIG DIAMOND RACEWAY

Pottsville - *(Near Forestville, off Rt. 901), 17901. Phone: (570) 544-6434.* **Web:** *www.bigdiamondraceway.com Hours: Fridays at 8:00pm (April-Labor Day).* Nascar - Winston Series Stock Car Racing.

SHAWNEE MOUNTAIN SKI AREA

Shawnee-on-Delaware - *PO Box 339 (Exit 309, Off I-80), 18356. Phone: (570) 421-7231. (800) VILLA-4-U. (Lodge). Snow Report: (800) 233-4218.* **Web:** *www.shawneemt.com* 22 Trails, Terrain Park, Snowboarding, "Pocono Plunge" Snow Tubing Park & Half-Pipe. Open Day & Night. Longest Run: 5100 ft. Comfortable rooms, dining, indoor pool and jacuzzi, and the only full-size indoor ice rink in the region.

SHAWNEE PLACE CHILDREN'S PLAY & WATER PARK

Shawnee-on-Delaware - *PO Box 339 (I-80, Exit 309, US 209 North, Follow signs), 18356. Phone: (570) 421-7231.* **Web:** *www.shawneemt.com Hours: Weekends (Memorial Day weekend*

- *Mid-June). Daily 10:00am-5:00pm (Mid-June - Labor Day). Admission: Participants $13.00, Spectators $10.50.* Ball pits, cable glide, cargo nets, water slides, wading pools, magic shows, arcade, snack bar. Children, ages 2 - 12.

MRS. T'S PIEROGIES

600 East Center Street (off SR61, turn right on Center Street - SR924 North), **Shenandoah** 17976

❑ Phone: (570) 462-2745. **Web: www.pierogy.com**

❑ Admission: FREE

❑ **NOTE: Mrs. T's tours schedule will be extremely limited in 2003 due to renovations. Full tour schedule resumes in January 2004.**

❑ Tours: (approximately 40 minutes) - By appointment only with 30 days notice. Ages 3rd grade+ (5-6 minimum - 15 maximum)

As you adorn hair nets and lab coats, you begin your tour seeing first the raw materials (mostly eggs, flour, and potato flakes) as they arrive and are prepared for cooking. You'll see hundreds of pierogies floating in boiling water, after they have been secretly prepared. The Secret Room (called the Black Box) has a special pierogy making machine. No one (except a few workers, sworn to secrecy) ever enters this room. The 9,500,000 unique pasta pockets made here weekly are flash frozen and packaged immediately. Every kid's favorite part of this tour has to be the complimentary warm pierogies offered at the end of the tour. We sampled the cheddar and potato variety and drank soft drinks from Mrs. T's souvenir mugs. The tour and personnel are wonderful. Ask for unique recipes - great new ways to use a classic ethnic food. Their snack line of "Rogies" are cute, bite sized pasta pockets (just right for kids!).

QUIET VALLEY LIVING HISTORICAL FARM

1000 Turkey Hill Road (I-80 to exit 304, US209 SW (Bus Rte), right at Shafer's School House Road, left on Business Route 209.

Stroudsburg 18360

❑ Phone: (570) 992-6161, **Web: www.quietvalley.org**

❑ Hours: Tuesday-Saturday 10:00am-5:30pm, Sunday 1:00-5:30pm (June 20-Labor Day).

- ❑ Admission: $7.00 adult, $4.00 child (3-12).
- ❑ Tours: 90 minute, costumed guided. Last tour leaves at 4:00 pm.

Meet a Pennsylvania Dutch family as they go about their numerous daily chores – pretend the time is the early 1800's. Daily activities include spinning, weaving, smoking and drying meats, vegetables and fruits; cooking, gardening, and tending to animals. Kids can touch barnyard animals and jump in a giant haystack! Usually one craft is highlighted weekly - ex. quilting, butter churning, candle dips, basket making, natural wool dying (how do they get color naturally?) and blacksmithing. Actual aunts, uncles, cousins, and siblings escort you around the farm & treat you like visiting relatives.

DELAWARE STATE FOREST

Swiftwater - *HC 1, Box 95A, 18370. Phone: (570) 895-4000* *www.dcnr.state.pa.us/forestry/stateforests/forests/delaware/delaware.htm* Messing Nature Center lead to Trails, Horse Trails, ATV Trails (35 miles), Fishing, Cross-Country Skiing.

CAMEL BEACH WATER PARK (CAMELBACK SKI AREA)

PO Box 168 (I -80, Exit 299), **Tannersville** 18372

- ❑ Phone: (570) 629-1661 **Web: www.camelbeach.com** or **http://skicamelback.com/**
- ❑ Hours: Waterpark open Daily at 11:00am (Summers). Weekends only (early Fall and late Spring). Skiing (December-March).
- ❑ Admission: See website for skiing. Spectator ~$11.00. General $21.00-$25.00. Save on Twilight (after 4:00pm) tickets.

Waterpark: 10 water slides, Wave Pool, Lazy River Ride, Family Play Pool, 3200 foot long Alpine Slide, bumper boats, go-carts, mini-golf, chairlift rides, Cameltop Restaurant (lunch only). Ski Area: Skiing, snowboarding and tubing. You'll find 33 trails, 13 lifts including 2 high-speed detachable quads, halfpipe, 2 terrain parks, night skiing and 100% snowmaking.

ECKLEY MINERS' VILLAGE

Route #2, Box 236 (I-80 West to Exit 40 - SR940 West - then follow signs), **Weatherly** 18255

- ❑   Phone: (570) 636-2070
  www.phmc.state.pa.us/bhsm/toh/eckley/eckley.asp?secid=14
- ❑   Hours: Monday-Saturday 9:00am-5:00pm, Sunday Noon-5:00pm. Closed State Holidays except summer holidays.
- ❑   Admission: $4.00 adult, $3.50 senior, $2.00 child (6-12).
- ❑   Tours: Guided tours available for small extra charge (recommended) in the summertime only.
- ❑   Miscellaneous: Great supplement to a nearby tour of a coal mine.

What is a Patch Town? A patch was a cluster of a few dozen company houses along a crooked, unpaved street built within the shadow of black silt ponds and strip mining pits. See an actual town (only slightly restored) just as it appeared in a movie (in the 1970's). Retired miners, miner's widows, and children still live here. Watch a 15 minute video at the Visitor's Center first, then walk by audio displays of a typical miner's day or week (including church on Sunday). School-aged kids will want to take the tour which includes going inside a house (1870's - 1890's - notice all of the updates!), a company store, and a doctor's office. Just imagine having to be a young boy then, helping to support the family by being a "breaker boy" in the smoky, dangerous mill. Boy, can you feel the coal miner ancestry here!

HICKORY RUN STATE PARK

White Haven - *RD 1, Box 81 (PA Route 534, 1-80 exit 274), 18661. Web: www.dcnr.state.pa.us/stateparks/parks/hickory.htm Phone: (717) 443-0400.* The Boulder Field, a striking boulder-strewn area, is a National Natural Landmark. This large park has over 40 miles of hiking trails, three natural areas and miles of trout streams. While at the park, learn about lumbering history at the Visitors Center, observe wildlife or see Hawk Falls. Beach & Swimming, Sledding, and numerous Campsites. LeHigh Gorge and mountain biking.

JACOBSBURG STATE PARK

Wind Gap - *835 Jacobsburg Road (PA 33), 18091. Phone: (610) 746-2801. www.dcnr.state.pa.us/stateparks/parks/j-burg.htm* Environmental Education Center offers many programs. Once the site where the famous Henry Rifle was made, the Jacobsburg National Historic District lies almost entirely within the park. Henrys Woods offers scenic hikes and the rest of the center grounds have multi-use trails. Horseback Riding and Mountain Biking are most popular here.

FRANCES SLOCUM STATE PARK

Wyoming - *565 Mt. Olivet Road (exit 170B of I- 81, take Rte. 309 North). 18644. www.dcnr.state.pa.us/stateparks/parks/slocum.htm Phone: (717) 696-3525.* The horseshoe-shaped lake provides 165 acres for boating and fishing. An environmental interpretive center located in the day use area features exhibits on American Indians and ecological topics. The park is named for a young girl who was kidnapped by a Lenni Lenape raiding party in 1778. Frances Slocum spent her first night of captivity in a rock shelter in the park. Pool, Campsites, Boat Rentals, and Sledding.

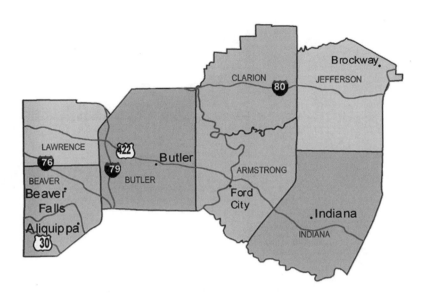

Chapter 3
Central West Area

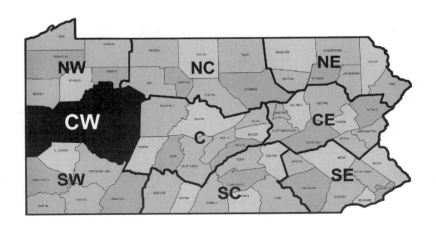

Our Favorites...

Cook Forest State Park

DeBence Antique Music Museum

Punxsutawney Groundhog Zoo

Raccoon State Park

Shadow or No Shadow ?

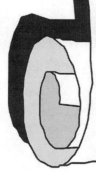

BUTLER COUNTY MUSEUMS

106 South Main Street, **Butler** 16003

❑ Phone: (724) 283-8116

www.butlercountyhistoricalsociety-pa.org/

❑ Hours: Call for current hours, mostly weekends (May-September).

Country life at 4 different sites:

❑ COOPER CABIN - (off Rte. 356, Cooper Rd.). The 1810 cabin is still furnished with family heirlooms and memorabilia as well as other period pieces. Out buildings include a spinning house, spring house and tool shed. A self-guided nature trail winds through the more than four acres of land surrounding the cabin. There is also a model oil well and an extensive herb garden.

❑ SHAW HOUSE - a summer residence for Butler's only U.S. Senator, Walter Lowrie (1828).

❑ LITTLE RED SCHOOLHOUSE - (1838) living history museum on 200 Jefferson St. which recreates the one-room school experience for visitors and school classes.

❑ HERITAGE CENTER - 119 West New Castle Street. Industry in the area including tin shop, Bantam Jeep, and Franklin glassworks.

COOK FOREST STATE PARK

River Road - PO Box 120 (I-80 exit 78, PA 36 north)

Cooksburg 16217

❑ Phone: (814) 744-8407

Web: www.dcnr.state.pa.us/stateparks/parks/cookforest.htm

Virgin white pine and hemlock timber stands nick-named the "Black Forest". Highlights are the Forest Cathedral, Log Cabin Inn Visitor Center, Sawmill Craft Center and Theater, the Fire Tower and Seneca Point Overlook. Log Cabin Inn: Cook Forest's environmental learning center is a large log building built in 1934 by the CCC. It is at one end of Longfellow Trail and contains a variety of displays, taxidermy animals and logging tools from early lumbering days. Near the entrance on Route 36 is Double Diamond

Deer Ranch, where deer are raised from birth. Children can bottle-feed fawns June -August.   Pool, Horseback Riding, Campsites, Rustic Cabins, Boating, Fishing, Skiing, and Snowmobiling. Several private canoe rentals are in the Cooksburg area.

DOUBLE DIAMOND DEER RANCH

Cooksburg - *(I-80, Brookville exit north on SR36, South of Cook Forest),   16217.   Web: www.doublediamonddeerranch.com Phone: (814) 752-6334. Hours: Daily 10:00am-Dusk (May-November), Weekends Only (December-April). Admission: $3.00+ (age 5+).* Photograph or watch white tail deer in natural habitats. Covered walkways, scenic trails, and a Museum & gift shop. Fawns are born early June. Come see how tiny they are. "Bottle times" and "Treat Times" are scheduled in June, July and August.

LOG CABIN INN

Harmony - *430 Perry Highway (US19 - 2 miles north of Zelienople), 16037. Phone: (724) 452-4155. Hours: Daily, Lunch & Dinner.* Rural and rustic 160 year old log cabin located near downtown historic Harmony community. The original dining room area floor is tilted and the logs are huge. All American fare with children's menu complete with coloring and crayons.

RACCOON STATE PARK

Hookstown - *RD 1, Box 900 (3000 SR 18, or enter from US 22 or US 30), 15050. www.dcnr.state.pa.us/stateparks/parks/racc.htm Phone: (724) 899-2200. Hours: 8:00am-Sunset.* A centrally located 100-acre lake provides opportunities for outdoor recreation like fishing, boating, and photographing and viewing waterfowl and other wildlife. Wild Flower Reserve (899-3611, Rte 30.) A 315 acre tract of land with over 500 species of wildflowers and wildlife. Frankfurt Mineral Springs - explore the reported "medicinal" properties of the water.   Beach/Swimming, Visitor Center, Boat Rentals, Horseback Riding, Sledding, Campsites, and Modern Cabins.

JIMMY STEWART MUSEUM

Indiana - *845 Philadelphia St (Indiana Public Library - 3rd Floor, corner of 9th), 15701.* Phone: *(724) 349-6112 or (800) 83-JIMMY* **Web: www.jimmy.org** *Hours: Monday-Saturday 10:00am-5:00pm, Sunday & Holidays Noon-5:00pm. Closed Christmastime and New Years time. Also closed Monday & Tuesday in winter. Admission: $5.00 adult, $4.00 senior, $3.00 child (7-17).* A legendary actor (every Christmas we still all watch "It's a Wonderful Life") who had accomplishments in film, radio and television plus civic and family roles. Displays of his great grandfather's uniform, baby photographs, furniture from the family hardware store, original movie posters, props and costumes. Watch films that are shown in a small 1930's vintage movie theatre.

HARLANSBURG STATION'S MUSEUM OF TRANSPORTATION

New Castle - *West Pittsburgh Road (US19 & SR108), 16101. Phone: (724) 652-9002. Hours: Tuesday-Saturday 10:00am-5:00pm, Sunday Noon-5:00pm. Weekends Only (March, April, May, November, December). Admission: $2.00-$3.00.* Olde time railroad station with display of real Pennsylvania railroad cars outside and memorabilia displayed inside the cars. Meet the mascot conductor and see lots of railroad uniforms. In the station are trains, cars, planes, trucks, and trolleys.

LIVING TREASURES ANIMAL PARK

New Castle - *US422, 16101. Phone: (724) 924-9571.* **Web: www.ltanimalpark.com** *Hours: Daily 10:00am-8:00pm (Summer). Weekdays 11:00am-5:00pm, Weekends 10:00am-6:00pm (May, September, October). Admission: $6.50 adult, $6.00 senior, $4.50 child (3-11).* Watch kangaroos, tigers and wolves and ride the miniature horses. Kids love the petting area (babies, reindeer, and camels) and feeding areas (bears, otters, monkeys, goats, sheep, and llamas).

NEW CASTLE REGIONAL BALLET COMPANY

New Castle - *1807 Moravia Avenue, 16101. Phone: (724) 652-1822.* **Web: *www.angelfire.com/pa4/ncrballet/*** Composed of approximately 30 youths performing classics like "The Nutcracker" and "Showcase". Ages 6+.

YELLOW CREEK STATE PARK

Penn Run - *170 Route 259 Highway (PA 422 or PA 259), 15765.* **Web: *www.dcnr.state.pa.us/stateparks/parks/y-crek.htm*** *Phone: (724) 357-7913.* Beach, Visitor Center, Boat Rentals, Sledding, Fishing, and Trails.

MCCONNELL'S MILL STATE PARK

Portersville - *RD 2, Box 16 (near the intersection of PA 19 and US 422), 16051.* ***www.dcnr.state.pa.us/stateparks/parks/mmill.htm*** *Phone: (724) 368-8091. Hours: Open 8:00am-sunset.* A 400 ft. deep gorge with giant boulders and unique eco-system. Slippery Rock Creek flows through the gorge. You can tour the restored rolling gristmill or the covered bridge. There is also scenic hiking, whitewater boating and two rock climbing and rappelling areas. Historical Center, sledding, boating, fishing, swimming, biking, camping, skiing, and snowmobiling.

MORAINE STATE PARK

Portersville - *225 Pleasant Valley Road (bisected by PA Route 422 running east/west and PA 528 running north/south), 16051.* **Web: *www.dcnr.state.pa.us/stateparks/parks/morain.htm*** *Phone: (724) 368-8811.* Moraine State Park features 3,225-acre Lake Arthur, an outstanding warm water fishery that is also great for sailing and boating. Visitors sometimes see osprey that were reintroduced to the park. Of special interest is the Frank Preston Conservation Area and a 7-mile paved bike trail that winds around the north shore of the lake. Beach, Visitor Center, Horseback Riding, Mountain Biking, Modern Cabins, Fishing, Trails, and Winter Sports.

PUNXSUTAWNEY GROUNDHOG ZOO

East Mahoning Street, Civic Center Complex (I-80 to exit 97,
US119), **Punxsutawney** 15767

❑   Phone: (800) 752-PHIL. **Web: www.groundhog.org**
❑   Hours: Museum: Tuesday-Saturday 1:00-4:00pm, Sunday 2:00-
     4:00pm. Zoo: Dawn to Dusk. Call first to confirm hours of
     museum.
❑   Admission: FREE
❑   Miscellaneous: At 401 West Mahoning Street, (814) 938-2555 is
     the Punxsutawney Museum devoted to groundhog history and
     legend.

On Groundhog Day (February 2), the world looks for
"Punxsutawney Phil" each year to peek out of his burrow on
Gobbler's Knob and see if his shadow appears.   His prediction
indicates how much of the winter season is left.   The legend was
brought to this country by German immigrants.   Phil and his
descendants have been popping out every year since February 2,
1887. He and his family reside at this zoo. We might suggest you
watch the movie "Groundhog Day" starring Bill Murray prior to
your visit to get into the spirit of things! By the way, Phil gets
almost as much mail as Santa Claus and on Groundhog Day up to
35,000 people come to see him each year! (they have pictures to
prove it).   It's worth a trip anytime of the year to meet a live
groundhog up close ... your family may be surprised how they can
change shape to fit the landscape.

CLEAR CREEK STATE PARK

Sigel - RR 1, Box 82 (1-80 to exit 73), 15860. Phone: (814) 752-
2368. Web: *www.dcnr.state.pa.us/stateparks/parks/clear.htm* Set
along the Clarion River, Clear Creek is a cozy getaway and a
canoeist's paradise. Whether you bring your own canoe or rent one,
a popular activity is the 11-mile trip from Clear Creek to Cook
Forest State Park. Rustic log and stone cabins are nestled among
ancient pines and hemlocks, making this park the perfect place to
spend a secluded, rustic vacation. Beach, Visitor Center, Historical
Center, Boat Rentals, Sledding, Campsites, Fishing, Winter Sports,
and Trails.

JENNINGS ENVIRONMENTAL EDUCATION CENTER

Slippery Rock - *2951 Prospect Road, 16057. Phone: (724) 794-6011. Web: www.dcnr.state.pa.us/stateparks/parks/jenn.htm Hours: Daily, Dawn - Dusk. Educational Center Monday-Friday 8:00am-4:00pm. Admission: FREE. Miscellaneous: Hiking trails. Picnic areas.* Surviving remnants of a Midwest Prairie. In late July, blooms of blazing star (wild prairie flowers) along with other assorted wildflowers of all varieties. Due to the glacial activity, the ground is mostly clay and only supports growth of thin grasses and plants.

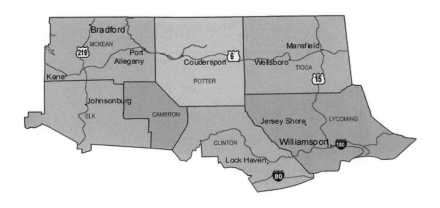

Chapter 4
North Central Area

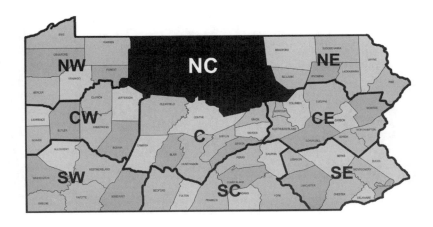

Our Favorites...

Children's Discovery Workshop

Draper's Super Bees Apiary

Holgate Toy Factory

Leonard Harrison State Park -
Grand Canyon of Pennsylvania

Pennsylvania Lumber Museum

Pennsylvania's Grand Canyon

SINNEMAHONING STATE PARK

Austin - *8288 First Fork Road (junction of PA 872 & US 6 or PA 120), 16720. Web: www.dcnr.state.pa.us/stateparks/parks/sinn.htm Phone: (814) 647-8401.* The diverse habitat supports the American eagle, black bear and white-tailed deer. Interpretive pontoon boat rides on George B. Stevenson Reservoir are available during the summer to allow a closer look at lake wildlife. Boating, Fishing, some Trails, Modern Campsites, and one Modern Cabin.

SKI DENTON

Coudersport - *PO Box 367 (on US 6), 16915. Phone: (814) 435-2115. Web: www.skidenton.com* With slopes ranging from the steepest in the Eastern states to long, gentle beginner trails, Ski Denton draws skiers of all levels. Addition of a lighted Snowboard Park and new tube slide. Longest Run: 1 mile; 20 Slopes & Trails. Located in Denton Hill State Park. There are five cabin chalets and hostel-style group lodging located on the Ski Denton grounds.

SUSQUEHANNOCK STATE FOREST

Coudersport - *PO Box 673 (north & south of US 6), 16915. Web: www.dcnr.state.pa.us/forestry/stateforests/forests/susquehannock /susquehannock.htm Phone: (814) 274-3600.* Hiking is available on many trails in the Susquehannock State Forest, though the main trail is the Susquehannock Trail System, an 85-mile loop through the forested hills and valleys of the region. 261,784 acres of Fishing, Trails, Winter Sports, and ATV Trails.

OLE BULL STATE PARK

Cross Fork - *Box 9 (PA Route 144), 17729. Phone: (814) 435-5000. Web: www.dcnr.state.pa.us/stateparks/parks/ole.htm* The park area is referred to as the Black Forest of Pennsylvania. Its dense tree cover and mountainous terrain attracts thousands of campers along Kettle Creek. The park is named after Ole Bornemann Bull, the famous Norwegian violinist who toured this country in the 1850s. Beach, Modern Cabin rental, Fishing, Trails, and Cross-Country Skiing.

BUCKTAIL STATE PARK

Emporium - *RD 1, Box 1-A (Route 120), 15834. Phone: (814) 486-3365. Web: www.dcnr.state.pa.us/stateparks/parks/b-tail.htm* Hemmed in by mountains, this state park scenic drive follows PA Route 120 as it winds from Lock Haven to Emporium along the West Branch of the Susquehanna River and the Sinnemahoning Creek. The scenic drive has no recreational facilities. In June, the mountain laurel is in bloom and in early October the fall colors are breathtaking. Boating permitted, Fishing, and some Trails.

ELK STATE FOREST

Emporium - *RR 1, Route 155, Box 327 (258 Sizerville Road), 15834.* ***www.dcnr.state.pa.us/forestry/stateforests/forests/elk/elk.htm*** *Phone: (814) 486-3353.* Quehanna Wild Area Trail System. Fish Habitat Project on Hick's Run. Known for high quality fishing.

SIZERVILLE STATE PARK

Emporium - *RD 1, Box 238-A (PA Route 155), 15834.* ***Web: www.dcnr.state.pa.us/stateparks/parks/s-ville.htm*** *Phone: (814) 486-5605.* Within the park, you will find beautiful white pines, hemlocks, spring wild flowers, a butterfly garden and flaming fall foliage in early October. Pool, Visitor Center, and Campsites.

CHERRY SPRINGS STATE PARK

Galeton - *RD 1, Box 136 (PA Route 44 - Potter County), 16922.* ***Web: www.dcnr.state.pa.us/stateparks/parks/cherry.htm*** *Phone: (814) 435-5010.* Cherry Springs State Park is nearly as remote and wild today as it was two centuries ago, a haven for campers who like to rough it and who can appreciate one of the finest scenic drives in Pennsylvania. Public Stargazing Saturdays.

LYMAN RUN STATE PARK

Galeton - *545 Lyman Run Road, 16922. Phone: (814) 435-5010.* ***Web: www.dcnr.state.pa.us/stateparks/parks/lyman.htm*** Lyman Run State Park has been carved from the Susquehannock State Forest. The shaded picnic area is popular for picnicking and hiking, and the lake is a fishing hot spot. Beach, Campsites, Fishing, Trails.

PENNSYLVANIA LUMBER MUSEUM

5660 US 6 West (just west of PA 449)

Galeton (Coudersport) 16922

- ❑ Phone: (814) 435-2652 **Web: www.lumbermuseum.org**
- ❑ Hours: Daily 9:00am-5:00pm (April-November). Closed fall state holidays.
- ❑ Admission: $4.00 adult, $3.50 senior (61+), $2.00 child (6-12)
- ❑ Miscellaneous: The museum is set in the heart of the Susquehannock State Forest, where an abundance of State Parks, campgrounds, rental cabins and motels are available for an overnight stay.

Pennsylvania once had a prosperous lumber heritage with its wealth of white pine and hemlock trees. Now on display, are 3000+ objects including old-fashioned logging tools and a logging locomotive. The best part of the visit is the short walk to the preserved remains of, a once very busy, logging camp. See the huge sawmill (buzzing logs that have floated down river), mess hall, dormitories, rails, and engines used for transport. The well kept operational facility is extremely interesting and educational.

CRYSTAL LAKE SKI CENTER

Hughesville - *1716 Crystal Lake Rd (off US 220), 17737. Phone: (570) 584-2698. Snow Report: (570) 584-4209.* **Web: www.crystallakeskicenter.com**   The facilities include an unusual natural setting of 960 acres of mountain woodlands at elevations from 1550 to 2100 feet, several lakes and ponds, dining facilities for up to 200 in a modern, fully winterized dining hall, lodging for up to 180 in the winter months, and recreational facilities. Cross-country skiing, ice skating and snowshoeing.

HYNER RUN STATE PARK

Hyner - *Box 46 (Hyner Run Road, PA 1014), 17738. Phone: (717) 923-6000.* **Web: www.dcnr.state.pa.us/stateparks/parks/h-run.htm** The terrain of the park is generally level and occupies the small valley created by Hyner Run, with steep mountains on both sides. The park is entirely surrounded by Sproul State Forest. Pool, Campsites, one Modern Cabin, Fishing, Winter Sports, and Trails.

BENDIGO STATE PARK

Johnsonburg - *533 State Park Road, 15845. Phone: (814) 965-2646. Web: www.dcnr.state.pa.us/stateparks/parks/ben.htm* Located in a valley on a bank of the East Branch of the Clarion River, a charming streamside picnic area sits amidst a mixture of hardwood trees. A trout stream provides ample opportunities for anglers and the swimming pool is a big hit in summer. Sledding. Kinzua Bridge (very high railroad bridge).

HOLGATE TOY FACTORY

One Holgate Drive (US6 to Kane, follow signs - west of downtown)

Kane 16735

- ❑ Phone: (800) 499-1929 or (814) 837-7600
  Web: www.holgatetoy.com
- ❑ Hours: Monday-Friday 9:00am-5:00pm, Saturday 10:00am-3:00pm, Sunday Noon-3:00pm (May-December). Closed Sundays (January-April).
- ❑ Admission: FREE
- ❑ Miscellaneous: Toy Store with discount seconds at great prices. Bring your infant/preschool kid's gift list.

This is where they make "Mr. Roger's Neighborhood" trolleys! What a fun, cute place to visit and learn! The colorful shop draws kids and parents in to explore. Grandparents will love the old pull toys in the museum. All the toys are made from wood - no plastic to break or batteries to replace - We like that! While the young kids may gravitate to the play areas with toys galore (try before you buy), the older kids and adults will want to watch the operations. During some weekdays, you can see actual operators make the different pieces of a toy. The giant computerized routers are the most fun to watch. Other times, the factory is silent, but you can watch a 25 minute video of the manufacturing process. Our favorite was watching the wood shapes "dance" for the paint sprayers. Although old-fashioned toys are their namesake, they are still progressive. Their toy, the G-Yo is a geometric wood Yo Yo shaped very differently. We thought the one shaped like Mr. Roger's trolley was the coolest - and it really works!

DRAPER'S SUPER BEE APIARIES

RR #1, Box 96 (SR15 & SR238. Follow signs)

Millerton 16936

- ❑ Phone: (570) 537-2381 or (800) 233-4273
  Web: www.draperbee.com
- ❑ Hours: Monday-Friday 8:00am-5:00pm, Saturday 8:00am-1:00pm.
- ❑ Admission: FREE
- ❑ Tours: Vary per day
- ❑ Miscellaneous: Gift shop with honey products galore and bee keeping equipment for sale. They even sell "bee" theme "knick knacks" which the owner said is also found in her house.

Every visit warrants a view of the observation hive (don't worry, it's enclosed in safety glass). On tour, you'll learn about different products produced from bee hives. Hopefully, you'll be able to get to a bee site, help extract some honey, and then take a taste test. If you call ahead, Mrs. Draper might make some baked goods and beverages (Kool-Aid with honey) for you to sample. TIDBITS YOU MIGHT LEARN - The White House Presidents use Draper Honey; Wildflower honey has the most nutrients (why? - Find out!); the Queen Bee lays 2000 eggs per day (the larva are what bears really love!). Speaking of bears, can you guess how they keep the "locals" away from their outdoor hives? Learn why honey is liquefied in a "hot room" and not boiled. Learn how to identify the difference between worker bees, male drones, and the Queen. This is an extremely family-oriented, educational, and helpful (health-wise) tour given by people who care deeply about what they do. Well worth the trip into the "Endless Mountains".

SKI SAWMILL MOUNTAIN RESORT

Morris - *PO Box 5 (Rte. 220 to Rte. 287), 19963. Phone: (570) 353-7521. Snow Report: (800) 532-SNOW. **Web: www.skisawmill.com***
They have 12 slopes and 3 lifts. Peak elevation is 2,215 feet and base elevation is 1,770 feet - giving a vertical drop of 515 feet. There is also a terrain park adjacent to our double chairlift. Beginner area and tubing area.

KETTLE CREEK STATE PARK

Renovo - *Box 96 (SR 4001), 17764. Phone: (717) 923-6004. Web: www.dcnr.state.pa.us/stateparks/parks/kettle.htm* Beach, Horseback Riding, Sledding, Campsites, Fishing, Trails, Winter Sports.

SPROUL STATE FOREST

Renovo - *HCR 62 Box 90, 17764. Phone: (717) 923-6011. Web: www.dcnr.state.pa.us/forestry/stateforests/forests/sproul/sproul.htm* Horse Trails, ATV Trails (32 miles). 279,636 acres of Fishing, Camping, Winter Sports.

LITTLE LEAGUE BASEBALL MUSEUM, PETER J. MCGOVERN

US 15, **South Williamsport** 17701

❏   Phone: (570) 326-1921
      Web: www.littleleague.org/museum/index.htm
❏   Hours: Monday-Saturday 10:00am-7:00pm, Sunday Noon-
      7:00pm (Memorial Day-September). Monday, Thursday, Friday
      10:00am-5:00pm, Saturday Noon-5:00pm, Sunday Noon-4:00pm
      (October-Memorial Day).
❏   Admission: FREE
❏   Miscellaneous: The museum is next to the Little League
      International Headquarters and overlooking the Howard J.
      Lamade Little League World Series Stadium.

The birthplace of Little League is host to the world championship (nationally televised-last weekend in August). From its humble beginnings in 1939 through today and its 3 million participants in over 90 countries, the museum is a tribute to Little League Baseball. Learn about the legends, swing the bat or test your arms. Actually "Play Ball" in the batting and pitching areas, and then watch your form on instant replay. Experience the running track, push-button quiz panels, and the opportunity to do your own play-by-play commentary on a World Series game. Learn about nutrition that will help you play your best. Watch videotaped highlights of the most exciting moments of the Little League World Series.

TIADAGHTON STATE FOREST

South Williamsport - *423 E. Central Avenue, 17701. Web: www.dcnr.state.pa.us/forestry/stateforests/forests/tiadaghton/ tiadaghton.htm Phone: (570) 327-3450.* Fishing, Camping, Trails, ATV Trails, and Winter Sports.

LITTLE PINE STATE PARK

Waterville - *Box 100 (four miles north of PA 44 at Waterville and eight miles south of PA 287), 17776. Phone: (570) 753-6000. Web: www.dcnr.state.pa.us/stateparks/parks/l-pine.htm* Little Pine State Park is located in one of the most beautiful sections of the Tiadaghton State Forest in the Appalachian Mountains. Beach, Boat Rentals, Sledding, Campsites, Fishing, Trails, and Winter Sports.

HILLS CREEK STATE PARK

Wellsboro - *RD 2, Box 328 (US Route 6 or PA Route 287), 16901. Web: www.dcnr.state.pa.us/stateparks/parks/hills.htm Phone: (717) 724-4246.* Osprey, loon and waterfowl visit the lake that boasts a variety of warm water fish species. Camping, modern cabins, swimming beach and picnicking. Visitor Center and Boat Rentals.

LEONARD HARRISON STATE PARK

RR 6, Box 199 (take PA Route 660 west from Wellsboro for 10 miles), **Wellsboro** 16901

❑   Phone: (717) 724-3061
        Web: www.dcnr.state.pa.us/stateparks/parks/leon.htm

Visitor Center at Pine Creek Gorge. The "Grand Canyon" of Pennsylvania begins just south of Ansonia, along U.S. Route 6 and continues south for about 47 miles. At Leonard Harrison and Colton Point State Parks, the depth of the canyon is about 800 feet and these park locations have the most spectacular scenic overlooks. Well worth the drive off the beaten path for the scenic views! If your children are able, we suggest hiking one of the trails up or down the gorge. The Pine Creek Trail runs through the bottom of the gorge and provides great bicycling. Bring along quarters (for viewers) or binoculars to get detailed views. Rustic camping and Canoe/Raft liveries threaded throughout the park system.

TIOGA STATE FOREST

Wellsboro - *One Nessmuk Lane Rte. 287 south), 16901.* ***Web: www.dcnr.state.pa.us/forestry/stateforests/forests/tioga/tioga.htm*** *Phone: (570) 724-2868.* Discover the three state forest picnic areas that are maintained, along with two Pine Creek access areas. Fishing, Camping, Trails, Winter Sports.

CHILDREN'S DISCOVERY WORKSHOP

343 West 4th Street (Runs parallel to I-180. In YMCA building - Downtown), **Williamsport** 17701

- ❑ Phone: (570) 322-KIDS
    Web: www.williamsportymca.org/cdw/
- ❑ Hours: Tuesday-Saturday 10:00am-4:00pm, Sunday 1:00-4:00pm (Summer). Tuesday-Friday 10:00am-5:00pm, Sunday 1:00-5:00pm, Saturday 11:00am-5:00pm (September - May).
- ❑ Admission: ~$4.00 general (over age 2).
- ❑ Miscellaneous: Educational Gift Shop

This hands-on children's museum is designed for kids ages 3-11. There are many rooms of exhibits but our favorite, most unique areas were the Kids' Clinic, Human Habitrail, Ice Cream Parlor, and Funnel. The Kids' Clinic was full of actual size equipment that got the kids into the act by pretending to be nurses, doctors, or x-ray technicians (with real x-rays to review - a real hospital bed too!). The Ice Cream Parlor featured life-size equipment that taught children how to be "soda jerks". The Human Habitrail and Funnel are giant-sized environments where you would usually find small animals - but now they're re-sized for human kids! The habitrail is like the one that your hamster might play in, and the FUN-nel is like a pipe a rodent might wander through underground. Both teach adaptation to a new environment and encourage strengthening large motor skills. Well done!

HIAWATHA RIVERBOAT TOURS

Susquehanna State Park (Docked at Arch Street - US220 to Reach Road Exit - Follow signs), **Williamsport** 17701

- ❑ Phone: (570) 326-2500 or (800) 248-9287
  Web: www.citybus.org/hiawatha
- ❑ Hours: Tuesday-Sunday, 1:00, 2:30, and 4:00pm. (Summer). Weekends Only in May, September & October.
- ❑ Admission: $7.50 adult, $6.50 senior (60+), $3.50 child (3-12).
- ❑ Tours: 1 hour

An old-fashioned paddlewheel boat cruises along the river as your narrator tells tales of the river when "lumber was king". Snacks and gifts are available on board. Tuesday night is "Family Night" during the summer (reduced family rates).

LYCOMING COUNTY MUSEUM

Williamsport - *858 West 4th Street, 17701. Phone: (570) 326-3326. Web: www.lycoming.org/lchsmuseum Hours: Tuesday-Friday 9:30am-4:00pm, Saturday 11:00am-4:00pm, Sunday 1:00-4:00pm. Closed Sundays (November-April). Admission: $5.00 adult, $4.00 senior, $1.50 child (2-12).* Over 12,000 square feet of exhibits include the history of lumbering, The LaRue Shempp model train exhibit, an American Indian gallery, and period rooms. See a one room schoolhouse and a working gristmill. A changing art gallery is on the premises, also.

WILLIAMSPORT SYMPHONY ORCHESTRA

Williamsport - *220 West Fourth Street or 2990 W. Fourth St. (Community Arts Center/ high School Auditorium), 17701. Phone: (570) 322-0227. Web: www.lycoming.org/wso/* Concerts feature international guest artists performing classical and contemporary works. The Youth Orchestra focuses on cultural presentations.

WILLIAMSPORT TROLLEYS

100 Pine Street (Trolley Gazebo across from Trade/Transit Ctr. - Downtown), **Williamsport** 17701

- ❏   Phone: (800) CITY-BUS or (570) 326-2500
  Web: www.citybus.org/trolleys.html
- ❏   Hours: Tuesday, Thursday, Saturday 10:45am & 12:15pm or 1:45pm (Summer) . Call ahead to confirm times -Only 10:45 am on Saturdays.
- ❏   Admission: $3.00 general.
- ❏   Tours: Taped narration in replica streetcars - lasts about 70 minutes.

Millionaires Row (impressive mansions built by lumber barons) is the focus of this tour. Kids enjoy Memorial Park (the site of the first Little League Baseball game). For fidgety children, there are several on and off stops throughout the trip.

Chapter 5
North East Area

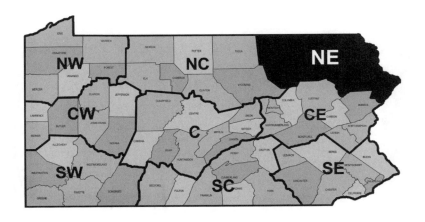

Our Favorites...

Bushkill Falls

"Claws N Paws"

Delaware Water Gap Recreation Area

Steamtown National Historic Site

Union Pacific "Big Boy" 4012

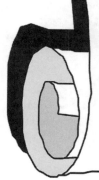

CAROUSEL WATER AND FUN PARK

Beach Lake - *Box 134 (Rte 6 East to Honesdale, then Rte 652 East), 18405. Web: www.carousel-park.com Phone: (570) 729-7532. Hours: Daily 11:00am-10:00pm (Summers) Weekends 11:00am-6:00pm (late spring/late summer). Waterslides close at 6:00pm. Admission: Pay one price ticket ($10.00-$15.00) or pay per activity ($1.50-$3.00).* Water slides (regular and juvenile), go-carts, bumper boats, Kiddie cars, wading pool, mini-golf, batting range, arcade, snack bar.

WYOMING STATE FOREST

Bloomsburg - *274 Arbutus Park Road, 17815. Phone: (570) 387-4255. Web: www.dcnr.state.pa.us/forestry/stateforests/forests/wyoming/wyoming.htm* Within the forest, visit 780 acres, first know as "Whil's Glen" due to its location at a narrow S-shaped gorge. Many ponds and overlooks.

BUSHKILL FALLS

Bushkill Falls Road (I-80 to Exit 52 - SR209 North)

Bushkill 18324

❑   Phone: (888) 628-7454 or (570) 588-6682
      Web: www.visitbushkillfalls.com
❑   Hours: 9:00am - 5:00-7:00pm (April-November). Basically
      closes before dusk sets in. Due to weather conditions, some trails
      may be restricted partly or in full.
❑   Admission: $8.00 adult, $7.00 senior, $4.00 child (4-12).
❑   Miscellaneous: Wildlife exhibit, gift shops, fishing, concessions,
      miniature golf, paddleboats.

Experience the Lenni Lanape Native Americans longhouse exhibit where kids can walk into an Indian home with "beds" - pretty neat! The main falls include Upper Canyon (craggy glen), Bridle Veil Falls (long, misty), Laurel Glen (mountain laurel wildflowers), Pennell Falls and Main Falls (over 100 foot cliff). Trails and bridges lace the area. Plan to spend at least one-half day here.

DELAWARE WATER GAP NATIONAL RECREATION AREA

(US209), **Bushkill** 18324

❑   Phone: (570) 588-2451 **Web: www.nps.gov/dewa**
❑   Admission: Only for guarded beaches (per vehicle).

Stretching over 37 miles along the Delaware River, you'll find extremely scenic roads and trails to wander along. Great canoeing & rafting (some short - kid friendly), fishing, skiing, and snowmobiling. (For updated brochures or information call 1-800-POCONOS or **www.800poconos.com**).

❑   DINGMAN'S FALLS - A flat boardwalk trail, accessible to
       wheelchair-users, leads through a hemlock ravine to the base of
       Dingmans Falls (1/2 mile round-trip, no climb.) From the base of
       the falls, a steep climb of 240 steps reaches the top of the falls.
       Rangers give guided walks to the falls on summer weekends at
       2:00 p.m. The visitor center at Dingmans Falls is closed
       indefinitely for construction. Dingmans Falls is on Johnny Bee
       Road, which is just south of the traffic light on Route 209 in
       Dingmans Ferry PA (milepost 13).
❑   BUSHKILL VISITOR'S CENTER - Daily 9:00am-5:00pm
       (summer). Weekends only in late spring and early autumn.

Both Visitor's Centers offer "ranger picked must sees" during each season. They also have a Junior Ranger program which includes a kid's self-guided exploring booklet. During the summer, rangers present programs just for kids, as well as family campfire programs and guided walks suitable for children as well as adults.

POCONO INDIAN MUSEUM

Bushkill - *PO Box 261 (SR209 North off I-80), 18324. Phone: (570) 588-9338. **Web: www.poconoindianmuseum.com** Hours: Daily 9:30am-5:30pm. Admission: $2.00-$4.00 (age 6+).* The museum recreates the life of the Delaware Indians from B.C. to the contact period with Europeans to post American Revolution. You will be given a cassette player which will guide you step by step through the museum in great detail. See their lifestyle through homes (some made of bark - and you thought they only lived in tee-pees!), weapons, and kitchen pottery. Most of these items were unearthed in the Delaware Water Gap. Boys like the "150 year old scalp" and buying an authentic "peace pipe".

FERNWOOD SKI AREA

Bushkill - *Route 209 North (20 Minutes from Camelback Ski Area), 18371. Web: http://resortsusa.com/tubing.php Phone: (888) FERNWOOD.* Spend the day snowtubing, horseback riding, ice skating or take a horse drawn sleigh ride. Longest Run: 1500 ft.; 2 Slopes & Trails. Lodging with gameroom and indoor/outdoor pools.

LACKAWANNA STATE PARK

Dalton - *RD 1, Box 230 (I-81 exit 60, travel 3 miles west on PA Route 524), 18414. Phone: (570) 945-3239. Web: www.dcnr.state.pa.us/stateparks/parks/lack.htm* Includes Salt Spring - a 36 acre natural area with old-growth hemlocks, streams and 3 waterfalls. Also Archbold Pothole - world's largest geological pothole - 38 ft. deep, 42 ft. wide. There is a campground, organized group tenting sites and a pool. Boaters and anglers enjoy the 198-acre Lackawanna Lake, and Kennedy Creek. This park is a favorite of canoeists, hikers, nature enthusiasts and campers. Biking, skiing, and snowmobiling.

WORLD'S END STATE PARK

Forksville - PO Box 62 (PA Route 42 from 1-80, then to Rte. 184), 18616. *Web: www.dcnr.state.pa.us/stateparks/parks/worlds.htm* Phone: (570) 924-3287. Virtually in a class by itself, this wild, rugged and rustic area seems almost untamed. Camping, rustic cabins and hiking on the Loyalsock Trail attracts many visitors. The scenery is spectacular, especially the June mountain laurel and Fall foliage. Canyon Vista, reached via Mineral Spring and Cold Run Roads, has outstanding views. Beach, Horseback Riding, Visitor's Center, Fishing, Boating, Horse Trails, and Winter Sports.

PROMISED LAND STATE PARK

Greentown - *RD 1, Box 96 (PA Route 390), 18426. Phone: (717) 676-3428. Web: www.dcnr.state.pa.us/stateparks/parks/p-land.htm* Promised Land lies in the heart of the Poconos. Two lakes, campgrounds, many hiking trails and beautiful scenery make the park popular in all seasons. A seasonal museum explores CCC contributions and area wildlife. Beach, Boat Rentals, Rustic Cabins, Fishing, Boating, Hiking, and Winter Sports.

CLAWS AND PAWS ANIMAL PARK

(SR590 East - then follow signs)

Hamlin 18427

- ❑ Phone: (570) 698-6154, **Web: www.clawsnpaws.com**
- ❑ Hours: Daily 10:00am-6:00pm (May-October).
- ❑ Admission: $10.95 adult, $9.95 senior (65+), $7.95 child (2-11).
- ❑ Miscellaneous: Snack bar. Gift shop. Picnic Area. Large walk-in petting zoo. Dino dig. Wild West Territory-pictures on a covered wagon, mining for gemstones and "gold" at the Gemstone Mining set-up, or see some interesting animals of the old west like buffalo (bison), prairie dog, coyote, and camel.

"Get Close to the Animals" is their theme...and you will! Many cages have glass front enclosures - so animals can walk right up to your face and you're still protected. During posted times, you can feed giraffes using a long stick or hand-feed fruits and vegetables to Lory Parrots (colorful, small, tame parrots). The animals are comfortable with visitors and they're not bashful about getting close to get a good nibble from your snack-filled hands. During the summer months they have unique Performing Parrot shows and Wildlife Encounter shows. When was the last time you saw a parrot ride a bike or you got to pet an alligator?

LAKE WALLENPAUPACK

US 6, **Hawley** 18428

- ❑　Phone: (570) 226-3191 Area Chamber
  Web: www.hawleywallenpaupackcc.com

Created as a project of the Pennsylvania Power and Light for hydroelectrics (see Visitor's Center on US6 - South of Hawley). While at the center, ask about Shuman Point, Lacawac, Ledgedale, and Beech House Creek natural and wildlife areas, all maintained for public use by PP & L. Notable attractions include:

- ❑　RITZ COMPANY PLAYHOUSE - (570) 226-9752.
- ❑　BOAT TOURS - US6, Gresham Landing. (570) 226-3293 or **www.eastshorelodging.com**. (June - October). Daily scenic tours for one half hour. Tours boats run daily from 11am to 7pm on weekends from May 1 through October and daily from June 15 through Labor Day.
- ❑　TRIPLE "W" RIDING STABLE RANCH - Beechmont Drive - off Owego Turnpike. (570) 226-2670 or **www.triplewstable.com**. Horse ranch and western riding trips from one hour to overnight camping ($25 - 100+). Overnight accommodations at Double "W" Bed and Breakfast. Year round except hunting season.

STOURBRIDGE RAIL EXCURSION

(I-84, exit 5 - SR191 north - to Main Street)

Honesdale 18431

- ❑　Phone: (570) 253-1960
  Web: www.waynecountycc.com/trhome.htm
- ❑　Hours: Sundays @ 1:30pm (Sunday before July 4th - Sunday before Labor Day), plus seasonal tours listed on their website.
- ❑　Admission: Start at $14.00 and up depending on excursion.

On the Great Train Robbery Run, see masked men from the "Triple W Ranch" ambush the train on a 3 hour round trip (includes a one-hour stop for sightseeing). Or, take a Fall Foliage Tour or one of the many holiday tours listed in Seasonal & Special Events.

HOLLEY ROSS POTTERY

LaAnna - *RR2, Box 1016 (SR191), 18326. Phone: (570) 676-3248. **Web: www.holleyross.com** Admission: FREE. Tours: Monday - Friday at 11:00am (demonstrations). Picnic area in wooded park.* Factory outlet.

SKI BIG BEAR

Lackawaxen - *HC #1 - 1A 353 Karl Hope Blvd, 18435. Phone: (570) 685-1400.* Longest Run: 6300 ft.; 10 Slopes & Trails. Skiing and Snowboarding.

MOUNT TONE SKI AREA

Lake Como - *Wallerville Road (Off Route 247), 18437. Phone: (800) 747-2SKI. **Web: www.mttone.com*** Unlike any other ski area, at Mount Tone families, youth organizations and children of all ages are their number one priority. Skiing and Snowboarding. Longest Run: 2500 ft.; 11 Slopes & Trails.

LERAYSVILLE CHEESE FACTORY

Le Raysville - *RR 2 Box 71A (Off SR467 - turn on dirt road 1/2 mile from town), 18829. Phone: (800) 859-5196 or (570) 744-2554 Hours: Daily 9:00am-5:00pm (March - December). Admission: FREE. Tours: Twice per week, they make cheese in 6000 pound vats. Call for viewing times.* The majority of the region's Amish community resides in the Le Raysville area. Their horsedrawn carriages are a common sight along the local roadways. This factory uses local milk from several local farms in the town. Specialize in traditional cheddar cheese. Store.

POCONO RACEWAY

Long Pond - *184 Sterling Road, 18344. Phone: (800) RACEWAY. **Web: www.poconoraceway.com*** NASCAR 2.5 Mile super speedway - NASCAR Winston Cup racing, 1st weekend in June, 4th weekend in July.

UPPER MILL WATERWHEEL CAFÉ

Milford - *(off US6 - follow signs), 18337. Phone: (570) 296-2383.* **Web: www.waterwheelcafe.com** *Hours: Daily 8:00am-5:00pm (May-October). Other times of year, by season. Weekend (Thursday-Sunday) evening dinner served by reservation.* An early 1800s water-powered 3 story gristmill still operates and you can watch the giant water wheel turn which drives a series of shafts, gears, and pulleys. Through the glass walls of the café, you can see the stones and grain milling equipment at work. Sit down and enjoy whole grain pancakes, muffins, and scones or multi-grain bread sandwiches.

ELECTRIC CITY TROLLEY MUSEUM

(at Cliff Street, on the grounds of the Steamtown National Historic Site, I-81 exit 185), Scranton 18503

❑　　Phone: (570) 963-6590. **Web: www.ectma.org/museum.html**

❑　　Hours: Daily (Wednesday through Sunday only - during the Winter) from 9:00am-5:00PM, except Christmas, New Years and Thanksgiving Day.

❑　　Admission: Average $3.00 museum fee. Additional average $4.00 fee for trolley ride.

A late 19th century mill building serves as the museum. Trolleys are exposed for viewing and rides. Interactive displays, where visitors will actually generate electricity and learn how this energy form is harnessed to serve transportation needs. The Electric City, a hands-on interactive kids exhibit, puts children in the operator's seat of a recreated open-style trolley car as they view a model trolley in operation on a suspended track.

❑　　TROLLEY EXCURSIONS: The scenic route follows a portion of the former Lackawanna & Wyoming Valley Railroad right-of-way as it parallels Roaring Brook and makes stops at the Historic Iron Furnaces and continues through the Crown Avenue Tunnel. At 4747 feet long, the tunnel is one of the longest interurban tunnels ever built.

LACKAWANNA COAL MINE

McDade Park (I-81, Exit 57B or 51 – follow signs)

Scranton 18503

❏ Phone: (570) 963-MINE or (800) 238-7245

Web: www.lackawannacounty.org

❏ Hours: Daily 10:00am–4:30pm (April–November). Closed Easter and Thanksgiving.

❏ Admission: $7.00 adult, $6.50 senior, $5.00 child (3-12).

❏ Company Store – souvenir coal jewelry and such. Food service. Constant 55 degrees F. below so bring along a jacket. McDade Park has excellent areas for picnics and play.

"Go down in history" where you descend (by railcar) 300 feet below the ground to see how men "hand harvested" coal. Actual miners are your guides as they share personal stories about the hard life, the work, and the dangers of digging for "black diamonds". A walking tour of three veins of mine floor.

LACKAWANNA STATE FOREST

Scranton - *401 Samters Building, 101 Penn Avenue, 18503*. ***Web: www.dcnr.state.pa.us/forestry/stateforests/forests/lackawanna/ lackawanna.htm*** *Phone: (570) 963-4561.* The name Lackawanna is the English spelling of an Indian word which means "a place where the river forks". This 6,711-acre woodland offers extensive outdoor recreational opportunities such as picnicking, hiking, backpacking, hunting, snowmobiling, cross-country skiing, fishing and nature walks.

STEAMTOWN NATIONAL HISTORICAL SITE

150 South Washington Avenue (I-81, exit 185 - toward downtown)

Scranton 18503

❏ Phone: (888) 693-9391or

❏ (570) 340-5200 **Web: www.nps.gov/stea**

❏ Hours: Daily 9:00am-5:00pm. Closed New Years Day, Thanksgiving Day, and Christmas Day.

❏ Admission: $6.00 adult, $5.00 senior (62+), $3.00 child (6-12).

❑ Tours: On Train ($10.00-$15.00 per person). 2 hours long. Reservations recommended - mostly Friday - Sunday (Late May - October).

"This is just like Thomas the Train" squealed our kids as we all saw the roundhouse come to life! This fully restored roundhouse and turntable are incredible to watch. As the Baldwin #26 enters the yard, it stops on the turntable and advances to the correct numbered house where it will "sleep" or receive maintenance. While you are out walking around the roundhouse, talk with the crew as they share stories about their jobs and the engines. The conductors love to wave and are good photograph opportunities. The Visitor's Center (mostly oriented for older kids) has both a Technology Center and History Museum of American Steam Railroading. Join a Park Ranger or a Volunteer for a walking tour through a portion of the former locomotive shops to see and learn what it takes to keep steam-era railroad equipment operational. When the train rides aren't running (Monday - Wednesday), yard shuttles operate several times daily. This is a short excursion best for younger children who can't endure a 2 hour train ride. Yard shuttles are seasonal (April - December).

PENNSYLVANIA ANTHRACITE HERITAGE MUSEUM

RD #1 - Bald Mountain Road (I-81 - Exit 57B or Exit 51 - Follow signs to McDade Park), **Scranton** 18504

❑ Phone: (570) 963-4804 or (570) 963-4845
www.phmc.state.pa.us/bhsm/toh/anthheritage/
anthraciteheritage.asp

❑ Hours: Monday - Saturday 9:00am-5:00pm, Sunday Noon-5:00pm (Closed holidays - except summer holidays).

❑ Admission: $4.00 adult, $3.50 senior (60+), $2.00 child (6-11).

Explore the culture created by life and work in the coal towns. Their collections include highlights of the mines, canals, railroads, mills, and factories. This was really hard work! To see a close-up of the mills producing iron "T" rails for America's railroads, stop over to the park setting of Scranton Iron Furnaces.

MONTAGE SKI AREA

Scranton - *1000 Montage Mountain Road, 18505. Phone: (570) 969-7669. Snow Report: (800) GOT-SNOW* **Web: www.skimontage.com** Longest Run: 1+ miles; 21 Slopes & Trails. Ice skating and snow tubing, too.

SCRANTON / WILKES-BARRE RED BARONS BASEBALL

Scranton - *225 Montage Mountain Road (Lackawanna County Stadium), 18507.* **Web: www.redbarons.com** *Phone: (570) 969-BALL.* AAA Class affiliate of the Philadelphia Phillies (April-August).

HOUDINI MUSEUM

1433 North Main Avenue (I-81 to exit 56)

Scranton 18508

❑ Phone: (570) 342-5555
   Web: www.microserve.net/~magicusa/houdini.html
❑ Hours: Weekends 1:00-4:00pm (Memorial Day – June), Daily 12:30-6:00pm (July, August – Labor Day Weekend).
❑ Admission: $7.95-$9.95 per person.
❑ Tours: Guided, thorough tours begin ~ 12:30pm and 3:00pm.
❑ Miscellaneous: Gift/Magic Shop. Admission includes video presentation and live magic shows (check website or call for exact times of shows). Very enthusiastic magicians answer questions and perform illusions before your eyes.

The world's only exhibit devoted entirely to Houdini. It helps to know the magic word if you want to get into the Famous Houdini Museum (Houdini Lives!). Houdini and his brother Hardeen toured through this area often. Now, nationally known magicians re-create these shows daily. Wander around and see Houdini's favorite trick props and photographs. How did he do it?

EVERHART MUSEUM

Scranton - *1901 Mulberry Street (Mulberry and Arthur Avenue), 18510. Phone: (570) 346-7186. Web: www.everhart-museum.org Hours: Generally, Daily Noon-5:00 pm. Closed Monday and Tuesday (Mid-October - March). PLEASE CALL FOR HOURS as they change each season. Admission: $5.00 adult, $3.00 senior, $2.00 child (6+).* Housing exhibits of American Folk, Native American, Oriental and primitive art. They also have fun exhibits for kids in the dinosaur hall and the bird collection. Children's store.

TANGLWOOD SKI AREA

Tafton - *PO Box 165 (Lake Wallenpaupack - on Route 390), 18464. Phone: (570) 226-SNOW. Snow Report: (888) 226-SNOW. Web: www.tanglwood.com* Longest Run: 1.25 miles; 10 Slopes & Trails.

TOBYHANNA STATE PARK

Tobyhanna - *PO Box 387 (accessible from I- 84 via PA Routes 507, 191 and 423), 18466. Phone: (570) 894-8336. Web: www.dcnr.state.pa.us/stateparks/parks/toby.htm* The 5,440-acre park includes the 170-acre Tobyhanna Lake. Tobyhanna is derived from an American Indian word meaning "a stream whose banks are fringed with alder." Beach, Boat Rentals, Campsites. Also in this location are Big Pocono and Gouldsboro State Parks. Trails and Winter Sports.

FRENCH AZILUM

RD #2, Box 266 (off SR187 - follow signs)

Towanda 18848

❑   Phone: (570) 265-3376
      Web: www.bradford-pa.com/sites/azilum
❑   Hours: Wednesday-Sunday 11:00am-4:00 pm. (June-August).
      Weekends 11:00am-4:30pm (May, September, October).
❑   Admission: $3.00-$5.00 (age 6+).
❑   Miscellaneous: Picnic pavilion. Nature trails.

Few sites in Pennsylvania address another country's historic events like this one does. Founded in 1793, 50 log cabins were created as a refuge for French nobility fleeing the Revolution. After Napoleon's pardon, most left the area. There are still a few log cabins standing and an 1836 LaPorte House containing period furnishings.

BRADFORD BASKET COMPANY

PO Box 157 (SR14 North - Go 1.1 miles off US 6)

Troy 16947

❑   Phone: (800) 231-9972 or (570) 297-1020
   Web: www.bradfordbaskets.com
❑   Hours: Monday-Saturday 9:00am-4:00pm.
❑   Tours: Self-guided. Monday-Friday 9:30am-1:30pm. Visitors are welcome to walk through the plant during the work day and see the baskets being made. Guided tours only for tour buses (pre-arranged with fee and souvenir)
❑   Miscellaneous: Don't look for factory seconds or discounts. They only allow first quality products to leave their facility.

See an old world craft brought back to modern day usefulness. Bradford and Bradford Wee baskets (so-o-o cute) are hand-woven maple baskets in 23 styles and trimmed in 7 colors. First watch the weavers as they form different shapes of baskets using hard maple veneer strips (2 at a time for strength). You'll see many of the different forms they use - some are really unusual shapes – like, the Millennium, the peanut, or the cloverleaf basket. It takes 6-16 weeks of training (on 3rd shift) to be good enough to be a weaver. You'll also see ladies dye strips of wood, shape and attach handles. They "hand dip" each basket individually. All baskets are personally hand-signed by the master weaver.

MT. PISGAH STATE PARK

Troy - *RD 3, Box 362 (2 miles north of US Route 6), 16947.* **Web: www.dcnr.state.pa.us/stateparks/parks/pisg.htm** *Phone: (570) 297-2734.* At the base of Mt. Pisgah and set along Mill Creek. Pool, Visitor Center, Fishing, Boating, Trails, and Winter Sports.

ELK MOUNTAIN SKI AREA

Union Dale - *RR 2, Box 3328 (I-81 exit 206), 18470. Phone: (570) 679-4400. Snow Report: (800) 233-4131 Web: www.elkskier.com* Skiing and Snowboarding. Longest Run: 1.75 miles; 27 Slopes & Trails.

WILKES-BARRE/SCRANTON PENGUINS HOCKEY

Wilkes-Barre - *415 Arena Hub Plaza, 18702. Phone: (570) 208-PENS. Web: www.wbspenguins.com* Kids Club activities, section and skate. AHL Hockey (October-early April).

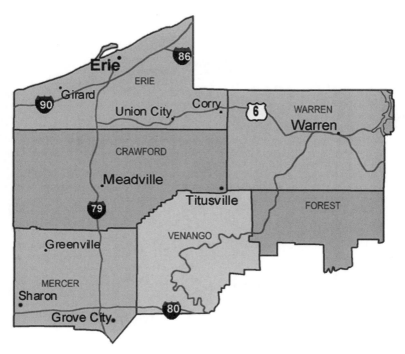

Chapter 6
North West Area

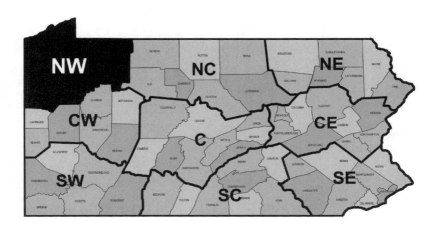

Our Favorites...

Daffins Candies

Drake Well Museum

Oil Creek & Titusville Railroad

Presque Isle State Park

Erie Maritime Area

Wendell August Forge

Drake Well Model

MOUNTAIN VIEW SKI AREA

Cambridge Springs - *14510 Mount Pleasant Road, 16403. Web: www.skiresortsguide.com/stats.cfm/pa16.htm   Phone: (814) 734-1641.* Longest Run: 2500 ft.; 9 Slopes & Trails (snowboarding and night skiing too).

CHAPMAN STATE PARK

Clarendon - *RD 2 Box 1610 (off US Route 6), 16829. Web: www.dcnr.state.pa.us/stateparks/parks/chap.htm   Phone: (814) 723-0250.* Chapman sits on the banks of the West Branch of Tionesta Creek. Among its many recreational offerings, the park boasts a 68-acre lake that provides swimming at a beach and warm and cold water fishing. Boat Rentals, Campsites, Fishing, Trails, and Winter Sports.

CLEAR CREEK STATE FOREST

Clarion - *158 South Second Avenue, 16214. Phone: (814) 226-1901. Web: www.dcnr.state.pa.us/forestry/stateforests/forests/ clearcreek/clearcreek.htm*   Points of interest within the State Forest are the Clear Creek State Park with overnight camping facilities, swimming, fishing, hiking trails, and day-use areas; Bear Town Rocks, a vista with an excellent view accessible by trail or automobile; and Hays Lot Fire Tower with a panoramic view of great distances. Visitors can tour the laurel fields located on Spring Creek Road during the early June wildflower season.

CONNEAUT LAKE PARK

Conneaut Lake - *12382 Center St (I-79, exit 147B west on Rte. 322, follow signs to PA 618), 16316. Phone: (814) 382-5115. Web: www.conneautlakepark.com   Hours: Wednesday-Sunday Noon-8:00 to 10:00pm (Memorial Day weekend-Labor Day weekend). Admission: FREE, pay for each ride or buy combo pkgs. For around $9.00.* Old-fashioned 100 year old park with rides, water attractions, kiddie land, restaurant, Camperland and beach/boardwalk. Conneaut Lake Park has over 80 rides, including the famous Blue Streak Wooden Roller Coaster (1938).

WOODEN NICKEL BUFFALO FARM

Edinboro - *5970 Koman Road (I-79 to exit 166 - go east - follow signs), 16412. **Web: www.woodennickelbuffalo.com** Phone: (814) 734-BUFF. Hours: Daily 11:00am-5:00pm (Friday-Sunday only in winter). Admission: $1.00-$2.00 per person ($10.00 per tour, minimum charge). Reservations required.* The owners loved the meat when they first tried it and decided to breed and sell buffalo products. The tour includes a talk on Bison as you view them in the pastures. You will: learn about their history and relationship with Native Americans, see the handling facilities, view authentic Native American art and Bison products in the Gift Shop. American Indian folklore and festival in July. Feel a real buffalo hide or admire cute baby bison (late July).

PRESQUE ISLE BOATS

Erie (see Presque Isle State Park, page 84)

❑ PRESQUE ISLE EXPRESS - 36 passenger water taxi departs Dobbins Landing on the mainland. (814) 881-2502. $3.00-$5.00.

❑ VICTORIAN PRINCESS - 149 passenger paddlewheel dinner cruises. (814) 459-9696.

❑ PRESQUE ISLE STATE PARK SCENIC BOAT TOURS –

- M/V Lady Kate - 110 passenger, 90 minute narrated cruises leaves several times daily (summer) and on weekends (late spring or early fall from the Perry Monument. **www.presqueisle.org/boat_tours.html** or (814) 836-0201 or $9.00-14.00 (ages 5+).

- Pontoon Boat Ride - Leaves from the Graveyard Pond Pontoon landing at 10:00am, 1:00pm, and 2:00pm. An hour long environmental excursion into the serene Lagoons. (814) 833-0351.

BICENTENNIAL OBSERVATION TOWER

Erie - *Dobbins Landing, 16501. Phone: (814) 455-6055. **Web: www.porterie.org/touring.html#tower** Hours: Open at 10:00am - closing varies seasonally between 6:00-10:00pm (April-October). Admission: $1.00-$2.00 (age 7+). Free admission on Tuesdays.*

185 foot tower with a view of Lake Erie, downtown, and Presque Isle. 210 stairs to the observation deck (or, yes, there is an elevator!). If you climb the stairs, follow the 16 stations that highlight various landmarks.

ERIE ART MUSEUM

Erie - *411 State Street, 16501. Phone: (814) 459-5477.* **Web: www.erieartmuseum.org** *Hours: Tuesday-Saturday 11:00am-5:00pm, Sunday 1:00-5:00pm. Admission: $1.00-$2.00 adult, senior, student. $0.50 child (under 12).* Art exhibits, concerts, tours and children's programs. Western and Asia; famous "The Avalon Restaurant" is a mini-sculpture of town diner and local residents.

ERIE COUNTY HISTORICAL MUSEUM

Erie - *417 - 422 State Street (I-79 to Bayfront Parkway), 16501. Phone: (814) 454-1813.* **Web: www.eriecountyhistory.org** *Hours: Tuesday-Saturday 9:00am-5:00pm. Admission: $2.00-$4.00.* Local history, architecture and industry. Cashiers House - life in Erie during the antebellum period. "Voices from Erie County History" offers glimpses into Erie County's rich heritage from the days of pre-settlement to the turn of the twenty-first century.

ERIE OTTERS HOCKEY

Erie - *809 French Street (office) (Louis J. Tullio Civic Center), 16501. Phone: (814) 452-4857 (Box Office) or 455-7779 (office)* **Web: www.ottershockey.com** *Admission: $6.00-$10.00.* Ontario Hockey League (players between the age of 16-20).

ERIE SEA WOLVES

Erie - *110 East 10th Street (office) (Jerry Uht Ballpark), 16501. Phone: (814) 456-1300.* **Web: www.seawolves.com** *Admission: $3.00-$8.00.* AA Class affiliate of the Detroit Tigers.

ERIE YOUTHEATER

Erie - *13 West 10th Street Erie Playhouse, 16501. Phone: (814) 454-2852.* **Web: www.erieplayhouse.com** Performances at playhouse and around town (Arts Festival in late June).

PRESQUE ISLE STATE PARK

PO Box 8510 (Lake Erie, reached by PA Route 832 or by boat)

Erie 16505. (see Presque Isle boat tours, page 82)

❑   Phone: (814) 833-7424

Web: www.dcnr.state.pa.us/stateparks/parks/presqueisle.htm

Seven miles of sandy beaches (Top 100 swimming holes) and it has the only surf beach in the Commonwealth. Because of the many unique habitats, Presque Isle contains a greater number of the state's endangered, threatened and rare species than any other area of comparable size in Pennsylvania. Canoe and Boat Livery. 321 species of birds. Lighthouses. Visitor Center, Year-round Education & Interpretation. Boating, Fishing, Swimming, Picnicking, Biking, Camping, Skiing, and Snowmobiling.

WALDAMEER PARK AND WATER WORLD

220 Peninsula Drive (Close to entrance of Presque Isle State Park)

Erie 16505

❑   Phone: (814) 838-3591 **Web: www.waldameer.com**
❑   Hours: Tuesday-Sunday (Mid-May - Labor Day)
❑   Admission: Per ride prices and General Admission ranging from $8.50 - $17.00.
❑   Miscellaneous: Restaurants. Tubes and life jackets are free.

Five incredible body slides, Three fabulous double tube slides, The Wild River single tube slide, A daring free fall slide, a speed slide, A refreshing Endless River innertube ride, A heated relaxing pool, Three tad pool areas with five great kiddie slides, and Beautiful parks. Thunder River log flume ride plus many more classic amusement rides in Waldameer Park. Puppet shows and concerts, too!

ERIE MARITIME MUSEUM / U.S. BRIG NIAGRA

150 East Front Street (I-79 North to Bayfront Parkway)

Erie 16507

❑   Phone: (814) 452-BRIG

Web: www.brigniagara.org/museum.htm

For updates visit our website: www.kidslovepublications.com

❑   Hours: Monday-Saturday 9:00am-5:00pm, Sunday Noon-
       5:00pm. Closed Monday-Wednesday (winter).
❑   Admission: $6.00 adult, $5.00 senior, $3.00 child (6-17).
       Reduced prices when Niagara is out of port.
❑   Miscellaneous: Shipwright gift shop.

New, artistic exhibits about the ship "Niagara" (including video),
Lake Erie ecology, the bow of the Wolverine, bilge pumps in
action, cannon fire, knots and sails surround you. Tour the flagship
"Niagara" (when in port) built to fight in the War of 1812 - the
Battle of Lake Erie - Commodore Perry. Once aboard, see over
200 oars, steered with a tiller instead of a wheel, sleeping quarters,
and rows of cannons. Do you know the difference between a Brig
(2 sails) and a ship (3 sails)? How do you preserve a ship? - Sink it
in freshwater! (it's the air & salt that causes deterioration) Why
can't cannons fire all at once on one side of the ship?

EXPERIENCE CHILDREN'S MUSEUM

420 French Street (Discovery Square) (I-79 North to Bay Front
Highway), **Erie** 16507

❑   Phone: (814) 453-3743
       www.tourerie.com/experience_childrens_museum.shtml
❑   Hours: Tuesday-Saturday 10:00am-4:00pm, Sunday 1:00-
       4:00pm. Closed Tuesday during school year.
❑   Admission: $4.00 general (ages 2+)
❑   Miscellaneous: Aimed at 2-12 year old children. The Much More
       Store gift shop.

The first floor is full of science - from giant bubble creations to
energy, light, and motion. Check out Radar Rooster weather, a
Bedrock Cave, or the New Circles and Cycles (pollution -
unregulated and innumerable, and its effects on the Lake Erie
watershed). Children are challenged to create a safe community.
The second floor is the "Gallery of the Human Experience" and
has career dress up areas, Rookie Reporter newsroom, the Corner
Store, Senses, Safety, Construction, and your heartbeat.

FIREFIGHTER'S HISTORICAL MUSEUM

Erie - *428 Chestnut Street (I-79 to Route 5), 16507. Phone: (814) 456-5969. Hours: Saturday 10:00am - 5:00pm, Sunday 1:00-5:00pm (May-August). Saturday - Sunday 1:00 - 5:00pm (September, October). Admission: $1.00 - $2.00 (students+).* The #4 Erie Firehouse has 1300+ items on display. Items include antique equipment, uniforms, badges, helmets, masks, fire extinguishers, hand pumps and horse drawn carts. They have the only display of an 1889 horse drawn fire engine and an understandable demonstration of the relay system in fire call boxes.

ERIE ZOO AND BOTANICAL GARDENS

423 West 38th Street (I-90 to exit 7)

Erie 16508

❑   Phone: (814) 864-4091, **Web: www.eriezoo.org**
❑   Hours: Daily 10:00am-5:00pm except Christmas Day and New Year's Day. Children's Zoo is open May-September.
❑   Admission: $5.50 adult, $4.75 senior (62+), $2.75 child (3-11). Slightly reduced admission in the winter.
❑   Miscellaneous: Train & Carousel rides ($1.25-$1.50 extra)

See over 300 animals (100 species). Children's Zoo - feed and pet babies - "Critter Encounters". Monkey and otter's habitats are especially fun to watch. Visit the new Kiboka Outpost with rhinos, cheetahs and warthogs. Various gardens include the Butterfly gardens, the Greenhouse, and the great gardens at Kiboka Outpost where the rhinos roam.

MARX TOY MUSEUM

Erie - *50 East Bloomfield Parkway, 16509. Phone: (814) 825-6500. Hours: Daily (except Tuesday) 1:00-5:00pm (June-September). Friday, Saturday, Sunday only (October-May). Admission: $1.00-$3.00 (age 5+).* Not all the monkeys are in the Zoo. The Marx Toy Museum, Inc. has a few monkeys on display as well as other toys. Parents, remember the Johnny West action figures you played with as a kid? Remember riding the world's first three-wheeled speed cycle: the Big Wheel? Or remember having fun on the Krazy Kar or the Rock'Em Sock'Em Robot? These toys plus hundreds more Marx Toys ranging from 1920 through 1970 are on display.

SPLASH LAGOON

Peach Street (I-90 exit 24, Rte. 19 south), **Erie** 16509

❑ Phone: (866) 3-SPLASH **Web: www.splashlagoon.com**
❑ Hours: Generally 9:00am-10:00pm.
❑ Admission: Waterpark passes are $15.00 each.
❑ Miscellaneous: 4 hotels are part of the indoor waterpark resort and are directly connected to Splash Lagoon (range $200-$300, include 4-6 waterpark passes and one or two complimentary meals).

A new indoor waterpark resort with a: Tree House packed with interactive water fun, 48-Ft Tall Tipping Bucket regularly dumps 1,000 gallons of water, 4 twisting & turning 4-story high Body Slides, A Swirling Body Coaster with speeds of over 40 MPH, Swirling Tube Coaster for 1 or 2 riders, Two 25 Person whirlpools, Laaaazy River, Activity Pool featuring 8 water basketball hoops, Dancing Water Play Area, Little People Activity Pool with zero depth entry, 6,000 Sq. Ft. Arcade, Lazer Tag Arena, and Food Court.

TRI-CITY SPEEDWAY

Franklin - *(7 miles north of Franklin on Route 417), 16248.* **Web: www.tricityspeedway.com** *Phone: (814) 473-4038 or (814) 676-1681.* Tri-City Speedway offers exciting stock car, sprint car, and modifieds racing in addition to special events like demolition derbys and school bus races.

DEBENCE ANTIQUE MUSIC MUSEUM

1261 Liberty Street (Downtown, off I-80 to exit 3)

Franklin 16323

❑   Phone: (814) 432-5668 or (888) 547-2377
       Web: www.debencemusicworld.com
❑   Hours: Tuesday-Saturday 11:00am-4:00pm, Sunday 12:30-
       4:00pm (mid-March - October). Long weekends in November
       thru before Christmas.
❑   Admission: $8.00 adult, $7.00 senior (60+), $3.00 child (3-12).

"To See and Hear Museum". 100+ antique, automated music machines from the gay 90's - roaring 20's. See and hear demonstrations of nickelodeons, Swiss & German music boxes, waltzes and polkas, merry-go-round band organs, calliopes, player pianos, and a variety of antique organs. We were most fascinated by the nickelodeons that had glass panel inserts showing the musical instrument "guts". This was the first time we have ever seen a violin or accordion playing as an accompaniment. Be sure grandparents are along for this visit.

BRUCKER GREAT BLUE HERON SANCTUARY

Greenville - *(SR18 - Thiel College), 16125. Phone: (724) 589-2117.* 400 Blue Herons nest here - the largest colony in Pennsylvania (over 200 nests). Most are over 4 feet tall with a 7 foot wingspan - and they can fly up to 35 MPH! Nesting (March - May). Fly ins (June - August). Fall migrations. FREE. Open dawn to dusk.

CANAL MUSEUM

Greenville - *60 Alan Avenue (Lock 22 - Alan Avenue, near Riverside Park), 16125. Phone: (724) 588-7540. Hours: Tuesday-Sunday 1:00-5:00pm (summer). Weekends only (May, September, October). Admission: Small admission for students+.* History of Erie Extension Canal - artifacts like tools and photographs. The Erie Extension Canal played a vital role as the first efficient transportation into northwestern Pennsylvania for settlers and commerce. Great Lakes iron ore was shipped on the canal, which was combined with coal at iron and steel mills. Small settlements along the canal grew, forming new towns. See a full size replica of an 1840s canal boat - Rufus Reed, and view a working model of a canal lock.

GREENVILLE RAILROAD PARK AND MUSEUM

Greenville - *314 Main Street - Rte. 358, 16125. Phone: (724) 588-4009. Web: http://members.tripod.com/~greenville/rrpark.html Hours: Daily 1:00-5:00pm (Summer). Weekends only (May, September, October). Admission: Free.* Climb aboard the largest switch engine - #604 - used in the steel industry. Plenty of railroad cars - hopper cars, cabooses, and a 1914 Empire auto touring car. World's first parachute invented by local Stefan Banie in 1914. Stationmasters quarters, dispatch office and displays of railroad uniforms.

BISON HAVEN RANCH

Grove City - *316 Elliott Road (I-80 exit 3A to SR173 North), 16127. Phone: (724) 458-9199. Hours: Monday-Saturday 9:00am-6:00pm, Sunday 1:00-6:00pm. Admission: $1.00-$2.00 per person (pre-arranged tour).* View farm raised bison that produce a low fat, nutritional meat used for food, clothing, shelter, and the focus of many folklores. 36+ bison are in an average herd.

WENDELL AUGUST FORGE

620 North Madison Avenue (I-79, exit 31 or I-80, exit 3A - follow signs), **Grove City** 16127

❑   Phone: (800) WAF-GIFT or (724) 458-8360
      Web: www.wendellaugust.com
❑   Hours: Monday-Saturday 9:00am-4:00pm (except several days
      surrounding holidays).
❑   Admission: FREE
❑   Miscellaneous: Country's oldest and largest forge producing
      aluminum, pewter, sterling silver, and bronze items by hand. Old
      time Nickelodeon, W.A. Parrot (who talks and does impressions,
      LGB train on a surrounding track up above and a 225 gallon
      ocean reef tank. These keep the kids amused while adults gift
      shop.

A self-guided tour of the production workshop is fascinating to watch as metal is taken through an eleven step process. The gift metal is hammered over a pre-designed template with random hand, or machine-operated hammer motions. At one point, you'll get a chance to pick up a hammer that is used - they weigh up to 3 pounds. You'll understand why a craftsman thought to automate the hammering process - tired, tired hands! Once the impression is set, the item is forged (put in a log fire) to produce smoke marks that bring out the detail of the design. The item is cooled and cleaned and finished by thinning the edges. Each piece is marked with a sign particular to the craftsman. This is a wonderful place to show children the balance between old world craft and new, automated craftsmanship.

PHILADELPHIA CANDIES

1546 East State Street (off SR18 North)

Hermitage 16148

- ❑   Phone: (724) 981-6341 **Web: www.philadelphia-candies.com**
- ❑   Hours: Daily 9:00am-4:00pm (lunch between 12:00-1:00pm).
- ❑   Admission: FREE
- ❑   Tours: Pre-arranged, 15-20 minutes around floor.

Have you ever tried chocolate covered potato chips? We have - and this is where you can see them being made! Here are some "fun" numbers for you: 30,000 square foot facility, 80 year old family business, 7000 pounds of chocolate are melted at one time, sugar comes in 50 pounds bags, & corn syrup is delivered in 55 gallon drums!

PYMATUNING DEER PARK

Route 58, East Jamestown Road (off US 322, 3 Miles South of Pymatuning Dam), **Jamestown** 16134

- ❑   Phone: (724) 932-3200
- ❑   Hours: Monday - Friday 10:00am-5:00pm, Saturday, Sunday, Holidays 10:00am-6:00pm (Summer). Weekends only in May, September & October (weather permitting).
- ❑   Admission: Average $4.00 per person.
- ❑   Miscellaneous: Train and pony rides.

Petting zoo plus other animals like lions, tigers, bears, camels, and kangaroos (and farm animals). 200 animals in all.

PYMATUNING STATE PARK

Box 425 (accessible by U.S. Route 6, U.S. Route 322, PA Route 18, PA Route 285, and PA Route 58), **Jamestown** 16134

❑ Phone: (724) 932-3141

   Web: www.dcnr.state.pa.us/stateparks/parks/pyma.htm

❑ Miscellaneous: Annual Snow Fun Days-ice fishing, ice skating, ice boating, cross-country skiing, and snowmobiling.

Flood control reservoir along the Ohio border. The largest body of water in the state. Wildlife Museum - state's largest colony of nesting eagles. The Lionsville water "spillway" is perhaps one of the best known locations in the park. The fish are so crowded that the ducks walk on the fishs' back to compete for the food fed by the visitors. Beach, Boat Rentals, Sledding, Campsites, Modern Cabins, Fishing, and Trails.

CORNPLANTER STATE FOREST

North Warren - *323 N. State Street, 16365. Phone: (814) 723-0262.* **Web: www.dcnr.state.pa.us/forestry/stateforests/forests/cornplanter/cornplanter.htm** 1,256 acres named for Chief Cornplanter, a famous Indian Chief of the Seneca tribe. Highlights include Hunter Run Demonstration Area and Lasure Trail. Winter Sports, ATV Trails.

OIL CREEK STATE PARK

Oil City - *RD 1, Box 207 (the main entrance to the park is off of PA Route 8), 16301. Phone: (814) 676-5915.* **Web: www.dcnr.state.pa.us/stateparks/parks/o-crek.htm** The site of the world's first commercial oil well, this park tells the story of the early petroleum industry by interpreting oil boom towns, oil wells and early transportation. Many sites can be seen while traveling the 9.5-mile paved bicycle trail through the scenic Oil Creek Gorge, or on an excursion train. Petroleum Centre - displays and programs on oil history. Wildcat Hollow - outdoor classroom and 4 theme trails. Boat Rentals, Sledding, Fishing, and Cross-Country Skiing.

VENANGO MUSEUM OF ART, SCIENCE, & INDUSTRY

Oil City - *270 Seneca Street, 16301. Phone: (814) 676-2007. Web: www.ibp.com/pit/venango Hours: Tuesday - Saturday, 10:00am-4:00pm, Sunday, 1:00-4:00pm. Admission: Adults $2.00, Children $0.75 (12 and under).* Learn about the various cultures that have inhabited this land, the industries that have shaped their economy, and the natural resources that this area provides. Kids will love the annual "Scientrific" hands-on elementary physics exhibit.

GODDARD STATE PARK, MAURICE K.

Sandy Lake - *684 Lake Wilhelm Road (I-79 exit 34, west on Rte. 358), 16145. Web: www.dcnr.state.pa.us/stateparks/parks/godd.htm Phone: (724) 253-4833.* The 1,860-acre Lake Wilhelm is an angler's paradise. The large lake, abundant wetlands, old fields and mature forests provide a diversity of habitats that attracts wildlife in all seasons. Boat Rentals, Sledding, Trails, and Winter Sports.

DAFFIN'S CANDIES

496 East State Street (Factory - 7 Spearman Avenue, SR60 in nearby Farrell)

Sharon 16146

❏ Phone: (724) 342-2892 **Web: www.daffins.com**

❏ Hours: Monday-Saturday 9:00am-9:00pm, Sunday 11:00am-5:00pm.

❏ Admission: FREE

❏ Tours: Monday - Friday 9:00am-3:00pm (lunch 12:00 - 1:00 pm). Tuesday or Wednesday only (summer). By reservations. 15+ people (add-ons to other groups accepted). 45 minutes long.

❏ Miscellaneous: Tours in the fall and winter are best - more activity preparing for Christmas and Easter Holidays. The Chocolate Kingdom is available to view whenever the store is open.

Start in the Chocolate Kingdom. The display is filled with giant rabbits, elephants, turtles and castles made of chocolate. Click a picture or pick up free postcard pictures of these unique creatures. Each giant figurine can require up to 700 lbs. of chocolate! As the tour continues, you'll learn how cocoa beans are removed from pods, mashed into paste, and finally processed into the chocolate forms we all know and love. Daffin's still hosts its annual event known as Swizzle Stick Day on the Sunday before Palm Sunday. The facility holds plant tours that day, drawing nearly 8,000 people during the four-hour session. Regular factory tours are also available year-round. At the Factory, the group will see a short video tape of Daffin's and the History of chocolates. The seven foot Rabbit and other artistic chocolate items are also on display at the factory. Then, the group will take a tour thru the factory and see how some chocolates are made. At the end of the tour, each person will receive a candy sample.

DRAKE WELL MUSEUM

East Bloss Street, 205 Museum Lane (I-80 to exit 3, off SR8 North)

Titusville 16354

- ❑ Phone: (814) 827-2797, **Web: www.drakewell.org**
- ❑ Hours: Monday-Saturday 9:00am-5:00pm, Sunday 10:00am-5:00pm (May-October). Tuesday-Saturday 9:00am-5:00pm, Sunday Noon-5:00pm (November-April). Closed most holidays except summer holidays.
- ❑ Admission: $5.00 adult, $4.00 senior (50+), $2.00 student (7-17). Reduced adult fares, winter hours.
- ❑ Miscellaneous: Head over to Pithole City (off SR227 between Pleasantville and Plummer) Visitor's Center (June-Labor Day). Within the park is a bike trail and tourist train ride depot. Magic Lantern Shows (old-fashioned movies using glass slides to illustrate stories, songs and comedy) and Blacksmith demos occasional Saturdays each month. Look at Calendar of Events.

The birthplace of the petroleum industry. Edward Drake drilled the first oil well in 1859 through layers of sandstone. Start your visit with a video about the challenges Drake and his driller, "Uncle" Billy Smith faced to succeed. The museum's indoor and outdoor exhibits explain the progress of the oil industry. Operating oil field machinery, historic buildings, and scale models demonstrate primitive and modern drilling processes. Many exhibits have "push buttons" and "cutaways" of the machinery in action (the kids will really like pushing the small button to make all the working parts move). And, they can "squeeze and sniff" oil samples from all over the world, make plastic, send telegraph messages, and find the only object NOT made from oil in the museum lobby. Some will surprise you (ex. Tape, aspirin, eggs). Be sure to purchase a souvenir vial of real crude Pennsylvania oil in the Museum Store and eat your ice cream on the patio.

OIL CREEK & TITUSVILLE RAILROAD

409 South Perry Street (I-80 exit Route 8 north to Perry Street Station), **Titusville** 16354

- ❑   Phone: (814) 676-1733 **Web: http://octrr.clarion.edu**
- ❑   Hours: Weekend departures at 1:00pm (June-September). Selected weekday runs in July, August and October. (October weekends at 11:00am and 3:00pm)
- ❑   Admission: $12.00 adult, $11.00 senior (60+), $8.00 child (3-12). $1.00 off admission if order tickets ahead of time.
- ❑   Tours: 2 1/2 hour narrated trip by guide and audio recording.
- ❑   Miscellaneous: Railroad memorabilia displays, souvenir area, and snack shop.

See the first oil fields in the world tell a story of the oil rush boom days in the valley (similar to the gold rush). Stop by Rynd Farm and Drake Well Park. Ride in restored 1930's passenger cars. One car is the only working railway Post Office car - have your postcard to grandma hand-stamp cancelled while on board.

ALLEGHENY NATIONAL FOREST

Warren - *PO Box 847, 222 Liberty Street, 16365. Phone: (814) 723-5150.   Web: www.fs.fed.us/r9/allegheny/*   Visit Pennsylvania's wilderness land with 400-year-old forests, 120 miles of trout streams, and where deer, elk, and bear roam the hills. 600 miles of trails. Hundreds of Mountain Laurel in June. 1/2 million acres of land. Twin Lakes and Loleta Recreation Areas. Black Cherry and Tracy Ridge trails. Longhouse Byway and Old Powerhouse. Rimrock Overlook, Jake's Rock, Buzzard Swamp and Owl's Nest.

KINZUA DAM/ BIG BEND VISITOR'S CENTER

Warren - *1205 Kinzua Road - Route 59 (I-79 to Route 6 east to Route 59 east), 16365. Phone: (814) 726-0661.* **Web:** *www.lrp.usace.army.mil/rec/lakes/kinzuala.htm*   Hours: Daily 10:00am-4:00pm (Summer). Weekends (September, October). Admission: FREE.*   A flood control dam has created a vast waterway known as the Allegheny Reservoir (within the Allegheny National Forest). Center features exhibits, displays, and slide programs which explain the purpose of the dam and power plant.

Chapter 7
South Central Area

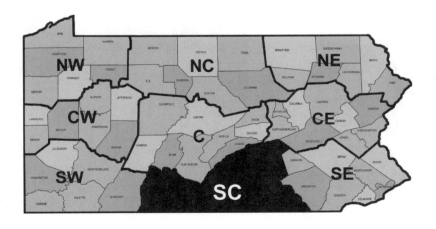

Our Favorites...

American Civil War Wax Museum
Gettysburg National Park
Hershey's Chocolate World & Park
Land of Little Horses
Lincoln Train Museum
National Apple Museum
Snack Food Tours (Utz, Snyder's)
State Museum & Capitol
Wolfgang Candy Company Tour
York County Heritage Museum

Kids Love Hershey's Chocolate World !

INDIAN STEPS MUSEUM

Airville - *205 Indian Steps Road (4 1/2 miles Northeast on SR425), 17302.* **Web:** ***www.fieldtrip.com/pa/77553777.htm*** *Phone: (717) 993-3392. Hours: Thursday-Sunday 10:00am-4:00pm (Mid-April - Mid-October). Admission: Donations. Miscellaneous: Nature Center Arboretum.* See Indian artifacts from 10,000 BC - Susquehanna Indians through Colonial times that are imbedded in rock. A 350 year old holly tree on the property has a unique story. Each year a twig is broken off and presented to the Pennsylvania Power and Light Company as payment for rent of the land behind the museum.

FORT BEDFORD MUSEUM

Fort Bedford Drive (I-76, exit 11, SR320 - Pitt Street - Downtown)

Bedford 15522

❑ Phone: (814) 623-8891 or (800) 259-4284
   Web: www.bedfordcounty.net/attract/fort

❑ Hours: Daily 10:00am-5:00pm (June-August). Daily except
   Tuesday (May, September, October).

❑ Admission: Generally $2.00-$3.00.

The French and Indian War fort site - "The Fort in the Forest". A blockhouse structure that houses the large scale model of the original fort along with Native American household artifacts. From flint rock rifles to hand tools to clothing – each help you explore pioneer and frontier days in western Pennsylvania. In order to secure the water and secure the banks of the stream, a gallery with loopholes extended from the central bastion on its north front down to the water's edge. A ladder-like arrangement of steps led down the river's bluff-like south bank. This enclosed gallery was a real military curiosity. The fort controlled the river gap and served a British stockade against the French for years.

OLD BEDFORD VILLAGE

220 Sawblade Road (1/2 mile south of PA Turnpike (I-70/76), exit
11- Route 220), **Bedford** 15522

- ❑   Phone: (814) 623-1156 or (800) 238-4347
      Web: www.oldbedfordvillage.org
- ❑   Hours: Daily (except Wednesday) 9:00am-5:00pm (Memorial
      Day-Labor Day). Thursday-Sunday 10:00am-4:00pm
      (September/October).
- ❑   Admission: $8.00 adult, $4.00 student (age 6+). Ask about senior
      discount.
- ❑   Tours: Self-guided. Guided tours are available with advance
      notice.
- ❑   Miscellaneous: Dress for walking on the natural roadways.
      Pendergrass Tavern.

Craftsmen are in action as you relive the past walking through 40
log homes and shops (see them making brooms, baskets, bread,
pottery). There are seasonal productions such as "Welcome to
Early America" - a recreated world of the 1790's Pioneer America
or summer theatre musical, comedies or mysteries (814-623-7555
for reservations).   In 1794, President George Washington led
federal troops with his battle headquarters here in Bedford. After
the troops left, the colonial industry flourished with blacksmiths,
attorneys, a doctor, distillers, innkeepers, soldiers, millers, and
farmers setting up shop in the village. In all, over 14 period skills
are represented at the Village, and many of the products made on
site can be found at the Village Craft Shop. And don't miss the
opportunity to learn one of the many crafts available through Old
Bedford Village's educational programs.

NATIONAL APPLE MUSEUM

154 West Hanover Street (US 30 west to York to SR234 & SR394 -
Look for big red barn), **Biglerville** 17307

- ❑   Phone: (717) 677-4556
      Web: www.uasd.k12.pa.us/upperadams/appmus/apple1.htm
- ❑   Hours: Saturday 10:00am-5:00pm, Sunday Noon-5:00pm (April-
      October). Call for special group arrangement during other times.

For updates visit our website: www.kidslovepublications.com

- ❑ Admission: $2.00 adult, $1.00 child (6-12).
- ❑ Tours: Guided every 2 hours (last one at 4:00pm). Self-guided audio tape tours.
- ❑ Miscellaneous: Picnic area. Gift shop - guess what…everything in there has apples on it!

What a treat this place is! America's favorite fruit (red delicious, the most popular) is highlighted here. Kids can get involved right from the beginning (they eat a snack of apple juice and cookies). As you sip on your juice, they show a film about apple varieties, picking, and production (bet you didn't know the apple is part of the rose family!). This film is very entertaining (not boring at all) and the kids are thrilled seeing thousands of apples in every scene. Because many apple production facilities don't give tours, you'll get a great video look at how they "produce" apples for applesauce. How do they keep apples unbruised and ripe all year long? Antique equipment displays and old town dioramas are upstairs. The bug displays really appeal to the kids. See the "apple biz" come to life when you drive just up the road through apple orchards. Do you know why orchards love bees, ladybug beetles, and dwarf trees?

TUSCARORA STATE FOREST

Blain - *RD 1, Box 42-A, 17006. Phone: (717) 536-3191.* **Web: www.dcnr.state.pa.us/forestry/stateforests/forests/tuscarora/tusca rora.htm** Derives its name from Tuscarora Mountain, and the mountain was named for the Tuscarora Indians, a tribe adopted by the Iroquois Nation. Horse Trails, Fishing, Camping, Trails, Winter Sports.

HOPE ACRES FARM, HOME OF THE BROWN COW

Brogue - *2680 Delta Road (PA Rte. 74 southeast off US 30), 17309. Phone: (800) 293-1054.* **Web: www.hopeacres.com** *Admission: $3.00-$6.00 per person. Includes a free ice cream cone at end of tour. Tours: Tuesday, Friday & Saturday at 10:00am and 2:00pm. Length of tour: 1 to 1 1/2 hour.* Tour the Brown Cow's processing facilities, then head to Hope Acres farm where you will see 100% automated robotic milking. They call them Astronauts machines. They are currently one of four farms in the country testing these robotics. You will also see our beef operation & grainery.

KINGS GAP STATE PARK

Carlisle - *500 Kings Gap Road, 17013. Phone: (717) 486-5031.*
Web: www.dcnr.state.pa.us/stateparks/parks/k-gap.htm Kings
Gap offers a panoramic view of the Cumberland Valley. Sixteen
miles of hiking trails interconnect three main areas and are open
year-round. Kings Gap offers environmental education programs
from the pre-school environmental awareness program to
environmental problem solving programs.

SKI LIBERTY

Carroll Valley - *78 Country Club Trail (Rte. 30 to Rte. 116,
Liberty Mountain Resort is 8 miles on the left), 17320. Phone:
(717) 642-8282. **Web: www.skiliberty.com*** Skiing, Snowboarding
and Snow Tubing. Longest Run: 5300 ft.; 16 Slopes & Trails.
Snow Monsters Kids club.

CALEDONIA STATE PARK

Fayetteville - *40 Rocky Mountain Rd (US Route 30), 17222.*
Web: www.dcnr.state.pa.us/stateparks/parks/caledonia.htm
Phone: (717) 352-2161. Known locally as South Mountain,
Caledonia located on the northern-most section of the Blue Ridge
Mountains fifteen miles west of Gettysburg via Route 30. The
Appalachian Trail passes through the central portion of the park. It
is a great place for family outings: Pool, Visitor Center, Campsites,
Modern Cabins, Fishing, Trails, and Cross-Country Skiing. Mr.
Ed's Elephant Museum (a collection of 6000 elephants) is open
daily just 2 miles east of the park on Rte. 30 (717-352-3792).

MICHAUX STATE FOREST

Fayetteville - *10099 Lincoln Way East, 17222. Phone: (717) 352-
2211. **Web: www.dcnr.state.pa.us/forestry/stateforests/forests/
michaux/michaux.htm*** The Michaux State Forest spans Adams,
Cumberland and Franklin counties. In 1785, a French botanist,
Andre Michaux, sent by France to gather plants for the Royal
Gardens, identified numerous flowers, shrubs and trees. From the
mid-eighteenth century to the early twentieth century, large iron
companies owned much of the forest. Iron furnaces processed iron
ore, which was forged into iron implements, cannonballs, and

stoves. The iron companies needed large tracts of woodland to cut and burn for the charcoal-fueled furnaces. There are miles of trout streams and many lakes and reservoirs for fishing. Camping, hiking, horseback riding, bicycling, cross-country skiing and snowmobiling are some recreational activities.

TOTEM POLE PLAYHOUSE

Fayetteville - *9555 Golf Road, Caledonia State Park (Junction of US 30 & PA233), 17222. Phone: (717) 352-2164.* **Web:** **www.totempoleplayhouse.org** *(June-August) Admission: Varies by performance, $20.00+ (Children under 5 not admitted).* Professional theatre featuring comedies and musicals plus Summer Theatre Camps.

COWAN'S GAP STATE PARK

Fort Loudon - *(PA 75 North to Richmond Furnace, follow signs), 17224.* **Web:** **www.dcnr.state.pa.us/stateparks/parks/cowansgap.htm** *Phone: (717) 485-3948.* Beach, Visitor Center, Boat Rentals, Campsites, Rustic Cabins, and Winter Activities. Buchanan's Birthplace State Historical Park nearby. Environmental Education and Interpretation (April-November).

PINE GROVE FURNACE STATE PARK

Gardners - *1100 Pine Grove Road (PA Route 233 & 34), 17324.* **Web:** **www.dcnr.state.pa.us/stateparks/parks/pine.htm** *Phone: (717) 486-7174.* This park was once the site of the Pine Grove Furnace Iron Works that dates from 1764. Historical buildings include the ironmaster's mansion, a gristmill, an inn and several residences. The self-guiding historical trail leads you through the remains of the iron works. The Appalachian Trail passes through the park. Beach, Visitor Center, Boat Rentals, Campsites, Kite-flying Area. Fishing, Trails, and Cross-Country Skiing.

AMERICAN CIVIL WAR WAX MUSEUM

297 Steinwehr Avenue (US15 - Business Route)

Gettysburg 17325

❑   Phone: (717) 334-6245 **Web: www.e-gettysburg.cc**

❑   Hours: Daily 9:00am-9:00pm (Summer), Daily 9:00am-7:00pm (mid-April - mid-June), Daily 9:00am-5:00pm (September - December, March - Mid-April), Weekends Only (Winter).

❑   Admission: $5.50 adult, $3.50 student (13-17), $2.50 child (6-12).

More than 200 life-size wax figures in 30 different scenes re-create crucial moments but also describe the cause and effects of the conflict. Besides strategic planning and battle scenes, voices from history blend with scenes and words to recreate the past. Jennie Wade bakes bread before being fatally shot in her sister's kitchen. John Brown, bound in ropes, walks to the gallows. Slaves using the Underground Railroad try to escape to freedom. And Abraham Lincoln sits in the theatre on that fateful day. The last scene is of an animated wax figure of Lincoln making his speech the night before his famous address. At the end of the tour, you'll enter the Battleroom Auditorium where the battle is re-enacted (with wax figures and lighting). It's an easy explanation of the three days of battle (not too technical for kids). Lincoln arrives and gives his address at the end.

BATTLEFIELD BUS TOURS

Gettysburg - *778 Baltimore Street, 17325. Phone: (717) 334-6296* **Web: www.gettysburgbattlefieldtours.com** *Hours: Daily 9:00am-9:00pm (Summer), 9:00am-7:00pm (Spring & Fall), 9:00am-5:00pm (rest of year). Weather permitting. Admission: $17.95 adult, $12.35 child (4-11). Tours: 23 mile tour of "The Battle of Gettysburg". 2 hour narration audiotape tours leave several times daily, depending on season. Call to reserve tickets for specific tour times.* A Hollywood cast of actors, technicians, and special effects recreate the Battle of Gettysburg as you tour the Battlefield from the famous Double Decker buses (seasonal, warm months) that have become a landmark in Gettysburg. Enclosed bus for other cold, rainy season tours.

BOYD'S BEAR COUNTRY

Gettysburg - *75 Cunningham Road (off Bus. Rte. 15, near Emmitsburg Rd.), 17325. Phone: (717) 630 - 2600.* **Web:** *www.boydsbearcountry.com Hours: Daily 10:00am - 6:00pm except New Years, Easter, Thanksgiving and Christmas. Admission: FREE. Miscellaneous: Restaurants on premises. Dress-your-own bears and seasonal crafts area.* The World's Most Humongous Teddy Bear Store and museum. Get a history of the Boyds Collection…its product and the life story of the founder. Your tour is led by Bennie B., an overstuffed (and overfed!) Boyd's Bear who serves as the resident historian. The museum includes a replica of Gary's father's butcher shop in New York City (where Gary learned business tricks and tips!); neat photos and memorabilia of Gary's growin' up years and experiences as a Peace Corps volunteer; displays of early Boyd's duck decoys, Gnomes Homes, early plush and resin, and other stuff that made Boyd's famous; and sections dedicated to QVC shows, collectors' club, and charitable activities. They've built a display of virtually every Boyd's plush critter ever made.

EXPLORE & MORE CHILDREN'S MUSEUM

20 East High Street (near the circle), **Gettysburg** 17325

❑ Phone: (717) 337-9151 **Web: www.exploreandmore.com**
❑ Hours: Monday-Saturday 10:00am-5:00pm (May–August). Hours vary slightly rest of year
❑ Admission: $3.50 adult (age 15+), $5.50 child (2-14).
❑ Miscellaneous: Toy store. Drop off child care service.

Located in an historic home, they have seven rooms where children can create a work of art, play house the way people lived around the time of the Civil War, make a bubble large enough to stand inside of, or experiment with mixing colors (make color explosions in milk!) and waterworks. Children can make puppets and then perform a show with them. More pretend play in the Hard Hat area (receiving, conveyor, shipping, recycling – clean up) or the Black Light Dress Up Room (wild!). At this place, you can even play with an overhead projector, just like teacher. Give your children a break from the battlefield nearby!

FARNSWORTH HOUSE INN

Gettysburg - *401 Baltimore Street, 17325. Phone: (717) 334-8838*
Web: www.farnsworthhousedining.com   *Hours: Lunch/Dinner -
Moderate lunch prices, fine dining dinner.*   A historic building
with 100 bullet holes from the battle. Gettysburg's only Civil War
dining. Tours are available. We recommend a lunch
(indoor/outdoor) because the menu at lunch is kid friendly and
casual.

GETTYSBURG BATTLE THEATRE

Gettysburg - *571 Steinwehr Avenue, 17325. Phone: (717) 334-
6296. Hours: Daily 9:00am-9:00pm (Summer), Daily 9:00am-
7:00pm (April, May, September, October), 9:00am - 5:00pm
(March, November, December). Admission: $3.50-$6.00 (age 6+).*
Begin with a viewing of a movie featuring a multi-media battle re-
enactment. To further visualize the battlement during the Civil
War, take a close look at the electronic map and a complete
Battlefield Diorama of 25,000 hand-painted miniature soldiers.
Learn what role your home state played in the Battle. See the
Armies arrival, battle lines forming, and the advances and retreats
of the struggling Armies. Jim Getty, who portrayed Abraham
Lincoln in the first person, occasionally can be still be seen at the
Gettysburg Battle Theatre.

GETTYSBURG HORSE / BIKE RENTALS

Gettysburg 17325

Artillery Ridge Camping Resort. 610 Taneytown Rd. (717) 334-
1288. Horseback riding rentals. Gettysburg Miniature Battlefield
Diorama - View the "Whole Battlefield" as it appeared in 1863.
Included is a light & sound show, with over 20,000 hand painted
miniatures. Blazing Saddles. **www.blazingsaddles.com** or (717)
337-0700. Bike rentals.

GETTYSBURG NATIONAL MILITARY PARK
97 Taneytown Road (SR134 or Steinwehr Ave. -Bus. 15)
Gettysburg 17325

❑   Phone: (717) 334-1124 Park or (717) 338-9114 Eisenhower Site
Web: www.nps.gov/gett

❑   Hours: Daily 8:00am-5:00pm. Closed Thanksgiving, Christmas
and New Years.

❑   Admission: *Visitor Center/Battlefield* - FREE.
Cyclorama/Electric Map - $2.00-$3.00 (age 6+) for each exhibit.
Eisenhower Site - $7.00 adult, $4.00 child (13-16) and $2.50
child (6-12)

❑   Tours: Park grounds and roads - Self guided tours 6:00am -
10:00pm. Eisenhower Site - All visits to the Eisenhower National
Historic Site are by shuttle bus from the National Park Service
Visitor Center. Buses run on a regular schedule throughout the
year to meet visitor demand. Ranger conducted programs, walks,
tours, campfire programs, living history programs, children's
program and Battle Walks through the summer months.

Here is the site of the major Civil War battle and Abraham
Lincoln's Gettysburg Address:

BATTLEFIELD - The most important major blow to the
Confederate Army and the most casualties (51,000) on the first few
days of early July 1863. See key places: Cemetery Hill and Ridge,
Culp's Hill, Little Round Top, and Observation Tower. (We
suggest the audio tape tour for kids).

NOVEMBER 19, 1863, CEMETERY - President Lincoln
dedicated the National Cemetery on the battlefield and delivered
his famous speech "The Gettysburg Address".

CYCLORAMA - A 30 minute description while standing in the
middle of a 360 degree circular wall painting of the battlefield and
Pickett's Charge, the climactic moment of the battle (a sight and
sound experience). 9:00 am - 4:30 pm (every 1/2 hour).

ELECTRIC MAP - A 30 minute show with highlights of strategic
moves of battle. (every 45 minutes)

Gettysburg National Military Park (cont.)

MUSEUM OF THE CIVIL WAR - A large collection of Civil War artifacts, especially weapons and uniforms.

EISENHOWER HISTORIC SITE SUMMER HOME - Visit the web site at **www.nps.gov/eise**. During his Presidency, President and Mrs. Eisenhower used the farm as a weekend retreat, a refuge in time of illness, and a comfortable meeting place for world leaders. From 1961 to 1969, it was the Eisenhower's home during a vigorous and active retirement.

GETTYSBURG SCENIC RAIL TOURS

106 North Washington Street (Near Lincoln Square - Downtown)

Gettysburg 17325

- ❑ Phone: (717) 334-6932. **Web: www.gettysburgrail.com**
- ❑ Admission: $10.00-$20.00 per customer.
- ❑ Tours: 22-mile trip from Gettysburg to Aspers and return. Special trains for Fall Foliage, Santa and Special Festivals. Departures generally at 2:00pm weekends and some summer weekdays. (Memorial Day - December)
- ❑ Miscellaneous: The "Famous" Civil War Train Raid: An exciting special drama unfolds as Civil War Re-enactors from the Union Army guard the train before departure and then board for the 22-mile trip to protect our train from possible attack by the Confederates.

Relax aboard one of the vintage rail coaches or the unique double-decker open car, pulled by classic railroad locomotives. Enjoy a nostalgic train ride, first passing the famous "railroad cut", through the countryside and then passing through the First Day Battlefield of the Gettysburg National Military Park.

HALL OF PRESIDENTS AND FIRST LADIES

Gettysburg - *789 Baltimore Street, 17325. Phone: (717) 334-5717* ***Web: http://gettysburgbattlefieldtours.com/hallofpresidents.htm*** *Hours: Daily 9:00am-5:00pm. Later hours in summer season. (March-Thanksgiving Weekend). Admission: $4.00-$6.00 (age 6+).* Watch life-sized reproductions tell the "Story of America" through taped messages. First ladies appear in the type of gown they wore at the inauguration of their husbands. They've also added a heartwarming "Eisenhower at Gettysburg" exhibit. If your children are studying Presidential history, this is the best way to learn or re-learn important facts about each man.

JENNIE WADE HOUSE & OLDE TOWN

547 Baltimore Street (Adjacent to Olde Town)

Gettysburg 17325

- ❑ Phone: (717) 334-4100
- ❑ Hours: Daily 9:00am-9:00pm (Summer), Daily 9:00am-5:00pm (March-Thanksgiving Weekend).
- ❑ Admission: $4.00-$6.00 (age 6+).
- ❑ Miscellaneous: Caution: Due to the dramatic nature and story of this tour - parents with children younger than 1st or 2nd grade should probably arrange to be part of a school tour. They only give brief descriptions of the events and not explicit details.

Jennie Wade was the only civilian killed during the battle of Gettysburg and the situations that led to her death were quite dramatic. While baking bread for the soldiers in her kitchen, a stray bullet hit and killed young 20 year old Jennie. (a realistic hologram of Jennie is seen in the kitchen - and you see the actual bullet hole). A soldier tells you all the details including the fact that her fiancé was killed just days later in battle, but never knew of Jennie's fate!

LAND OF LITTLE HORSES

125 Glenwood Drive (3 miles West on US30, then follow signs)

Gettysburg 17325

- ❑ Phone: (717) 334-7259 **Web: www.landoflittlehorses.com**
- ❑ Hours: Monday-Saturday 10:00am-5:00pm, Sunday Noon-5:00pm (April-Labor Day). Weekends only (September, October).
- ❑ Admission: $7.00 (age 2+).

Land of Little Horses (cont.)

❏   Miscellaneous: Air-conditioned arena. The Gift Horse Shop.
    Carousel, train tram, petting farm. Put on a "feed bag" at the
    Hobby Horse Café.

As you enter, you'll be greeted by those adorable small horses
(most only a few feet tall) that seem to be just the right size for
kids to enjoy. Many are in separate pens throughout the park, some
are in the barn, others are getting ready for the show in the arena.
We took in the Barn Show first and loved the chance to see the
horses prance around and be gently petted. Especially cute are the
mothers with their young. The highlight of this farm is the
Performing Animals Show. They get the kids involved by "kissing
a pig" (there's a trick involved - 2 kids volunteered and did it!), or
helping with the animal tricks. "Something Special" is a daily
event at the Land of Little Horses. The event changes every day,
and can be anything from Miniature Horse costume parades (where
you dress up horses and show them off to the entire park), fun
games with prizes for the winners, goat milking & sheep sheering,
photo opportunities with the stars of our daily Arena Performances,
and much more! They also have cart races, saddle kids, and host
the "Bacon Downs" pig races - so cute, pick your favorite pig and
cheer it on! A great attraction for children of all ages.

LINCOLN ROOM MUSEUM

Lincoln Square (US15 - Business Route and US30 - Wills House)

Gettysburg 17325

❏   Phone: (717) 334-8188
    Web: www.gettysburg.com/lincolnbedroom
❏   Hours: Daily 9:00am-7:00pm (Summer). 9:00am-5:00pm
    (March-Thanksgiving Weekend).
❏   Admission: Donations

Home of the friend Lincoln stayed with in 1863 and where he
completed his Gettysburg Address. Original furnishings. He gave a
brief speech from the front door of this home the night before the
cemetery dedication. His words were brief because he feared that

he might say something foolish! Photographic views of all five drafts of the "Gettysburg Address" can be seen in the museum. Hear Jeff Daniels (actor) recite the "Gettysburg Address" during the Lincoln Bedroom presentation. Pose with the statue of Lincoln outside. Can you imagine his thoughts that night?

LINCOLN TRAIN MUSEUM

425 Steinwehr Avenue

Gettysburg 17325

- ❑   Phone: (717) 334-5678
- ❑   Hours: Daily 9:00am-9:00pm (Summer), Daily 9:00am-5:00pm (March-Thanksgiving).
- ❑   Admission: $4.00-$6.00 (age 6+).
- ❑   Miscellaneous: Events (in the diorama display) that led up to this historic train ride. Large train collection layout that reproduces the Civil War Era.

A simulated 1836 train ride with Lincoln and statesmen on a 12 minute trip. See Civil War grounds and overhear conversations that might have occurred on that trip. They project actual footage of a steam train ride as your seat and floorboards move to the straights, curves, and rumbles of the track. Statesmen speak of this time, in the still present war, Mr. President's ill son, and thoughts of re-election. We suggest this stop for young kids (all ages for that matter) because it easily and uniquely illustrates the emotion/history behind the Gettysburg Address.

SOLDIER'S NATIONAL MUSEUM

Gettysburg - *777 Baltimore Street, 17325. Phone: (717) 334-4890. Hours: Daily 9:00am-9:00pm (Summer) 9:00am-5:00pm (March-Thanksgiving Weekend). Admission: $4.00-$6.00 (age 6+).* 10 dioramas depict battles of the Civil War. There's also a life-sized, narrated confederate encampment. The building was once General Howard's headquarters and later the Soldier's National Orphanage.

LAKE TOBIAS WILDLIFE PARK

760 Tobias Drive (Rt. 322/22 West to Dauphin. Rt. 225 North to
Halifax. Four miles on Rt. 225 North to Fisherville)

Halifax 17032

❑   Phone: (717) 362-9126 **Web: www.laketobias.com**
❑   Hours: Monday-Friday 10:00am-6:00pm, Saturday & Sunday
     11:00am-7:00pm (Summer), Weekends only (May, September,
     October). Note: Park closes at 6:00pm in October.
❑   Admission: $1.00-4.00 per activity - adult, $1.00-3.00 per
     activity, child (2-12).
❑   Tours: Last safari tour one hour before closing.

Hundreds of wild and exotic animals - alligators, buffalo, llamas,
monkeys and reptile animal shows. Specially designed cruisers
take you across 150 acres of rolling land where you see herds of
wild and exotic animals from around the world. Tour guides travel
with you giving expert information on the various species and their
habitats. You will be surprised at how close you come to these
animals. Also a petting zoo and fishing ponds for "tamer" activity.

CODORUS STATE PARK

Hanover - *1066 Blooming Grove Road (PA Route 216), 17331.*
Web: www.dcnr.state.pa.us/stateparks/parks/codorus.htm Phone:
(717) 637-2816. The 1,275-acre Lake Marburg is popular with
fishermen, boaters and swimmers. Codorus is also an excellent
place to observe spring and fall migrations of waterfowl and
warblers. The park offers interpretive programs and hikes. Boat
rentals are available and a restaurant is convenient to the park.
Pool, Visitor Center, Horseback Riding, Sledding, Campsites,
Fishing, Trails, Winter Sports.

HANOVER SHOE FARMS

Hanover - *Route 194 South, 17331. Phone: (717) 637-8931.* ***Web:***
www.hanoverpa.com *Hours: Monday-Saturday 8:00am-3:00pm.*
Best time is spring when the foals are being born (April and May
are really good months). Admission: FREE. One of the largest
Standard bred horse breeders in the world. 1800 horses roam the
4000 acre grounds - many horses are record-breaking pacers and

trotters. The self-guided brochure tour lets your family wander at your leisure.

UTZ POTATO CHIPS

900 High Street (SR94 North and Clearview Streets)

Hanover 17331

- ❑ Phone: (717) 637-6644 **Web: www.utzsnacks.com**
- ❑ Hours: Monday-Thursday 8:00am-4:00pm. Occasional Fridays, by appointment.
- ❑ Admission: FREE
- ❑ Tours: Self-guided. (20 minutes)
- ❑ Miscellaneous: Outlet store just down the road. Lots of sampling and buying goes on there.

Walk along an elevated, glass enclosed observation gallery to observe potato chips in production. View close up TV monitors and listen to the descriptions of each step of the process. This is a modern and very clean facility. We probably got the closest to large conveyors of fried chips here (behind glass of course!). A new experience was watching home-cooked kettle chips being made. As you study family history photographs, enjoy a free bag of chips! We especially liked the "platform bridges" that they had throughout the tour so the "little ones" could see too!

SNYDERS OF HANOVER

1350 York Street, **Hanover** 17731

- ❑ Phone: (800) 233-7125 ext. 8592 **Web: www.snyders-han.com**
- ❑ Admission: FREE
- ❑ Tours: Tuesday, Wednesday, Thursday at 10:00am, 11:00am & 1:00pm. (24 hour notice is needed - approximately 35 minutes)

Meet at the factory storefront (where you'll no doubt be nibbling on samples before touring). It's no wonder that Pennsylvania is the "snack food" capital of the US. Watch a short video covering the company history starting with potato chips made at home in the early 1920s to the 1970s when they established sourdough hard pretzels. The differences you'll notice on this snack food tour are the numerous and extra large baking ovens and highly automated packaging systems. Machines build boxes while another machine fills the bags and yet another machine boxes the bags and then seals the cases shut. Kids love all the automation!

HARRISBURG SYMPHONY

Harrisburg - *5th and Walnut Streets, 17101. Phone: (717) 545-5527.* **Web: www.harrisburgsymphony.org** The "Crayon Concert" is a family series that features the theatrical retelling of children's stories with narration and song.

STATE CAPITOL BUILDING

Third & State Streets, **Harrisburg** 17101

❑   Phone: (800) TOUR-N-PA
     Web: www.legis.state.pa.us (CLICK the WELCOME button)
❑   Hours: Monday-Friday 8:30am-4:00pm, Saturday, Sunday, & Holiday 9:00am, 11:00am, 1:00pm, & 3:00pm. Closed major holidays.
❑   Admission: FREE
❑   Tours: Guided - every 1/2 hour, weekdays (except lunch - 12:00 - 1:00 pm). Specific times listed for weekends above.
❑   Miscellaneous: Stop at the Information Center first for a brochure on the self-guided tour. Welcome Center is open weekdays only.

The 272-foot dome will stun everyone as you stand underneath it and look up. Your neck could get sore because you'll be staring a good while. As you pass though bronze and ornately carved wooden doors, you can climb the stairs to the second and fourth floors to view the elegant and handsome Senate and House chambers. The favorite (and most educational) area is the Welcome Center. From the Ben Franklin video in miniature, to Hello History (take a telephone call from famous Pennsylvania leaders and athletes) to the glass window case full of colored balls (representing the number of bills that a state legislator considers in a year - there's a lot!). Other exhibits that encourage learning about laws (for kids and adults) are interactive displays of a "Day in the Life of a Legislator" (try to get your birthday as a holiday), voting (actually sit in a voting desk) and the making of a law (presented through a colorful display - like the game "Mousetrap" full of tracks, pulleys, and chains that follow a funny course). What a wonderful way to teach government!

WHITAKER CENTER FOR SCIENCE AND THE ARTS

222 Market Street (Downtown - Diagonal to the State Capitol)

Harrisburg 17101

❏   Phone: (717) 214-ARTS **Web: www.whitakercenter.org**

❏   Hours: Monday-Saturday 9:30am-5:00pm. Sunday 11:30am-5:00pm.

❏   Admission: $6.75 adult, $5.25 senior (55+), $5.25 child (3-12). IMAX additional charge. Combo discounts offered.

❏   Miscellaneous: IMAX Theatre - call (717) 214-IMAX for showtimes. Center closed Thanksgiving and Christmas Day. Food court attached by walkway. In addition to hands-on interactive exhibits, the Harsco Science Center also features Stage Two, a "black box" theater; and Big Science Theatre productions.

Their motto is "Question Everything". Nine different themed exhibit areas use performing arts to teach science concepts. How is dancing linked to science and physics? What are backstage secrets of how lighting and special effects contribute to the theater experience? Have you ever "walked through" a kaleidoscope? (you can here!). The younger kids will spend most of their time in the "kids hall" (ages 8 and below) where they too, get to experiment with light and sound! Other exhibits: Health and Wellness which includes The Gallery of Anatomy, The Five Senses, Medical Technology, and Wellness; The Gallery of Mathematics in Nature and Art; People and Diversity which includes Genetics, and Culture and Communication; Environment and Ecology which includes Global Environment, Watersheds, and Pennsylvania Environments; Physics which includes Forces and Motion, Simple Machines, Bodies In Motion: The Physics of Human Movement, and Backstage Science. Kids Hall which includes Sound and Music, Light and Color, Gizmos, the Theater, ArtWorks, and Kids Garden.

NATIONAL CIVIL WAR MUSEUM

1 Lincoln Circle at Reservoir Park

Harrisburg 17103

- ❑   Phone: (717) 260-1861 or (866) BLU-GRAY
  Web: www.nationalcivilwarmuseum.com
- ❑   Hours: Monday-Saturday 10:00am-5:00pm, Sunday Noon-5:00pm. (Closed Thanksgiving, Christmas & New Year's Day). Closed Mondays in the winter.
- ❑   Admission: $7.00 adult, $6.00 senior, $5.00 student, $25.00 family.

Mission Statement: The only museum in the United States that attempts to portray the story of the Nation's Civil War - Equally balanced presentations are humanistic in nature without bias to Union or Confederate causes. Dioramas, digital videos and simply displayed showcases ease you through the facts. Tours are educational, entertaining and sometimes emotional.

CITY ISLAND

Walnut & Market Street Bridges (Susquehanna River)

Harrisburg 17104

- ❑   Hours: Dawn-Dusk

Enjoy 63 acres of parkland developed as a recreational center. Once ashore, a miniature train provides a leisurely round-the Island tour of all the sights and attractions. Some of the Island's most popular activities are located on its north end, where the unique Water Golf miniature golf course awaits. Nearby, the distinctive Harbourtown Children's Play area beckons visitors with a scaled-down re-creation of an 1840's canal town. Playhouse-type structures include a pirate ship, lighthouse and stores. Within feet are large sandboxes and volleyball courts, and the city's historic Beachhouse and Beach. (one of the cleanest rivers in the Nation). Skyline Sports Complex & Riverside Village Park eateries (east shore) include crab cakes, burgers, fries, ice cream and more. This mid-19th Century-themed retail village contains a variety of picnic facilities, gazebos, scenic decks and plenty of places to feed the

Island's ever-hungry ducks and geese. Nestled against the Walnut Street Bridge is the City Island Arcade. Elegant horse-drawn carriage rides are offered in-season along the waterfront. What a treat for locals and a nice appeal to visitors!

JOHN HARRIS MANSION (DAUPHIN COUNTY HISTORICAL MUSEUM)

Harrisburg - *219 South Front Street, 17104. Phone: (717) 233-3462. Web: www.dauphincountyhistoricalsociety.org Admission: $7.00 adult, $6.00 senior (60+), $4.00 student (5-16). Tours: Tours for individuals and small family groups (fewer than 15 people) are normally conducted on Tuesday and Thursday afternoons at 1:30pm, but advance reservations are required.* John Harris Sr. chose the area on the Susquehanna River near where the Mansion is located to build a cabin and a trading post in the early 1700's. Harris later began a ferry business on the river, and the community became known as Harris' Ferry. Later, his son would build this home and become the founder of Harrisburg.

PRIDE OF THE SUSQUEHANNA RIVERBOAT TOUR

(Docked at City Island), **Harrisburg** 17104

❑   Phone: (717) 234-6500. **Web: www.harrisburgriverboat.com**
❑   Hours: Tuesday-Sunday Noon-3:00pm (May-October).
❑   Admission: $4.95 adult, $3.00 child (3-12). Wednesday has reduced fares.
❑   Tours: Indoor and outdoor seating. 40 minute narrated cruise leaves on the hour.

Pass under 6 bridges and by the grave of the city's founder, John Harris on an authentic paddlewheel boat. Take your children and their special friends back to yesteryear, and experience a unique method of transportation that was used over 150 years ago. The boat is docked on the wonderful city park, City Island, which is situated in the middle of the Susquehanna River. History tells us that the Susquehannock Indians lived on the islands in the river and fished the waters of the Susquehanna River in the 17th Century.

HARRISBURG SENATORS BASEBALL

Harrisburg - *PO Box 15757 Riverside Stadium (City Island), 17105. Phone: (717) 231-4444.* **Web: *www.senatorsbaseball.com*** *Admission: $3.00-$9.00.* AA Class affiliate of the Montreal Expos. Meet Riverside Rascal, the mascot on Sunday afternoons.

STATE MUSEUM OF PENNSYLVANIA

3rd & North Streets - PO Box 1026 (Downtown)

Harrisburg 17108

- ❑ Phone: (717) 787-4978. **Web: www.statemuseumpa.org**
- ❑ Hours: Tuesday-Saturday, 9:00am-5:00pm., Sunday 12:00-5:00 pm. (Closed holidays except Memorial Day and Labor Day)
- ❑ Admission: FREE
- ❑ Miscellaneous: Planetarium (additional charge) shows. Gift shop
  - *We bought some neat "Dinosaur DNA Dust" (cherry or grape flavor) to commemorate our Dino Lab experience.*

The Official Museum of the Commonwealth features 4 floors of historical exhibits: Geology, Archeology (pretend to dig like the professionals - what types of things are found at a typical site?), Military (Gettysburg, etc.), Industry, The Arts, Technology. Our favorite was the Dino Lab - a real paleontology lab tech at work carving a skeleton from a fossil rock. It is a fascinating experience - and you can even ask questions while they work! The original charter granted to William Penn by King Charles II in 1861 is also on display. CURIOSITY CORNER - Interactive Computer and dress up. Kids will want to check out activities that correspond to the displays in the museum. There is a small charge per child for this area open Wednesday-Sunday, 1:00-4:00pm.

WILDWOOD LAKE SANCTUARY

100 Wildwood Way (Lucknow Industrial Park, north of Harrisburg Area Comm. College), **Harrisburg 17110**

- ❑ Phone: (717) 221-0292 **Web: www.wildwoodlake.org**
- ❑ Hours: Dawn to dusk.
- ❑ Admission: FREE general admission, small fee for special programs.

It's a 212 acre lake with wonderful walkways through marshes, meadows and woodlands. The nature center has great interactive displays for children...they take a card through the exhibit and get stamps at various stations which teach them about the wetlands while creating a picture. There's also a Discovery Room with quick, easy arts and crafts. The pathways outside are well marked, paved or mulched, and lend themselves to a lot of discovery...turtles on logs, butterflies, etc. Gift shop with exploration toys. *Our relatives from Pennsylvania love this place!*

HARRISBURG HORIZON BASKETBALL

Harrisburg - *Union Center @ Penn State, 17111. Phone: (717) 986-0499. Web: www.harrisburghorizon.com Admission: $4.00-$8.00.* Central PA's Pro Basketball Team. Eastern Basketball Alliance, 2002 Champion team!

HERSHEY BEARS HOCKEY

Hershey - *100 West HersheyPark Drive (Giant Arena), 17033. Web: www.hersheybears.com Phone: (717) 534 - 3911. Admission: $14.00 - $20.00. Family Four Packs w/ food offered at a discount.* AHL, Colorado Avalanche affiliate. Join CoCo the Bears Kids Club.

HERSHEY GARDENS

Hershey - *170 Hotel Road (on the grounds of the Hotel Hershey), 17033. Phone: (717) 534-3492. Web: www.hersheygardens.org Hours: Daily 9:00am-5:00pm (April-October). Extended summer evening hours. Admission: $3.00-$6.00 (age 3+).* This 23-acre botanical gem has over 7,000 roses and seasonal flower displays, 25,000 tulips in the spring, a Japanese garden and an outdoor Butterfly House with 400 butterflies. The Butterfly House Opens first weekend in June and will remain open through the third Saturday in September, weather permitting. The Children's Garden provides opportunities for hands-on learning, self-discovery, and fun with water features, hideaways, creatures, surprises, whimsical characters, and more all within nearly 30 themed areas.

HERSHEY MUSEUM

170 West Hersheypark Drive (next to arena)

Hershey 17033

❑   Phone: (717) 534-3439 or (800) HERSHEY
   Web: www.hersheypa.com
❑   Hours: Daily 10:00am-6:00pm (Summer). 10:00am-5:00pm
   (Winter).
❑   Admission: $6.00 adult, $5.50 senior (62+), $3.00 child (3-15).

Learn how Mr. Hershey failed as a candy maker in Philadelphia and New York - but became a millionaire manufacturing caramels in Lancaster, Pennsylvania. He sold that business to start a chocolate factory in his birthplace farmland. See how it developed as Hershey, Pennsylvania. (Also exhibits on Pennsylvania German and Native American clothing, tools, art). We also fell in love with the Apostolic Clock Procession which performs at 20 minutes before each hour. Notice which Apostle doesn't greet Christ. Look for the "Marys" or try to find the Devil. They've enhanced the Discovery Room - now there are more "rooms" to play 1830's Victorian Home, Kitchen, and General Store. Elsewhere in the museum, kids can "punch a real time clock" or sit in an original HersheyPark roller coaster car (kind of virtual reality).

HERSHEY TROLLEY WORKS

Hershey - *(Departs at entrance to Hershey's Chocolate World), 17033. Phone: (717) 533-3000.* **Web: www.hersheypa.com** *Hours: Rain or Shine. Same hours as the park. Last tour is 1 hour before closing. Admission: $9.95 adult, $9.45 senior (62+), $4.95 child (3-12).* Family adventure through America's sweetest town. Old time songs and visits throughout from famous "characters" plus lots of little-known facts about the town as you pass historic sites.

HERSHEYPARK

100 W. Hersheypark Drive (Off SR 743 & US 422), **Hershey** 17033

- ❑ Phone: (800) HERSHEY **Web: www.hersheypa.com**
- ❑ Hours: Daily - Opens at 10:30am (May-September). Weekends only (May, September).
- ❑ Admission: Range $16-$35.00 (Ages 3+)
- ❑ Miscellaneous: Hershey Lodge, West Chocolate Avenue. (717) 533-3311 or **www.hersheypa.com**. A very family-friendly way to stay in the area comfortably. With lodging rates in the $100-$150 range, it includes a free shuttle to HersheyPark and other attractions, plus free admission to Hershey Gardens (Butterfly House) and Hershey Museum (Discovery Room). You have the opportunity to make reservations for Breakfast in the Park with Hershey Characters, too. On site (at the lodge) are tennis courts, basketball courts, miniature golf, gameroom, bocce ball, bike rentals, and their fabulous pools – indoor and outdoor. Kids will like to eat at Lebbie Lebkichers casual buffet or the Bears' Den hockey-themed sports café. Watch the game on a 9'x12' video wall, check out the game room, and order from the Kids Menu (we recommend the Bear Puck Dessert). Great way to enjoy Hershey, PA without a lot of hassle.

Begin by "measuring up" for size. From "Kisses" on up, the rides are rated by candy type. 110 acre theme park with 50 rides and attractions. You'll also find: German Area, English Area, Penn Dutch Area (and food to match), a SeaLion & Dolphin Show, Night Lights Musical Laser Spectacular. 21 kiddie rides and live entertainment at Music Box Theater or the Amphitheatres.

Rollercoasters you'll find include:

- ❑ GREAT BEAR - inverted looping roller coaster.
- ❑ SUPER DOOPER LOOPER - is a milder form of Great Bear.
- ❑ ROLLER SOAKER - an awesome interactive water coaster.

HERSHEY'S CHOCOLATE WORLD VISITORS CENTER

800 Park Blvd, **Hershey** 17033

- ❑ Phone: (800) HERSHEY
  Web: www.hersheyschocolateworld.com
- ❑ Hours: Daily 9:00am-5:00pm (everyday but Christmas). -
  Extended hours for special events.
- ❑ Admission: FREE.
- ❑ Miscellaneous: Free sample. 8 unique gift shops. Food court.
  Chocolate Town Café. HERSHEY'S Really Big 3-D Show, an
  immersive three-dimensional musical featuring the HERSHEY'S
  Product Characters as they come to life for the first time on the
  big screen (movie charges fee).

A factory tour on an automated tram into the simulated world of chocolate production! Start at the cocoa bean plantation (rainforests and tropic) to dairy farms to making chocolate through the years at Hershey. Actual video footage of a real factory and the wonderful scent of chocolate pervades. It even gets warmer as you pass through the "roaster oven" part of the ride. Souvenir photographs are taken of the passengers in each car. You can purchase them for around $10.00 at the end of the tour. Learn why different chocolate manufacturers have different flavors (the secret is where the cocoa beans came from).

ZOO AMERICA NORTH AMERICAN WILDLIFE PARK

Hershey - *Park Avenue (opposite HersheyPark), 17033. Phone: (717) 534-3860. Web: www.hersheypa.com Hours: 10:00am-5:00pm. (Open until 8:00 pm in the summer). Admission: ~$6.00-$7.00 (age 3+). FREE with paid admission to HersheyPark.* An eleven acre North American attraction that hosts wildlife from 5 regions (200+ species). "Desert of Night" area is unique and wonderful. "Visit" with creatures of the night like owls, snakes and bats. The American crocodile exhibit and interactive Maze learning stations are newer to the zoo.

INDIAN ECHO CAVERNS

368 Middletown Road (Off I-283 and US 322 at Hummelstown /
Middletown Exits), **Hummelstown** 17036

- ❏ Phone: (717) 566-8131. **Web: www.indianechocaverns.com**
- ❏ Hours: Daily 9:00am-6:00pm (Summer). 10:00am-4:00pm
  (Spring/Fall). Call for times (Winter).
- ❏ Admission: $9.00 adult, $8.00 senior (62+), $5.00 child (3-11).
- ❏ Tours: 45 minutes, guided.
- ❏ Miscellaneous: Gift shop - Southwestern, Rocks. Pan for gems at
  Gem Mill Junction (open seasonally). Wagon ride to the Petting
  Barnyard. Playground with Indian Tepee and Conestoga Wagon.

You'll walk the same paths that the Susquehannock Indians did
hundreds of years ago and be entertained with many stories and
legends surrounding Indian Echo. Check out the Wilson Room
and the Story of William Wilson who lived in the caverns for 19
years - "the Pennsylvania Hermit". The Indian Ballroom is the
largest room. There are 3 lakes and a variety of stalactites,
stalagmites, and flowstone.

BLUE KNOB STATE PARK

Imler - *RR 1, Box 449, 16655. Phone: (814) 276-3576.* **Web:**
www.dcnr.state.pa.us/stateparks/parks/b-knob.htm Bob's Creek
is great for trout fishing and Blue Knob boasts the second highest
peak in the state, which gives great views of up to 42 miles. All
park trails are open to mountain biking. Pool, Horse-back Riding,
Down-hill Skiing, Campsites, Fishing, Winter Sports.

GIFFORD PINCHOT STATE PARK

Lewisberry - *2200 Rosstown Road (Route 177), 17339.* **Web:**
www.dcnr.state.pa.us/stateparks/parks/giff.htm Phone: (717) 432-
5011.* Pinchot Lake is a great warm water fishery and is popular
for sailing. Beach, Visitor Center, Boat Rentals, Horseback Riding,
Sledding, Campsites, Modern Cabins, Fishing, Trails, and Cross-
Country Skiing.

SKI ROUNDTOP

Lewisberry - *925 Roundtop Road, 17339. Phone: (717) 432-9631. Snow Report: (717) 432-7000* **Web: www.skiroundtop.com** Magic Mountain area is set aside just for kids. With its own Magic Carpet lift, your children can learn in a secure area physically separated from the other slopes. Longest Run: 4100 ft.; 15 Slopes & Trails - Skiing and Snowtubing.

BUCHANAN STATE FOREST

McConnellsburg - *440 Buchanan Trail, 17233. Phone: (717) 485-3148.* **Web: www.dcnr.state.pa.us/forestry/stateforests/forests/buchanan/buchanan.htm** The Buchanan State Forest was named in honor of James Buchanan, 15th President of the United States. The area consists of five principle tracts that cover seventy-five thousand acres of Commonwealth owned forest lands. In Bedford County, there is a saltpeter cave within the Sweet Root Natural Area where saltpeter had been produced for gunpowder before and during the American Revolution. ATV Trails (26 miles), Fishing, Camping, Trails, and Winter Sports.

WHITETAIL SKI RESORT AND MOUNTAIN BIKING CENTER

Mercersburg - *13805 Blairs Valley Road, 17236. Phone: (717) 328-9400.* **Web: www.skiwhitetail.com** Longest Run: 4900 ft.; 17 Slopes & Trails. Terrain Park: 1 rail, 8 snow features, and a fun box for snow tubing and snow boarding. SnowMonsters kids program.

MIDDLETOWN AND HUMMELSTOWN RAILROAD

136 Brown Street (SR283 to Middletown exit - Race Street Station)

Middletown 17057

- ❑   Phone: (717) 944-4435 **Web: www.mhrailroad.com**
- ❑   Hours: Memorial Day Weekends - October. July & August - Tuesday and Thursday also.
- ❑   Admission: $4.50-$9.00 (age 3+).
- ❑   Tours: Generally departures at 11:00am, 1:00pm and 3:00pm. Check schedule for detailed times. You don't want to miss the train.

For updates visit our website: www.kidslovepublications.com

❑   Miscellaneous: Special event trains (see seasonal chapter).
      Reservations suggested.

The yard has several rail cars on display. During the ride, the train follows the towpath of the historic Union Canal and alongside the peaceful Swatara. The narrator relates the history of the Canal (completed in 1827) and the location of Canal Lock #33, as well as a century old limekiln and Horse Thief Cave. Passengers will want to have their cameras out while crossing a 35-foot bridge above the Swatara Creek. On the return trip from Indian Echo Cave Platform, you will enjoy a "sing-a-long" of tunes from the railroading days, as well as fun songs for young and old alike. Can you still "Chicken Dance"?

LITTLE BUFFALO STATE PARK

Newport - *RD 2, Box 256A (PA Route 34), 17074. Phone: (717) 567-9255. Web: www.dcnr.state.pa.us/stateparks/parks/buffalo.htm* Explore historical features including a covered bridge, restored grist mill, an old farm house built on the site of a colonial tavern, and a narrow gauge railroad. Programs are offered year-round. Many programs feature Shoaff's Mill. Over 12,000 people visit the mill annually. Today the Perry County Historical Society operates and maintains a museum and library in the farmhouse. Members volunteer to open the museum every Sunday during the summer months. For more detailed information on programs contact the park office. Pool, Visitor Center, Year-round Education & Interpretation Center, Boat Rentals, Sledding, Fishing, and Trails.

COLONEL DENNING STATE PARK

Newville - *1599 Doubling Gap Road (Doubling Gap, North Cumberland County, along PA Route 233), 17241. Phone: (717) 776-5272. www.dcnr.state.pa.us/stateparks/parks/coloneldenning.htm* The wooded park area nestles at the side of a mountain and has a scenic lake and excellent hiking trails. A hike on a 2.5 mile trail rises to Flat Rock for a beautiful vista of the Cumberland Valley. Beach, Visitor Center, Campsites, Fishing, and Cross-Country Skiing.

SHAWNEE STATE PARK

Schellsburg - *Box 67 (Ten miles west of historic Bedford along Route 30), 15559. Phone: (814) 733-4218.* **Web:** *www.dcnr.state.pa.us/stateparks/parks/shawnee.htm* Of particular interest is Shawnee's long sand and turf beach that receives ample use between Memorial Day and Labor Day. The lake is popular for boating and fishing. Boat Rentals, Mountain Biking, Sledding, Campsites, Modern Cabins, Trails, and Winter Sports.

STEWARTSTOWN RAILROAD

Stewartstown - *Pennsylvania Avenue, 17363. Phone: (717) 993-2936. Hours: Sundays, and some Saturdays (April - early Fall). Call for current schedules. Admission: $8.00 adult, $4.00 child (3-11).* The Stewartstown Railroad consists of a seven-mile stretch of tracks ending at New Freedom, where, in 1885 it made an important connection with the main line of the Northern Central Railway (now Conrail). Vintage equipment travels through rural scenic areas. Mighty Mo, a favorite of children today, is a 35-ton Plymouth locomotive. A 1915 Depot features the original waiting room and ticket office; the Freight House exhibits historical memorabilia; and an 1870 Iron Truss Bridge is a marvel to see.

MARTIN'S POTATO CHIPS

Thomasville - *5847 Lincoln Highway (US Route 30), 17364.* **Web: www.martinschips.com** *Phone: (717) 792-3565 or (800) 272-4477. Admission: FREE. Tours: Monday-Thursday 9:00am-Noon by reservation only. 45 minutes long. Closed-toe shoes required. Cameras permitted.* Enjoying the benefit of the rich loamy soil, farmers had to find ways to use their excess crops. From the farm kitchen of Harry and Fairy Martin in 1941, a unique potato chip found its way into homes. All potato chips and popcorn are made in their 40,000 sq. ft. Thomasville facility which produces over one million bags each month.

HARLEY-DAVIDSON MOTORCYCLE MUSEUM TOUR

1425 Eden Road (on US30 or Exit 21 East of I-83), **York** 17402

- ❑   Phone: (877) 883-1450 **Web: www.harleydavidson.com**
- ❑   Admission: FREE
- ❑   Tours: Tours begin at regular intervals between 9:00am and 2:00pm, Monday through Friday. Tickets are distributed on a first-come, first-served basis. It is recommended that you arrive early in the day. Modified tours may be conducted due to manufacturing requirements. Tours are not offered on weekends, major holidays, during the week of July 4th or during production changes and year-end maintenance. (Plant tour is for ages 12+, however, there are no age restrictions on the museum tour)
- ❑   Miscellaneous: Tours are wheelchair accessible. Souvenir Shop.

What little traveler hasn't seen (or better yet - heard) a Harley-Davidson motorcycle pass by? Founded in 1903, Harley-Davidson has become a passion of the American dream. See over 20 vintage and famous Harleys (Malcolm Forbes' custom bike) on the museum tour that is available for all ages (even a Kids Rally area for the little tykes). You will see photographs and videos of the 24 step manufacturing process that produces a completed motorcycle every 6 minutes! They are so confident in their quality and reliability that the first time an engine is started (it contains over 400 parts!) is when the bike is completely finished. An associate takes a few spins around the 1 mile long test track (what a great job!) to be sure that it meets all the standards and expectations of the waiting customer. More than 3,000 employees work around the clock assembling Touring and Softail® models, as well as limited production, factory-custom motorcycles. They perform a variety of manufacturing operations - from machining, polishing and chrome plating, to forming, welding and painting. What does a doctor, a lawyer, machine operator, actor, business owner, and pastor all have in common... a Harley-Davidson motorcycle!

YORK YOUTH SYMPHONY ORCHESTRA

York - *50 North George Street, 17402. Phone: (717) 846-1155 tickets / (717) 843-4481 youth.* **Web: www.yorksymphony.org** *or* **www.yorkyouthsymphony.org**   York Symphony has Classic as well as Summer Pops in July. All Youth concerts will be held in the York County School of Technology's auditorium (3x per year).

AGRICULTURAL & INDUSTRIAL MUSEUMS

480 East Market Street / 217 West Princess Street (US30 to George Street exit, Rte. 462 into downtown)

York 17403

- ❑   Phone: (717) 852-7007 **Web: www.yorkheritage.org**
- ❑   Hours: Tuesday-Saturday 10:00am-4:00pm.
- ❑   Admission: $6.00 adult, $5.00 senior (65+) & student (age 12+). One ticket for Ag & Industrial, Fire & Historical Museums. We recommend the Industrial Museum (Princess Street) for sure.

A lot of products produced here have clothed, sheltered, transported, fed, and entertained the nation. Learn how the modern day farm evolved from the time of Native Americans. Then, go a few streets away to explore the numerous products made in York. Begin in an old gristmill (still working - you'll see), pull a factory whistle (time to go home!) or use an old rotary phone to dial up a friend next door (watch the mechanics of the operation station tapping out the numbers). The Pfaltzgraff pottery exhibit is well done with several stages of pottery being made (sometimes a potter comes in for live demonstrations). Since the Pfaltzgraff tour has age restrictions and is rather long, you may vote this exhibit more family-friendly than an actual tour. Don't forget about CAT trucks (get in the cab) and York Peppermint Patties!

YORK COUNTY HERITAGE MUSEUMS

250 East Market Street (US 30 to George Street exit, follow signs to downtown), **York** 17403

- ❑   Phone: (717) 848-1587 **Web: www.yorkheritage.org**
- ❑   Hours: Tuesday-Saturday 10:00am-4:00pm, Sunday Noon-4:00pm. Winter hours only weekends.

❑   Admission: $6.00 adult, $5.00 senior (65+) & student (age 12+).
      One ticket for Ag & Industrial, Fire & Historical Museums.

When you venture downtown, be sure to visit the campus of historical buildings on West Market Street. These buildings include a replica of the courthouse where the Second Continental Congress met, as well as an authentic tavern dating back to 1741. A reproduction of original York village square with Bonham House (beautiful home), General Gates House, and Bobb Log House. The Golden Plough Tavern (c. 1741), the city's oldest structure, gives a taste of life during the years when the Tavern housed travelers and served local residents. The General Horatio Gates House (c. 1751): this English-style house was the General's home while he attended the Continental Congress, and is said to have been the site of LaFayette's famous toast to Washington that sent a signal to conspirators that the French would not support a plot to replace Washington with Gates. The Bobb Log House (c. 1812) is an example of the simple structures popular along the Pennsylvania frontier at the turn of the 19th century. The Horace Bonham House, with original furnishings of the artist, reveals the social and cultural changes that took place between the Civil War and the turn of the century.

YORK LITTLE THEATRE

York - *27 South Belmont Street, 17403. Phone: (717) 854-3894.* **Web: www.ylt.org** Family hits like Scrooge, Pooh, Annie Get Your Gun. Many productions include youth performers.

YORK COUNTY FIRE MUSEUM

York - *757 West Market Street, 17404. Phone: (717) 843-0464.* **Web: www.yorkheritage.org** *Hours: Saturday 10:00am-4:00pm. Closed winter. Admission: $6.00 adult, $5.00 senior (65+) & student (age 12+). One ticket for Ag & Industrial, Fire & Historical Museums.* The Fire Museum of York County displays more than 200 years of firefighting. All seventy-two fire companies of York County are represented here, with some of them dating back to before the American Revolution. The beautiful turn-of-the-century fire house contains a series of displays of how firefighters progressed from the early Leather Bucket Brigades to Hand Drawn Carts and Pumps, to Horse Drawn Apparatus, and finally to Motorized Equipment. All of the equipment is original and full-size. Pull a Fire Alarm Box or visit an old fashioned Fire Chief's Sleeping Quarters, complete with brass slide pole.

WOLFGANG CANDY COMPANY

50 East 4th Avenue (SR30 to North George Street - south to Fourth Avenue), **York** 17405

❑ Phone: (717) 843-5536 or (800) 248-4273
   Web: www.wolfgangcandy.com

❑ Hours: Monday-Friday 8:00am-5:00 pm, Saturday 9:00am-4:00pm.

❑ Admission: FREE

❑ Tours: Monday - Friday 10:00am and 2:00pm. 1/2 hour long. Groups by appointment only.

❑ Miscellaneous: Candy shoppe and soda fountain (Das Sweeten Haus Center). Relax on an antique stool (and watch the girls make hand dipped raisin clusters) as you enjoy a dish of Wolfgang's ice cream and sip a coffee or hot chocolate.

When you enter the Bavarian style shop to wait for your tour, you undoubtedly first glance at the antique truck parked in the middle of the main floor. This was the original delivery truck used to sell chocolate candies door to door back in the 1920's. It is also the truck that helps "Candy Dan" in his flying video tour of the factory. If you choose not to go on the tour at all, this video is a great "birdseye view" of a tour but with a children's twist. The actual facility started in the back of the Wolfgang house and grew and grew. You'll pass retired family members' homes as you adorn a white hair net and walk up to the factory. Their corn starch machine is still used and original to the factory. Smell and taste samples as you go. The guide kept the kids' attention by pointing out lessons they learn in school. The girls and guys on the line must pick partners and pay attention (sound like school?). We recommend Fall through Easter as the best time to see candy and fillings actually made on the line (it's easier to understand the tour during full production). Summertime has minimal production.

Chapter 8
South East Area

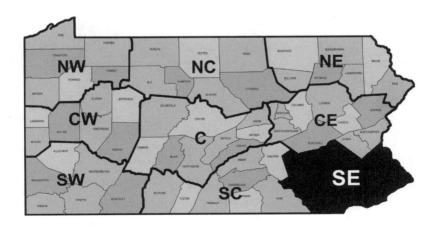

Our Favorites...

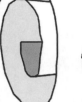

American Helicopter Museum

Amish Homes & Farms

Independence Park (esp. Liberty Bell)

Mercer Museum

QVC Broadcast Studios Tour

Roadside America

Snack Tours (Sturgis, Wilbur, Herr's)

Strasburg Railroad & Train Museums

Valley Forge

Weavertown One Room Schoolhouse

A snack food tour with Chipper

MILL GROVE, THE AUDUBON WILDLIFE SANCTUARY

Audubon - *Audubon & Pawlings Roads, 19407. Phone: (610) 666-5593. Web: www.methacton.k12.pa.us/audubon/mill_grove/ mill_grove2.html   Hours: Tuesday-Saturday 10:00am-4:00pm, Sunday 1:00-4:00pm. Admission: FREE.* Early 1800's home of noted artist, author and nature lover, John James Audubon. The house displays Audubon's paintings of birds and a complete set of his greatest work, "The Birds of America". Kids seem to admire the stuffed bird collection and birds' eggs. Grounds with nature trails and bird sanctuary are open dawn to dusk.

NESHAMINY STATE PARK

Bensalem - *3401 State Road (State Road and Dunks Ferry Road), 19020. Web: www.dcnr.state.pa.us/stateparks/parks/nesh.htm Phone: (215) 639-4538.* Neshaminy State Park provides boating access to the Delaware River. The picnic areas and swimming pool are the most popular park attractions. Fishing, Boating, Hiking, Cross-Country Skiing.

ABE'S BUGGY RIDES

Bird-In-Hand - *2596 Old Philadelphia Pike (Route 340), 17505. Phone: (717) 392-1794. Web: www.800padutch.com/abes.html Hours: Daily (except Sundays) 10:00am-3:00pm. Admission: $5.00-$10.00 (age 3+). Tours: 20 minutes.* Take a 2 mile tour in an Amish family carriage.

PLAIN & FANCY FARM

3121 Old Philadelphia Pike (7 miles east on SR340)

Bird-In-Hand 17505

- ❏ Phone: (717) 768-4400 or (800) 441-3505
  Web: www.millerssmorgasbord.com
- ❏ Hours:) Monday-Saturday 8:30am-5:00pm, Sunday 10:30am-6:00 pm (April-October). Extended summer hours. Monday-Sunday 10:00am-5:00pm (November-March).
- ❏ Admission: $4.00-$7.00 per person/ per activity (Depending on Activity).

❑   Miscellaneous: Plain & Fancy Restaurant - all you can eat home
      style meals.

Here's what you can do (choose one or a combo):

"THE AMISH EXPERIENCE" - Only one of three "experimental"
F/X theatres in North America - they use actual props, 5 projectors,
3D imagery, dramatic stage lighting and "surround sound" to tell a
story. The story is of an Amish family and their teenage son who is
in a "runabout time" - trying to decide which world he wants to
embrace. (85% of Amish teens stay within the church even after
experiencing the outside world). It tells a great Amish story (past
and present) and is very dramatic - probably best for ages 8 and
older. **www.amishexperience.com.**

AMISH COUNTRY HOMESTEAD - see how Amish live today
through a 9-room house. Learn about Amish living, furniture,
chores and clothing.

AARON & JESSICA'S BUGGY RIDES - 3.5 mile buggy ride
tour of Amish farmlands. Sleigh rides too (winter)! (717) 768-8828
or **www.amishbuggyrides.com.**

WEAVERTOWN ONE ROOM SCHOOLHOUSE

SR340 (between Bird-In-Hand and Intercourse)

Bird-In-Hand 17505

❑   Phone: (717) 768-3976
      Web: www.800padutch.com/wvrtown.html
❑   Hours: Daily 10:00am-5:00pm (April-October). Weekends only
      (March & November).
❑   Admission: $3.25 adult, $2.75 senior, $2.25 child (4-12).
❑   Tours: 15 minute presentation

See the full-sized animated teacher and class having a typical
school day in this authentic Amish schoolhouse. The bell, desk,
and blackboard are original and the school building was used for
nearly 100 years until it closed in 1969. The teacher asks questions
and the children answer. We learned that kids brought potatoes
from home that were baked on the cast iron heater (the only source

of heat in back of the room) all morning until lunch. Kids also brought lunch boxes. Extra desks are left open so visitors can sit among Amish students after the presentations for great photo and video opportunities. Note: Visitors to Lancaster County aren't normally permitted to enter one-room schoolhouses while actual classes are in session. This is your only opportunity to get a glimpse of this unique school room.

DANIEL BOONE HOMESTEAD

400 Daniel Boone Road (off US422 - 1 mile north)

Birdsboro 19508

❑ Phone: (610) 582-4900
   www.phmc.state.pa.us/bhsm/toh/boone/danielboone.asp?secid=14
❑ Hours: Tuesday - Saturday 9:00am-5:00pm, Sunday Noon-
   5:00pm. Closed non-Summer holidays. Reduced schedule
   January & February
❑ Admission: $2.00-$4.00 (age 6+).

Born here in 1734, the birthplace interprets the colonial Pennsylvania rural life of Daniel Boone. A restored 10 room Boone homestead (originally a log cabin), a similar cabin, sawmill, smokehouse, spring kitchen, blacksmith, and barn are on site. Be sure to watch the video presentation (re-enacted) to get a sense of the Boone family's life here and out-of-state.

BOYERTOWN MUSEUM OF HISTORIC VEHICLES

28 Warwick Street (SR73 and 562 - South to Warwick)

Boyertown 19512

❑ Phone: (610) 367-2090
   Web: www.berkscounty.com/museum/Boyertow.htm
❑ Hours: Daily 9:00am-4:00pm (except Monday), Sunday 9:30am-
   4:00pm.
❑ Admission: $2.00-$4.00 (age 6+).

See Pennsylvania's transportation heritage - carriages, wagons, trucks, bicycles, and cars. Also on display are 18th and 19th century vehicles built by Pennsylvania Dutch craftsmen and the tools that were used to assemble them. See rare vehicles, learn about some of America's earliest auto manufacturers. See custom bodied cars by Fleetwood, steam and electric vehicle technology, high wheel bicycles, children's vehicles and tools of the craftsman.

TERRY HILL WATERPARK

Breinigsville - *10000 Hamilton Road (SR222), 18031. Phone: (610) 395-0222.* **Web: www.terryhill.com** *Hours: Daily Noon-6:00pm (June), Monday-Friday Noon-7:00pm, Weekends until 8:00 pm (July & August). Admission: $10.00 -$16.00.* A family waterpark with nine different water slides, three pools, and kiddie waterplay area. Snack bars.

BRANDYWINE BATTLEFIELD PARK

Box 202 (US1, 1 mile east of SR100)

Chadds Ford 19317

❑   Phone: (610) 459-3342 **Web: www.ushistory.org/brandywine**
❑   Hours: Tuesday - Saturday 9:00am-5:00pm, Sunday Noon-5:00pm.
❑   Admission: Grounds FREE (building tours $1.50-$3.50 per person)
❑   Tours: Maps for self-guided tour at Visitor's Center.
❑   Miscellaneous: Museum shop. Plenty of picnic areas. Battle re-enactment every September.

Giant park and museum focused on actual Revolutionary War events. Watch the audiovisual introduction to the park first, then drive along a tour that includes 28 historic points taking you back to 1777. Remember, this defeat of American forces (led by George Washington) left the Philadelphia area open to attack and conquest by the British.

BRANDYWINE RIVER MUSEUM

Chadds Ford - *US 1 & PA Rte. 100, 19317. Phone: (610) 388-2700.* **Web: www.brandywinemuseum.org** *Hours: Daily 9:30am-4:30pm. Closed Christmas. Admission: $6.00 adult, $3.00 student/child (age 6+).* American art in a 19th century gristmill. Known for collections by three generations of Wyeths. The house where N.C. Wyeth raised his extraordinarily creative children and the studio in which he painted many of his memorable works of art have been restored to reflect their character in 1945, the year of the artist's death (House & Studio Tour $3.00 extra, April-November).

BYERS' CHOICE LTD

Chalfont - *4335 County Line Road (Just north of Rt.309 & Rt. 202), 18914. Phone: (215) 822-0150.* **Web: www.byerschoice.com** *Hours: Monday-Saturday 10:00am-5:00pm, Sunday Noon-5:00pm (Closed major holidays).* Family and friends (employees) hand sculpt precious Caroler figurines. By a walk-through observation deck, you can watch them mold delicate faces and then apply makeup (paint) to add dimension and features. See all the costumes and background landscapes available to make each singing doll unique. What you don't see in production that day, you can watch by pre-taped video.

EVANSBURG STATE PARK

Collegeville - *851 May Hall Road (off US Route 422), 19426.* **Web: www.dcnr.state.pa.us/stateparks/parks/evansburg.htm** *Phone: (610) 409-1150.* This park is a haven for hikers, equestrians and folks who want to picnic and relax. You can take a walk along Skippack Creek or visit the Friedt Visitor Center that provides insight into German Mennonite living in the 18th and 19th centuries. Fishing, Hiking, Cross-Country Skiing.

NATIONAL WATCH & CLOCK MUSEUM

514 Popular Street (off US30 west - follow signs)

Columbia 17512

❑　Phone: (717) 684-8261　**Web:**
　　www.nawcc.org/museum/museum.htm
❑　Hours: Tuesday-Saturday 10:00am-4:00pm (year round). Sunday
　　Noon-4:00pm (April-December). Open Tuesday-Saturday until
　　5:00pm (April-December).
❑　Admission: $4.00-$6.00 (age 6+).
❑　Miscellaneous: "Yours, Mine and Hours" Museum Shop. Library.

National Watch & Clock Museum (cont.)

You've got the time, they've got the place! The National Association of Watch and Clock Collectors have a school (of horology), offices, and this fabulously renovated museum. One staff member described it as the "Disneyland of Clocks and Time". Start at the beginning, Stonehenge, then travel through time as you browse past displays of time-keeping history. You'll see thousands of watches (many still working), unique water and candle clocks, sundials and even an alarm clock that pinches you when it rings! Bells, chimes, music boxes, and organs sound on the hour.

WRIGHT'S FERRY MANSION

38 South 2nd Street (US30 - Columbia/Marietta Exit SR 441 South)

Columbia 17512

- ❑ Phone: (717) 684-4325
- ❑ Hours: Tuesday & Wednesday, Friday & Saturday 10:00am-3:00pm, Closed July 4 (May- October).
- ❑ Admission: $5.00 adult, $2.50 child (6-18). Group tours (Call for reservations - 30 days in advance).

Discover the fascinating and visionary life of Susanna Wright, a bright, creative Quaker woman whose diverse talents have benefited many. She ran a ferry here, was an unofficial doctor and lawyer, launched the silk industry in this region, and shared ideas with people like Ben Franklin with whom she corresponded regularly. The 1738 house reflects Quaker lifestyles prior to 1750 and its collections are one of the most complete and representative in the country. Because this is an "open" museum (no velvet ropes separating you from the displays) you certainly get the feeling that the occupants have just left for a little while…and may be returning shortly! We recommend close supervision for younger children, or better yet only bring them if your children are age 8 or older.

CORNWALL IRON FURNACE

Rexmont Road - PO Box 251 (4 miles North of US76 off SR 72 on SR 419), **Cornwall** 17016

❑   Phone: (717) 272-9711

www.phmc.state.pa.us/bhsm/toh/cornwall/cornwalliron.asp?s ecid=14

❑   Hours: Tuesday-Saturday 9:00am-5:00pm, Sunday Noon-5:00pm (summer). Tuesday-Saturday 10:00am-4:00pm, Sunday Noon-4:00pm (September-May). Closed most holidays, except Summer holidays.

❑   Admission: $2.00-$4.00 per person (age 6+).

A 1742 - 1833 iron making complex. The preserved facility once produced farm tools, kitchenware, stoves, cannons and ammunition. You can see the original furnace stack, blast machinery, blowing tubs, and a Great Wheel (76 feet around). Remember this site was water-powered. An ironmaster's mansion and the Charcoal House Visitor's Center are on the premises.

KEYSTONE STATE PARK

Derry - *RD 2, Box 101 (on SR 1018, the park is three miles from SR 981/SR 22), 15627. Phone: (724) 668-2939. Web: www.dcnr.state.pa.us/stateparks/parks/key.htm*   Beach, Visitor Center, Year-round Education & Interpretation Center, Boat Rentals, Horseback Riding, Sledding, Campsites, Modern Cabins, Fishing, Trails, and Winter Sports.

MARSH CREEK STATE PARK

Downingtown - *675 Park Road (two miles west of the village of Eagle on PA 100), 19335. Phone: (610) 458-5119. Web: www.dcnr.state.pa.us/stateparks/parks/m-crek.htm*   Marsh Creek Lake is especially popular with sailboaters and windsurfers who take advantage of the prevailing wind to enjoy their sport. Nature lovers will enjoy a pleasant walk on hiking trails or the Larkins covered Bridge located in the northeast section of the park. Pool, Boat Rentals, Sledding, and Fishing.

SPRINGTON MANOR FARM

Downingtown - *RD #2, Box 455K (off US322 - Springton Road), 19343.* **Web: *www.chesco.org/ccparks/parks_yrparks.html*** *Phone: (610) 942-2450. Hours: Daily 10:00am-4:00pm. Admission: FREE.* Visit a casual demonstration farm once used to raise sheep (they're still plenty there). The giant Great Barn has an agricultural exhibit that follows the development of farm equipment from the late 1700's to the early 1900's. A catch and release pond lets kids fish for bass and blue gills. Petting zoo. Picnic areas.

MERCER MUSEUM

84 South Pine Street (off SR202, rear SR313 and SR611)

Doylestown 18901

❑   Phone: (215) 345-0210

      Web: www.mercermuseum.org/mercermuseum/index.html

❑   Hours: Monday-Saturday 10:00am-5:00pm, Sunday Noon-5:00pm (open until 9:00 pm on Tuesdays).

❑   Admission: $6.00 adult, $5.50 senior (60+), $2.50 child (6-17).

❑   Miscellaneous: Museum Shop.

The receptionist promised us that the best part of the self-guided tour was the walk into the Center Court. It's amazing! Artifacts are hanging everywhere! While searching through junk in a barn, Henry Chapman Mercer found a jumble of objects made obsolete by the Industrial Revolution. His collection, housed in a "cement castle", represents more than 60 crafts and trades - pre 1850. Called "The Tools of the Nation Maker", play a game to try to find one tool from at least 50 trades. Some are easy to see, but over 40,000 pieces of "junk" are in every nook and cranny. This is the most eccentric, yet curiously fun, museum you'll ever find! By the way, the cement and leaded glass windows truly give that medieval feeling inside and out.

MORAVIAN POTTERY AND TILE WORKS & FONTHILL

130 Swamp Road/East Court Street (Court St. and Swamp Rd., off of Rte. 313, which runs north/south of Doylestown)

Doylestown 18901

- ❑ Phone: (215) 345-6722

  Web: www.cr.nps.gov/NR/travel/delaware/mor.htm
- ❑ Hours: Daily 10:00am-5:00pm, except Sunday Noon-5:00pm.
- ❑ Admission: Averages $2.00-$3.00 per person for Tile Works or $2.50-$7.00 per person for Fonthill.
- ❑ Tours: Self-guided - every 1/2 hour. Last tour at 4:00 pm. Tower Tours for Families (explore basement to tower) the first Saturday morning of every month.
- ❑ Miscellaneous: Tile Shop.

This facility, beginning in 1912, produced tiles and mosaics for floors, walls and ceilings. Mercer's artistic floor tiles adorn the rotunda and halls of the Pennsylvania State Capitol, depicting 400 scenes in the Commonwealth's history. Today, the facility makes reproductions of Mercer's original line of tiles. Mercer was a visionary architect who was one of the first designers to work with reinforced concrete as a building material. Watch the clay being prepared, then stamped with designs, then fired, glazed and fired again. Kids will appreciate "Fonthill" (Mercer's mansion/castle that is next door - **www.mercermuseum.org/fonthill/**) or the Mercer Museum a little more if they understand what made him rich and famous. His mosaics are probably the prettiest to look at.

FRENCH CREEK STATE PARK

Elverson - *843 Park Road (off Route 345), 19520. Phone: (610) 582-9680. Web: www.dcnr.state.pa.us/stateparks/parks/french.htm* French Creek offers two lakes--Hopewell and Scotts Run, extensive forests and almost 40 miles of hiking trails. Adjacent to the park lies Hopewell Furnace. Pool, Boat Rentals, Horseback Riding, Mountain Biking, Campsites, Modern Cabins, Fishing, and Cross-Country Skiing.

HOPEWELL FURNACE NATIONAL HISTORIC SITE

2 Mark Bird Lane (PA Rt. 724 East, turn right onto PA Rt. 345
South), **Elverson** 19520

☐ Phone: (610) 582-8773. **Web: www.nps.gov/hofu/home.html**
☐ Hours: Daily 9:00am-5:00pm. Closed most holidays.
☐ Admission: $4.00 adult (over 17). Children FREE.
☐ Tours: Self-guided tours enhanced by recorded voices of workers
and their families.
☐ Miscellaneous: Younger children would prefer summers when
living history actors are in costume throughout the village. Older
kids really get into the stories told on the tour.

The Visitor's Center features an audio visual program and exhibits
of the original iron castings and tools used in Colonial cold blast
charcoal furnaces. See a restored cast house, water wheel cooling
shed, tenant houses and ironmaster's mansion (The Big House).
Learn about "pig iron" (formed in troughs), and stoves and
weapons produced here - recreated by actual blacksmiths shaping
the hot slabs of iron alongside molders. This is mostly a living
history village (summers and special events) and the "villagers" are
well educated on iron casting. Call ahead to be sure you get to see
live demonstrations during your visit.

EPHRATA AREA COMMUNITY THEATRE

Ephrata - *124 East Main Street (I-76 Exit 21, Route 222 South),
17522. Phone: (717) 738-2ACT. Hours: Mornings June - August.*
Other productions vary in showtimes. "The Ephrata Story" (an
unusual community-how it developed) and other musicals year-
round.

DOUGH BOYS PRETZEL FACTORY

Feasterville - *1801 Bridgetown Pike, 19053. Phone: (215) 357-
8590. **Web: www.doughboyspretzels.com** Tours: Groups of 10 or
more, by appointment.* Tours of soft pretzel factory. Dress as a
baker and twist and bake your own pretzel. Become an "Official
Dough Boys Twister".

FORT WASHINGTON STATE PARK

Fort Washington - *500 Bethlehem Pike (2 miles from PA Turnpike exit 26), 19034. Phone: (215) 646-2942. Web: www.dcnr.state.pa.us/stateparks/parks/ft-was.htm* This beautiful park interests historians of the American Revolution. The park takes its name from the fort built by George Washington's troops in the fall of 1777, before heading to Valley Forge. The park is popular with hikers and bikers. Hawks, Washington Encampment, Fishing, Trails, Winter Sports.

NEWLIN GRIST MILL PARK

Glen Mills - *US 1 & 219 South Cheyney Road, 19342. Phone: (610) 459-2359. Web: www.newlingristmill.org Hours: 8:00am-5:00pm (March-September).* A 1704 restored gristmill, the miller's house, a blacksmith shop, springhouse, and log cabin are in the park. Call first to inquire about upcoming Summer Discovery Programs or Heritage Workshops. These programs explore traditional colonial skills, crafts, and games. Have you taken a "dip" lately (dipping candles in wax that is!)? Small admission for guided tours of working mill. Ground corn sold on premises.

MEMORIAL LAKE STATE PARK

Grantville - *RD 1, Box 7045 (I- 81 at exit 29 /Fort Indiantown Gap, take PA Route 934 North), 17028. Phone: (717) 865-6470. Web: www.dcnr.state.pa.us/stateparks/parks/mem.htm* This quaint park has a lake for canoeing, wind surfing, fishing, hiking trails, & beautiful scenery. Boat Rentals, Fishing, Cross-Country Skiing.

INTERCOURSE PRETZEL FACTORY

3614 Old Philadelphia Pike (at Cross Keys) (at the intersection of Route 340 and Route 772 East), **Intercourse** 17534

- ❑ Phone: (717) 768-3432
     www.amishnews.com/Attractions/intercoursepretzelfactory.htm
- ❑ Admission: FREE
- ❑ Tours: When weather permits factory production Tuesday-Saturday 9:00am-3:00pm (Easter - Columbus Day). Mondays in July & August.
- ❑ Miscellaneous: Snack Bar

Intercourse Pretzel Factory (cont.)

How do you like your pretzels? Soft, stuffed, or hard? Plan on visiting this factory for a lunch/dessert treat. As you watch all the pretzels being made by hand and learn to twist your own pretzel...try to decide which flavors you're going to try now and which you'll take home. Their stuffed pretzels are wrapped around cheeses, meats, relishes, and jams. Soft and hard pretzels come in a variety of seasonings (doesn't brown butter topping sound warm and cozy?) and their chocolate covered varieties are smothered in Wilbur's (our favorite Pennsylvania chocolate) chocolate. Do you see why we suggest to save "tummy room" for snacking?

PEOPLE'S PLACE

3513 Old Philadelphia Pike (SR340), **Intercourse** 17534

❑   Phone: (800) 390-8436 **Web: www.thepeoplesplace.com**

❑   Hours: Daily (except Sundays) 9:30am-8:00pm (Summer), until
       5:00pm (rest of year).

❑   Admission: $5.00 adult, $4.00 senior, $2.50 child (5-11) per
       activity. Discount combo pricing available.

Educational center about Amish/Mennonites. "Who Are the Amish?" - a three screen documentary (30 minutes, especially delightful for kids that can sit still), slide show with music and narration. Younger, fidgety kids will prefer the pace of the "20Q" - imaginative museums with the "Feeling Box", the Barn Raising Book, the Energy Guy, and the Dress Up Room (getting dressed for school), puzzles, & an Alphabet Game (look thru view finder).

HAWK MOUNTAIN

1700 Hawk Mountain Road (I-78, exit 9B north to Route 895 east)

Kempton 19529

❑   Phone: (610) 756-6961 **Web: www.hawkmountain.org**

❑   Hours: Daily 9:00am-5:00pm (most of year), 8:00am-5:00pm
       (September-November).

❑   Admission: Trail Fees (to get to lookouts): $5.00-$7.00 adult,
       $4.00-$7.00 senior, $3.00 child (6-12).

Between mid-August and mid-December an average 18,000 hawks, eagles, and falcons fly past this site. Bookstore. Wildlife viewing windows. Exhibits. Trails. FREE Live-raptor programs on weekends (April-November).

W.K. & S. STEAM RAILROAD

Kempton - *PO Box 24 (SR143 or SR737 into Kempton. - follow signs), 19529. www.kemptontrain.com/pages/741740/index.htm Phone: (610) 756-6469. Hours: Sundays (May-October), Saturdays also (July, August, October). Departures from 1:00pm-4:00pm leave every hour on the hour. Admission: $3.00-$6.00 (age 3+).* Scenic train ride on the Hawk Mountain Line. Passengers enjoy a three-mile ride to Wanamaker through Pennsylvania's picturesque countryside, passing several historic sites and structures. Nice short ride (40 minutes) where you can get off at picnic groves throughout the countryside and get back on later. Gift shop. Snack bar.

LONGWOOD GARDENS

US Route 1, PO Box 501 (NE of town), **Kennett Square** 19348

❑   Phone: (610) 388-1000 **Web: www.longwoodgardens.com**
❑   Hours: Daily 9:00am-5:00pm (open later during peak Spring / Summer & Holiday seasons)
❑   Admission: $14.00 adult, ($10.00 on Tuesdays) *(no discount during holidays)*, $6.00 youth (ages 16-20), $2.00 child (ages 6-15), Under age 6 FREE.

Special children's programs like Peter Rabbit and Friends, Christmas and Mazes. 1,050 acres with 40 indoor/outdoor gardens. Conservatory and rainbow fountains. Terrace Restaurant. Special too, are the water platters, Topiary garden and Idea Garden.

MIDDLE CREEK WILDLIFE MANAGEMENT AREA

Kleinfeltersville - *Hopeland Road - PO Box 110, 17039. Web: www.dep.state.pa.us/dep/deputate/enved/mcreek.htm. Phone: (717) 733-1512. Hours: Tuesday - Saturday 8:00am-4:00pm, Sunday Noon-5:00pm (March-November). Admission: FREE.* Approximately 6300 acre habitat for migrating waterfowls and wildlife includes Visitor Center and Nature Trails.

CRYSTAL CAVE

Kutztown - *Crystal Cave Road (Off US 222. Follow signs), 19530. Phone: (610) 683-6765.* **Web: www.crystalcavepa.com** *Hours: Daily 9:00am-5:00pm (March-November) Summer to 6:00 or 7:00pm. Holidays & Weekends to 6:00pm. Admission: $5.00-$8.50 (age 4+). Tours: 45 minutes includes video about cave formation.* Food. Gift shop. Rock shop. Mini-golf. Museum and nature trails. Look for the Giant's Tooth and the Ear of Corn formations.

RODALE INSTITUTE FARM

611 Siegfriedale Road (off US222, just northeast of town)

Kutztown 19530

- ❑ Phone: (610) 683-1400 **Web: www.rodaleinstitute.org**
- ❑ Hours: Monday-Saturday 9:00am-5:00pm, Sunday 10:00am-3:00pm (early May - mid-October).
- ❑ Admission: Average $3.00 per person (age 5+)
- ❑ Tours: Monday-Friday morning (By appointment).
- ❑ Miscellaneous: International Café features organic light fare and beverages. Gift shop - suggest you try homemade organic apple sauce or butter.

Regenerative Organic Farming and Gardening - Do you know what that means? If you've eaten one too many frozen or fast food meals this week - start feeling healthier here. Learn the connection between healthy soil, healthy food, and healthy people, all through demonstrations and children's gardens. A tour highlight for children is watching how earthworms help aerate and fertilize the soil. Initial shrieks turn to keen interest as the children handle the subterranean workers, feed them kitchen scraps and watch them burrow. They can then take a trip through a child-size "Earthworm Tunnel™" for a first-hand experience.

DUTCH APPLE DINNER THEATRE

Lancaster - *510 Centerville Road (off US 30west), 17601. Phone: (717) 898-1900.* **Web: www.dutchapple.com** *Admission: Tickets range $18.00-$33.00.* Children's matinee and Sunday twilight. Dine while watching children's musicals like Sleeping Beauty.

HANDS-ON HOUSE CHILDREN'S MUSEUM

2380 Kissel Hill Road (US 30 to Oregon Pike N exit-next to Landis Valley Museum), **Lancaster** 17601

- ❑ Phone: (717) 569-KIDS **Web: www.handsonhouse.org**
- ❑ Hours: Tuesday-Saturday Open 10:00 or 11:00am-4:00 or 5:00pm , Saturday 10:00am-5:00pm, Sunday Noon-5:00pm. Open Mondays in the summer. Closed major winter holiday times.
- ❑ Admission: $5.00 general.
- ❑ Miscellaneous: Recommended for ages 2-10. Everything is simply explained to allow parents and kids' imagination to explore possibilities.

Favorite "spaces" include: a Lancaster Farming Area and Art Smart Fun. In Marty's Machine Shop, you'll wear safety goggles to work on an assembly line or sort and deliver mail at a kid-friendly factory. The Space Voyage Checkpoint takes kids on a spaceship ride to learn about health and wellness as earthlings get a checkup before their journey into space. At Feelings, talk to a giant stuffed bear.

LANDIS VALLEY MUSEUM

2451 Kissel Hill Road (3 miles north on Oregon Pike - SR272)

Lancaster 17601

- ❑ Phone: (717) 569-0401 **Web: www.landisvalleymuseum.org**
- ❑ Hours: Monday-Saturday 9:00am-5:00pm, Sunday Noon-5:00pm.
- ❑ Admission: $9.00 adult, $7.00 senior (60+), $6.00 child (6-17).
- ❑ Miscellaneous: Weathervane gift shop.

The largest Pennsylvania German museum in the U.S. (100 acres). See 20 buildings including the craft shop, schoolhouse, country store, leather crafts, farmstead, blacksmith, transportation building, hotel, pottery shop plus others. Exhibits interpret rural life prior to 1900 through artisans and demonstrations of traditional skills. Special performances, craft demonstrations and living history programs change monthly. Don't forget about the traditional walkways of dirt, pebble or brick.

AMISH FARM AND HOUSE

2395 Route 30 East,

Lancaster 17602

- ❑ Phone: (717) 394-6185 **Web: www.amishfarmandhouse.com**
- ❑ Hours: Daily 8:30am-6:00pm (Summer). 8:30am-5:00pm (Spring & Fall), 8:30am-4:00pm (November-March).
- ❑ Admission: $6.95 adult, $6.25 senior (60+), $4.25 child (5-11)
- ❑ Tours: 35 minutes long.
- ❑ Miscellaneous: Dutch Food Pavilion (April - October). Weekend craft demonstrations (branch carvings for example). Nighttime lamp tours (late September -late October). Buggy rides.

Guided tours of Amish home (10 rooms) - learn the history, religious customs and a simple way of life. Self-guided tour of a working farm with local crops, barns, and farm animals. Most interesting is a unique Lancaster County device - a water wheel powered pump (smaller pump in meadow) operates a larger pump via wire. In the Spring House, a large water wheel powers a pump which forces cold spring water into a kitchen refrigerator. A limestone quarry on the property supplied stone to build this barn and house.

BIBLICAL TABERNACLE REPRODUCTION / MENNONITE INFORMATION CENTER

2209 Millstream Road - Off US30

Lancaster 17602

- ❑ Phone: (717) 299-0954 **Web: www.mennoniteinfoctr.com**
- ❑ Hours: Monday-Saturday 8:00am-5:00pm (April-October). 8:30am-4:30pm (November-March).
- ❑ Admission: FREE (Center). $2.50-$5.00 (Tabernacle).
- ❑ Tours: Guided group tours can be arranged for a small fee per person.
- ❑ Miscellaneous: Gift shop featuring crafts (reproduction) from biblical times & craft kits to recreate tabernacle.

Film and displays explaining the faith and culture of Amish and Mennonites called "Postcards From a Heritage of Faith". Shown every half hour. Included is a reproduction of a Hebrew Tabernacle with lecture tours given on the history, construction, function, and significance on the hour (every 2 hours in the Winter). Most kids leave with an understanding of the Arc of the Covenant and can answer as to why the 66 lumps in the candleholder were prophecy of the future.

DISCOVER LANCASTER COUNTY HISTORY MUSEUM
2249 Route 30 East, **Lancaster** 17602

❑   Phone: (717) 393-3679 **Web: www.discoverlancaster.com**
❑   Hours: Daily 9:00am-8:00pm (Summer), 9:00am-5:00pm (Winter/Spring/Fall). Open until 8:00pm Saturdays in May/December.
❑   Admission: $6.95 adult, $6.25 senior (60+), $4.25 child (5-11).
❑   Miscellaneous: Gift shop.

See 32 life-like (some with audiovisuals) scenes of historic events in Pennsylvania from the 1600's to the present. Example: Indian Treaty, Ephrata Cloister, "Penn's Woods" and early settlers. Watch a 10 minute animatronics of an Amish Barn Raising - actually it takes one day in real life - a major accomplishment until you learn about their consistent, organized teamwork. Recently updated, the museum is equipped with several interactive areas relating to the scenes you see. For example, cut a log and see how old the tree was or look through a mirror to see yourself grown up (just like Daniel Boone).

DUTCH WONDERLAND FAMILY AMUSEMENT PARK
Lancaster - *2249 Route 30 East, 17602. Phone: (717) 291-1888. Web: www.dutchwonderland.com Hours: Daily 10:00am-7:00pm (Memorial Day-Labor Day), Weekends only 10:00am-6:00pm (Spring & Fall). Admission: Range $19.00-$26.00 (ages 3+). Discount packages available adding nearby attractions.* 48 acres with 28 rides, high diving shows, and botanical gardens. Rides include: Roller Coaster, Giant Slide, Double Splash Flume, Flying Trapeze, Space Shuttle, Lady Riverboat rides, Mini-Train rides, Sky ride, and Voyager motion simulator.

HERITAGE CENTER MUSEUM
OF LANCASTER COUNTY

Lancaster - *13 West King Street (Penn Square - Downtown), 17603. **Web:** www.lancasterheritage.com   Phone: (717) 299 - 6440. Hours: Tuesday - Saturday 10:00am - 5:00pm (mid-April - December). Admission: FREE.* You'll find out why Amish dolls have no faces, why there's an ever-watchful eye peering down from the ceiling and why the face in the tall-case clock changes from sun to moon. Focuses on local furniture, folk art and toys. Children's activity area (summertime) and self-guided Children's Guide available.

NORTH MUSEUM OF NATURAL HISTORY & SCIENCE

Lancaster - *400 College Avenue (Franklin Marshall College), 17603. Phone: (717) 291-3941.   **Web:** www.northmuseum.org Hours: Tuesday-Saturday 9:00am-5:00pm, Sunday Noon-5:00pm. Admission: $5.50 adult, $4.50 senior (65+) and child (3-12).* From the foundations of our earth to the wonders of space, dinosaurs to Native Americans, hands-on discovery for children to live snakes and turtles, the North Museum offers fun learning experiences about science and the natural world. Child's Discovery Room. Planetarium shows weekend afternoons.

WHEATLAND

1120 Marietta Avenue (PA 23 off US30west)

Lancaster 17603

- ❑ Phone: (717) 392-8721 **Web: www.wheatland.org**
- ❑ Hours: Daily 10:00am-4:00pm (April-October) plus long weekends in November (Friday-Monday).
- ❑ Admission: $5.50 adult, $4.50 senior, $3.50 student, $1.75 child (6-11).
- ❑ Tours: Costume guides for general or pre-arranged hands-on tours.
- ❑ Miscellaneous: Gift shop. Snack bar.

The Federal Style mansion was home to the nation's 15th President (and the only President from Pennsylvania), James Buchanan. Tours begin in the carriage house where you view a film about Mr. Buchanan and see the actual carriage his family used to travel around town. Also see the library that served as a headquarters for his Presidential campaign. Kids are invited to dress in top hats or hoop skirts and may be asked questions like, "How often did people take baths in the mid-1800's?" Guess? (Answer - An average of 2 times per year!) His response to inquiries about "Wheatland" was..."I am now residing at this place, which is an agreeable country residence...I hope you may not fail to come this way...I should be delighted with a visit..."

AMERICAN MUSIC THEATRE

Lancaster - *2425 Lincoln Highway East (US 30), 17605. Phone: (717) 397-7700 or (800) 648-4102. Web: www.amtshows.com Spring – Fall.* American Sights. American sounds. American Songs. American spirit. Musicals plus 30+ celebrity concerts year round. Morning, matinee and evening shows.

DONEGAL MILLS PLANTATION

Lancaster (Mount Joy) - *1190 Trout Run Road (SR772 to Musser Road - Follow signs), 17552. Phone: (717) 653-2168. Hours: Weekends Noon-6:00pm (Mid-March - December). Admission: $2.00-$4.00 (age 6+). Tours: Guided.* Visitors can tour this plantation which includes a 250 year old mansion, a mill, miller's house, bake house, and garden and wildlife area. Look for special seasonal events here. Many activities during these times are family-oriented.

NATIONAL CHRISTMAS CENTER

3427 US 30 (Lincoln Highway), **Lancaster (Paradise)** 17562

- ❑   Phone: (717) 442-7950
- ❑   Hours: Daily 10:00am-6:00pm (Early May-January 2).
- ❑   Admission: $5.00-$9.00 (age 3+).
- ❑   Miscellaneous: Santa visits November 20th - December 23rd. Gift shop.

As you enter, you're greeted by a cute 1950's Christmas morning scene as a little boy opens and tries on his new cowboy outfit. Another scene depicts "Yes Virginia, There is a Santa Claus". Can you find Santa patiently waiting for a little girl to go to bed? This scene depicts a Christmas 100 years ago. Life cast artists create theme walk-thru displays with story lines. "Tudor Towne" is of Jolly Old England, a Once-Upon-A-Time World. "Return to Christmas Past" features antiques dating back to the early 1800's . "The First Christmas" probably has the most impact as you walk down a life-size recreation of the journey of Mary and Joseph to Bethlehem. It's very touching.

WHITE CLAY CREEK STATE PARK

Landenberg - *PO Box 172 (off Route 896), 19350. Phone: (610) 255-5415. Web: www.dcnr.state.pa.us/stateparks/parks/w-clay.htm* White Clay Creek Preserve is managed for low intensity recreational day use activities throughout the year. Day use areas are open daily from 8:00am to sunset. Horseback Riding, Fishing, Trails.

STURGIS PRETZEL

219 East Main Street (Route 772 - off Route 501)

Lititz 17543

❑ Phone: (717) 626-4354 **Web: www.sturgispretzel.com**
❑ Hours: Monday-Saturday, 9:00am-5:00pm
❑ Admission: General $2.00 (A pretzel is given as your admission ticket. Be careful not to eat it all before the tour starts!)
❑ Tours: Every half hour.
❑ Miscellaneous: Gift shop with all sorts of fresh baked pretzels (flavorings, galore!) to purchase.

Boy, did the memories flow at this place! Over 20 years ago, my family *(Michele's)* took the same tour, in the same building and I still have my "Official Pretzel Twister" certificate. (By the way, they still do that - our daughter now has one too!). This is the first pretzel bakery in America (1861) and they still make their original soft pretzel by hand in the original 200 year old ovens. Julius Sturgis started the pretzel industry with a recipe he learned from a hobo. Learn the history of the "pretiola" derived from monk's gifts to nearby children if they said their prayers. As you learn to fold your own pretzel, you'll learn how each step is related to prayer or marriage or the trinity. Definite "must see" while in Amish country.

WILBUR CHOCOLATE AMERICANA MUSEUM

48 North Broad Street - (Route 501), **Lititz** 17543

- ❏   Phone: (717) 626-3249 **Web: www.wilburbuds.com**
- ❏   Hours: Monday-Saturday 10:00am-5:00pm.
- ❏   Admission: FREE
- ❏   Miscellaneous: Gift shop - suggest chocolate pretzels or Wilbur Buds (free sample).

Candy Americana Museum - antique metal molds, tin boxes, advertisements. View Video – "The World Of Wilbur Chocolate" - see smooth chocolate made from the start. Pass by the Candy Kitchen where specialty candy is hand-made right before your eyes. Pick up a "lucky" cocoa bean as you walk in (don't eat it though!). Everyone walks out with a bag full of store bought variety chocolates. P.S. for a walk back in time, try their hot cocoa mix that you prepare over a stove - it's worth shoveling snow to enter the warm house full of an aroma of rich liquid chocolate.

MEDIA THEATRE

Media - *321 West State Street, 19063. Phone: (800) 568-7771 or (610) 566-4020.* **Web: *www.mediatheatre.com*** World-class children's music theatre with productions like the Secret Garden.

RIDLEY CREEK STATE PARK

Media - Sycamore Mills Road (entrances on PA3, PA 252 or PA352), 19063. *www.dcnr.state.pa.us/stateparks/parks/r-crek.htm* Phone: (610) 892-3900. Shaded equestrian, hiking and bicycling trails lace the woodlands and old meadow. Within the park is the Colonial Pennsylvania Plantation that depicts a Delaware County Quaker farm prior to the American Revolution. On weekends from April to November, visitors can observe the farm family cooking over the open hearth, preserving foods, processing textiles, tending field crops and performing other chores necessary for survival in the 18th century world (small fee, 610-566-1725). Fishing and Winter Sports.

MAPLE GROVE PARK RACEWAY

Mohnton - *RR #3 Box 3420, 19540. Phone: (610) 856-7200, Web: www.maplegroveraceway.com (April-October). Admission.* 320 mph NHRA drag racing. Keystone Nationals in September.

PENNSBURY MANOR

400 Pennsbury Memorial Lane (on the Delaware River),

Morrisville 19067

- ❑   Phone: (215) 946-0400
      Web: www.pennsburymanor.org/PennInPa.html
- ❑   Hours: Tuesday-Saturday 9:00am-5:00pm, Sunday Noon-5:00pm (open Summer holidays).
- ❑   Admission: $5.00 adult, $4.50 senior, $3.00 child (6-17) .
- ❑   Tours: 90 minutes long - a little difficult for pre-schoolers.
- ❑   Miscellaneous: Best for kids to visit (April - October) Sundays for living history days. Picnic areas.

A quaint, Quaker, simple homestead of William Penn, the founder of Pennsylvania. See a replica of the boat Penn used to "commute" to Philly. They may be baking bread (up to 30 loaves at one time!) in the bake house or checkout the farm where sheep and geese roam. Inside the Visitor's Center try writing with the original "pen" - a quill pen. You can also learn about Colonial James writing style here.

NEW HOPE AND IVYLAND RAILROAD

PO Box 634 (Depot at West Bridge/Stockton St.) **New Hope** 18938

- ❑   Phone: (215) 862-2332 **Web: www.newhoperailroad.com**
- ❑   Hours: Daily (April-November). Weekends (rest of year).
- ❑   Admission: $10.00 adult, $9.00 senior (62+), $7.00 child (2-11), $1.50 Children under 2.
- ❑   Tours: Departure times vary, phone or visit website for schedule. 9 miles round trip-45 minutes.

This ride is famous for the trestle called "Pauline" upon which actress Pearl White was bound to in the 1914 silent film "The Perils of Pauline". It might be the best way to expose young kids to the silent movies era (pictures available at the depot, too).

NEW HOPE BOAT RIDES

New Hope 18938

❑ CORYELL'S FERRY HISTORIC BOAT RIDES. 22 South Main Street at Gerenser's Ice Cream. (215) 862-2050 or **www.spiritof76.com** - 1/2 hour tours on path once used to commute passengers by canoe (now they use paddleboats). (April - October)

❑ WELLS FERRY - Ferry Street and River Road. (215) 862-5965. Guided tour on a 36 passenger boat highlighting history of river and canal plus famous homes and wildlife. Admission. (May - October)

TYLER STATE PARK

Newtown - *101 Swamp Road (Follow I-95 north to the Newtown-Yardley exit 30), 18940. Phone: (215) 968-2021. **Web:** www.dcnr.state.pa.us/stateparks/parks/tyler.htm* The meandering waters of Neshaminy Creek flow through the park along with 10 miles of paved bicycling trails, a playhouse--Spring Garden Mill, and several children's play areas. Boat Rentals, Horseback Riding, Fishing, Trails, Winter Sports.

ELMWOOD PARK ZOO

1661 Harding Blvd (I76 to Rte. 202 to Johnson Hwy.)

Norristown 19401

❑ Phone: (610) 277-BUCK **Web: www.elmwoodparkzoo.com**
❑ Hours: Daily 10:00am-5:00pm. Closed major winter holidays.
❑ Admission: $7.25 adult, $5.50 senior (65+), $4.95 child (2-12).
❑ Miscellaneous: Pony rides add $2.00. Snack shop. Gift shop. Picnic area.

Highlights of the zoo include: Petting Barn (goats & sheep), Duck Lake, Prairie Dog exhibits, and Aviary Wetland (waterfowl, beaver, otters), The Bayou (murky home to lovely alligators, turtles, and snakes - everything that hisses or snaps!). There's also your basic natural Grasslands (bison, elk, and new "bears" area). Animal shows on Summer weekends.

HERR'S SNACKS VISITOR'S CENTER

PO Box 300 (US 1 and SR272 to Herr Drive), **Nottingham** 19362

- ❑ Phone: (800) 63-SNACK, **Web: www.herrs.com**
- ❑ Hours: Monday-Thursday, 9:00am-3:00pm, Friday, 9:00-11:00am (Extended summer hours)
- ❑ Admission: FREE.
- ❑ Tours: Reservations recommended
- ❑ Miscellaneous: Gift shop. Chippers Café with crunch and munch lunchroom. Very reasonable snack bar prices.

"Watch a groovy-chip movie" starring "Chipper" your tour guide and mascot. Whimsical (combination guide and TV monitor) tour takes you through the simple process of snack food production. Lots of hot oil and hot air drying, moisturizing and "spritzing" going on - a salon for snacks! Try samples warm off the "beltway" - those were a favorite point of the tour. Yes, you can have more than one! Also see other snacks made like cheesepuffs (corn meal dollops filled with air), tortilla chips, popcorn (huge poppers!) and pretzels. Your kids will be amused at the sideway mixers churning out 10 pound mounds of pretzel dough. The dough takes a long trip on a conveyor and then a "dough-bot" (robot) removes them to be shaped & baked. An excellent, organized tour - voted our best pick of snack food tours.

PHILLY TRANSPORTATION TOURS

Philadelphia - *(Downtown), Admission: Call for rates. Pay as you board.*

- ❑ AMERICAN TROLLEY TOURS - (215) 333-2119. The complete trolley tour loop is 2 hours. On/off privileges.
- ❑ 76 CARRIAGE COMPANY - (215) 923-8522. Victorian carriage rides. Leave at 2nd and Lombard Streets. 20 minute daytime tours for up to four people.
- ❑ PHILADELPHIA TROLLEY WORKS - (215) 925-TOUR. Narrated tours with on/off privileges.
- ❑ PHILLY PHLASH - (215) 4-PHLASH. Purple and teal buses run in a loop around downtown.
- ❑ RIVERLINK FERRY - (215) 925-LINK. Passenger ferry across the Delaware River between Penn's Landing and the Camden waterfront sites.

PHILADELPHIA ORCHESTRA

Philadelphia - *260 South Broad Street, 16th Floor (most performances at Kimmel Center), 19102. Phone: (215) 893-1900.* **Web: www.philorch.org** Sound All Around Series (ages 3-5), learn about the different families of instruments. Family Concert Series (ages 6-12) - music featuring puppets, magicians, storytellers, and young soloists. (Saturday mornings).

ACADEMY OF NATURAL SCIENCES

1900 Benjamin Franklin Parkway (off I-76 and corner of 19th Street), **Philadelphia** 19103

❑ Phone: (215) 299-1000 **Web: www.acnatsci.org**

❑ Hours: Monday-Friday 10:00am-4:30pm, Saturday, Sunday & Holidays 10:00am-5:00pm. Closed Thanksgiving, Christmas, and New Year's Day.

❑ Admission: $9.00 adult, $8.25 senior (65+), $8.00 child (3-12). Part of CityPass discount card.

❑ Miscellaneous: Ask for Scavenger Hunts sheets (age appropriate) when you enter. The kids stay focused this way. Films show daily. Ecology Café and gift shop.

The oldest dinosaur and natural science exhibit in the world is here. Actually peer into, or walk under, dinosaurs. You're greeted by a roaring robotic dinosaur at one entrance. A giant dinosaur skeleton hangs over the information desk at the main entrance. Most families' favorite area is the Dinosaur Hall. This is hands-on paleontology including a fossil dig (child equipped with goggles and tools), fossil prep lab, and Time Machine (get your picture image appearing with dinosaurs!). You'll also meet T-Rex, plus 11 friends, and even get to climb into a dinosaur skull. The North American Hall has some stuffed large animals that are almost 200 years old. By request only (and specific times), there are live animals shows and "Outside In"... hands-on, touching mice, snakes, frogs, and huge bugs. There's also a crystals and gems exhibit that features a 57 pound amethyst and "Living Downstream" - a showcase of life in a watershed or Egyptian Mummies.

FRANKLIN INSTITUTE SCIENCE MUSEUM

222 North 20th Street, **Philadelphia** 19103

- ❑ Phone: (215) 448-1200. **Web: www.fi.edu**
- ❑ Hours: Daily 9:30am-5:00pm.
- ❑ Admission: $12.75 adult, $10.00 child (4-11) & senior 62+.
  Sci-Pass includes museum, science demos, planetarium & 3D Theater.
- ❑ Miscellaneous: Ben's Restaurant - Lunch, Milky Way Café,
  Scoops & Slices, Museum Stores. Special exhibits change in the
  Mandell Center. IMAX Theatre (additional charge). Science Park
  out back (open May-October).

What began as a national memorial to Ben Franklin is now a
hands-on exhibit and demonstration complex. At the entrance are
displays of some of Franklin's personal effects and a famous statue
by James Earle Fraser. Some exhibits have been there forever.
Walk through a "Human Heart" - hear a heart beating as "blood"
races through the arteries. Also, see a full-size train or airplane
cockpit! Here's a look at other areas:

- ❑ SPACE COMMAND - Visit a research station right here on
  Earth! Locate your house using a satellite home-tracking device!
  Travel through time to uncover what our ancestry thought about
  space! Embark on a mission to discover a lost, unmanned space
  probe! Check out equipment used by real astronauts to explore
  space!
- ❑ KIDSCIENCE CENTER - Flight and optical illusions.
  Planetarium. Interactive Franklin…he's electric! Liquid air show
  - weather.
- ❑ OMNIVERSE THEATER - 180 degree field of view motion
  picture made for all age groups. Titles vary seasonally.

PLEASE TOUCH MUSEUM

210 North 21st Street (21st and Race Streets), **Philadelphia** 19103

- ❑ Phone: (215) 963-0667 **Web: www.pleasetouchmuseum.org**
- ❑ Hours: Daily 9:00am-4:30pm. Open until 5:00pm during the
  summer.
- ❑ Admission: General $8.95 (over age 1).

❑   Miscellaneous: Strollers are not permitted (inside parking area for
      strollers is available). Education Store - take ideas from the
      museum home as souvenirs or projects. Special areas for kids 3
      and under.

A hands-on museum for kids 8 and under with activities that are
educational, fun, and safe. Here are the highlights to look forward to:

❑   SENDAK - You probably recognize the name - does "Where the
      Wild Things Are" book ring a bell? Maurice Sendak's
      (Philadelphia native) popular books come to life as Max's giant
      bedroom is filled with jungle life. Children use fantasy play and
      daydreams to respond to feelings like anger and joy.
❑   MOVE IT! - Hop in a real full-sized bus or monorail. Learn to
      sail a boat or fill up your tank at the service station.
❑   SUPER MARKET SCIENCE - Shop and cook in a child sized,
      fully stocked grocery store, kitchen, and food science lab. Use a
      microscope or magnifying glass to examine those foodstuffs
      more closely.
❑   STUDIO PTM - Be in front of or behind a camera on TV. Try
      making sound effects like thunder. This is the easiest hands-on
      TV studio we've been in.
❑   ALICE IN WONDERLAND - The tale is explained in miniature
      (little doors to peek through) and then full size. Try on cover ups
      and pretend you're the Queen of Hearts ready for a tea party with
      Mad Hatter & rabbit (great photo op).

Although the setups are classic in here, the fresh aspects of
creativity through role playing are really different. It's pricier than
most kid's museums we've been to in our travels, but its uniqueness
is worth it - be sure to take advantage of science park (free with
admission) across the street.

SCIENCE PARK

Philadelphia - *(21st Street between Winter & Race Streets),
19103. Hours: During Franklin Institute hours, weather permitting
- (May-October). Admission: Included with either "Please Touch
Museum" or "Franklin Institute Museum" admission.* A 38,000
square foot learning playground. Climb on and over high tech

learning structures like mazes and optical illusions. Sky bike, miniature golf, radar detector and echo chambers. Its bright colors and unusual shapes entice kids.

PHILADELPHIA ZOO

3400 West Girard Avenue (I-76, exit 36)

Philadelphia 19104

❑   Phone: (215) 243-1100 **Web: www.phillyzoo.org**
❑   Hours: Daily 9:30am-5:00pm (February-November). Daily 9:30am-4:00pm (December-January). Closed Thanksgiving, December 24, 25 and 31 plus New Years Day.
❑   Admission: $9.95 (ages 2+) Zoo. $9.95 Zooballoon Ride. Parking $6.00.
❑   Miscellaneous: Zoo shop. McDonald's restaurants. Victorian picnic groves. Stroller and wheelchair rentals. Camel, elephant and pony rides and "Treehouse" interactive areas have additional fees. Behind-the-Scenes tours available occasionally.

The first zoo in the country - now has 1600 animals on 42 acres of beautiful landscape. Favorites include the famous white lions, Jezebel and Vinkel, the first white lions ever to be exhibited in North America. Presently, there are no white lions in the wild. Carnivore Kingdom has the country's only giant otters. Bear Country allows you to interact (viewing , that is) with playful bears that love to show off. The Children's Zoo has your typically petted animals plus cow-milking and other live demonstrations in the pavilion. The first passenger carrying balloon in the world to be located at a zoo is available for rides (Zooballoon).

UNIVERSITY OF PENNSYLVANIA MUSEUM OF ARCHAEOLOGY & ANTHROPOLOGY

3260 South Street (I-76 to South Street exit to 33rd and Spruce Streets), Philadelphia 19104

❑   Phone: (215) 898-4001. **Web: www.upenn.edu/museum**
❑   Hours: Tuesday-Saturday 10:00am-4:30pm, Sunday 1:00-5:00pm (Closed Mondays, Holidays, and summer Sundays from Memorial Day to Labor Day)

❑ Admission: $5.00 adult, $2.50 senior (62+) and student (age 6+).

❑ Tours: Guided on Weekends at 1:30 pm during the school year.

❑ Miscellaneous: Snack café. Pyramid Gift Shop. Most fun to come during a Family Fun Day Event (215) 898-4890.

Exhibits outstanding findings from Ancient Egypt, Asia, Central America, North America, Mesopotamia, Greece, and Africa, uncovered by University staff and student expeditions. See a giant Sphinx and real mummies. The stories of the archeologists' thoughts and accompanying pictures of "digs" might inspire a budding career.

BETSY ROSS HOUSE

239 Arch Street (Between 2nd & 3rd Streets), Philadelphia 19106

❑ Phone: (215) 686-1252. **Web: www.ushistory.org/betsy/**

❑ Hours: Tuesday-Sunday & Monday Holidays 10:00am-5:00pm. Also open summer Mondays. Closed Thanksgiving, Christmas and New Years.

❑ Admission: Donations, $1.00-$2.00 suggested.

❑ Tours: Self-guided.

❑ Miscellaneous: Ask for the "house hunt" sheet for kids.

In 1777, the first American flag made by Colonial Mrs. Ross was sewn here. You can tour her modest, working class home. Did she design the flag? Each room has a description, in Betsy's words (in old English), of what led up to her sewing the flag. She and the fellas that made the Liberty Bell were just ordinary folks who had a skill needed to enhance the cause of Independence. What was considered a routine job lead to national recognition many years later!

CARPENTER'S HALL

Philadelphia - *320 Chestnut Street, 19106. Phone: (215) 925-0167.* **Web: www.ushistory.org/carpentershall/** *Hours: Tuesday-Sunday 10:00am-4:00pm (Closed January & February Tuesdays). Admission: FREE.* Displays of early carpenters' chairs and tools used by the First Continental Congress in 1774. A 10 minute video chronicles the history of the carpenter's company (they still own and operate the hall).

CHRIST CHURCH

20 North American Street 2nd Street (between Arch & Market Streets), Philadelphia 19106

- ❑ Phone: (215) 922-1695 **Web: www.christchurchphila.org**
- ❑ Hours: Monday-Saturday 9:00am-5:00pm, Sunday 1:00-5:00pm (March-December). Wednesday-Sunday (Rest of year).
- ❑ Admission: Donation.
- ❑ Miscellaneous: Services (Episcopal) held on Sunday mornings and Wednesday at 12:00pm.

Fifteen signers of the Declaration of Independence worshiped here including George Washington and Benjamin Franklin. A brass plaque marks each pew of famous Colonists including Betsy Ross. The church was built in 1727 and originally had dirt or wood floors. Ask a guide what those marble rectangles are in the floor. Careful - though they won't mind…you may be stepping on the memory of a notable patron of the church!

CITY TAVERN

Philadelphia - *138 South 2nd Street, 19106. Phone: (215) 413-1443. Web: www.citytavern.com Hours: Daily, Lunch & Dinner Miscellaneous: Children's menu. Casual dress. Fine dining prices.* Based on a Colonial theme in a 1774 structure, the restaurant serves traditional beef and pork pie or stew plus modern favorites (mostly meat and potatoes). Paul Revere, General Washington, Benedict Arnold, and John Adams have all stopped here. Costumed wait staff serve you as you eat and drink from pewter utensils and cups.

DECLARATION (GRAFF) HOUSE

Philadelphia - *7th & Market Streets, 19106. Phone: (215) 597-8974. Web: www.nps.gov/inde/declaration-house.html Hours: Generally 10:00am-1:00pm. Vary by season. (Call ahead). Admission: FREE.* Catch the short video and then see the rooms that Continental Congress delegate, Thomas Jefferson rented in this building where he penned the actual Declaration of Independence. Like the other buildings in this national park, our history studies come alive in these authentic places where great men once walked, worked, and lived.

FIREMAN'S HALL

Philadelphia - *147 North 2nd Street (Historic district near Elfreth's Alley), 19106. Phone: (215) 923-1438.* **Web:** ***www.angelfire.com/pa4/firemanshall/*** *Hours: Tuesday-Saturday 9:00am-5:00pm. Admission: FREE.* An 1876 firehouse depicts the history of firefighting. See memorabilia, films, and early equipment. Did your kids know Benjamin Franklin founded the first Philadelphia Fire Department in 1736? See old-fashioned leather buckets, fire wagons and an "around the world" display of firefighter helmets. Play pretend in the re-created living quarters or steer a fireboat. Taped firemen's stories recall high level exciting moments on the job. The Spider Hose Reel (1804) has a chariot look with brass bells and shiny mirrors. Also be on the lookout for the fire pole and injured firemen's hats (charred & broken).

FRANKLIN COURT

3rd, 4th, Chestnut & Market Streets (Chestnut or Market Street entrance), **Philadelphia** 19106

- ❑ Phone: (215) 597-8974
  Web: www.ushistory.org/tour/tour_fcourt.htm
- ❑ Hours: Usually daily 10:00am-5:00pm but can vary. Call for details.
- ❑ Admission: FREE

Hear "voices" of historic men such as Thomas Jefferson and Mark Twain talk about Franklin and how they felt about his character. "Bump into" Mr. Franklin as you roam his court and he'll invite you to gather around to hear stories of his life. Once owned by Ben Franklin who lived in Philadelphia from 1722-1790, the complex of buildings includes:

- ❑ UNDERGROUND THEATER AND MUSEUM - See "Portrait of a Family" - tells of his family life.
- ❑ NEWSPAPER OFFICE - Working reproduction of 1785 printing press and bindery.
- ❑ POST OFFICE - In 1775, Ben Franklin was appointed as the first Postmaster General. The name "Free Franklin" was used as the hand cancellation signature because Mr. Franklin was referring to America's struggle for freedom. See actual hand-canceled letters, then, purchase a post card & send it from this working post office!

INDEPENDENCE HALL

5th & 6th Streets on Chestnut

Philadelphia 19106

- ❏ Phone: (215) 965-7676 **Web: www.independencehall.org**
- ❏ Hours: Daily 9:00am-5:00pm.
- ❏ Admission: FREE
- ❏ Tours: Guided tours only throughout the day. Long lines move pretty fast. You must reserve a free timed ticket from the Visitor Center or **http://reservations.nps.gov** ($1.50 handling fee per ticket if ordered in advance) to enter spring, summer and fall.
- ❏ Miscellaneous: Congress Hall (where the first US Congress met and inaugurations of Presidents occurred) and Old City Hall (Supreme Court original house) are across the street. Hours vary but it is a must see for kids studying the setup of the United States Government.

Hey…this is the place that we see in countless movies and pictures. You will get a patriotic chill as you enter the hall where the Declaration of Independence was adopted and the U.S. Constitution was written. The Assembly Room looks just as it did in 1776 (you'll feel like you're in a movie) and you can see the original inkwell the Declaration signers dipped quills in to sign the famous freedom document.

INDEPENDENCE SEAPORT MUSEUM

211 South Columbus Blvd (I-95 exit 20)

Philadelphia 19106

- ❏ Phone: (215) 925-5439 **Web: http://seaport.philly.com/**
- ❏ Hours: Daily 10:00am-5:00pm. Closed major winter holidays.
- ❏ Admission: $8.00 adult, $6.50 senior (65+), $5.00 child (5-12).
- ❏ Miscellaneous: The Museum Store. Ask about the Philadelphia Citypass - it's a great value if you're seeing more than just historic area.

Displayed here are the Delaware River and Bay maritime artifacts and interactive exhibits. History lessons are woven between these exhibits:

For updates visit our website: www.kidslovepublications.com

- **WHAT FLOATS YOUR BOAT?** - Climb into a boat that sits on a waterbed, put weights in different places on a model boat to study its center of gravity, or pull different shapes through a ten-foot tank of water to examine how drag affects speed. Assemble a four-foot wooden boat puzzle. And further on, the curious can walk or crawl through a full size replica of a 22-foot 19th century Delaware River Shad Skiff.
- **WORKSHOPS ON THE WATER**- Actual boatbuilder crafting new boats. Numerous models and small boats on display. If your kids are older, they can be apprentices.
- **DIVERS OF THE DEEP** - Diving gear and underwater archeology.
- **SHIP ZONE** - USS Becona & USS Olympia - Submarine from South Pacific and flagship during the Spanish American War. This is what the kids really come for! Self-guided tour lets kids "feel" like sailors, captains, or pirates.

INDEPENDENCE VISITOR CENTER (FOR THE NATIONAL HISTORICAL PARK)

One North Independence Mall West (northeast corner of 6th & Market Sts - across from the Liberty Bell), **Philadelphia** 19106

- Phone: (215) 597-8974. **Web: www.nps.gov/inde**
- Hours: Daily 8:30am-5:00pm. Extended summer hours.
- Admission: FREE
- Miscellaneous: This is where to park (below center) and purchase tickets or schedule times for tours. Plan to spend 5-8 hours in the Independence Historical Park. Audio Walk & Tour Historic Philadelphia CDs and players are available to rent.

Start here before you explore the well-known sites. See award winning historical and tourism films shown throughout the day. Ben Franklin, George Washington, John Adams and others come back to life to tell the Independence story. Older children will want to sign up for the walking tour here (little ones up to grades 1 or 2 will want to wander at their own pace and usually aren't interested enough to stay with the group). To keep attention spans high, we noticed they create a theme (seasonally) of historical significance. Actors called "Town Criers" present impromptu conversations and "street stage" presentations along with that theme. They admired our "carriage" (known to you and me as a wagon) and our "horse" that was pulling it (Daddy!) Most events are daily in the summer and weekends the rest of the year.

LIBERTY BELL

6th Street, between Market and Chestnut Streets (across from Independence Hall, entrance on Market St), **Philadelphia** 19106

- ❑   Phone: (215) 597-8974 **Web: www.nps.gov/inde**
- ❑   Hours: Daily 9:00am-5:00pm.
- ❑   Admission: FREE
- ❑   Tours: Given by park rangers, relates the bell's history. Long lines (for security checks) - but they move fast.
- ❑   Miscellaneous: Glass encased bell is viewable 24 hours a day. Interpretive kiosk displays explain details of the Bell.

Made a few blocks away by two crafters who only made pots and pans (usually), its famous "crack" has many folklore stories associated with it. It would be nice to believe that each crack was the result of zealous ringing; however, it just wasn't cast properly to withstand its large size and temperature variances. Initially, it was just a bell ordered to be placed in the tower of the meeting hall (now called Independence Hall). Later, abolitionists used it as a symbol of freedom for slaves and proclaimed it the Liberty Bell (not until 1840 though!) - and the name stuck! It'll give you goosebumps to stand inches from it. Be sure to take advantage of the photo opportunity time provided by park rangers.

LIGHTS OF LIBERTY

Philadelphia – *PELO Energy Liberty Center (6th and Chestnut Streets), 19106. Phone: (215) LIBERTY or (877) GO-2-1776.* **Web: www.lightsofliberty.org** *Hours: At Dark (April-September). See website for schedule. Admission: $17.76 adult, $16.00 senior (65+), $12.00 child (6-12). Tours: 60 minutes.* A nighttime sound-and-light show that takes visitors on a walk through five historic sites as a drama unfolds in Independence National Historic Park. A 3-D sound system and enormous five-story images projected on buildings immerse visitors into events leading up to the Colonists' fight for freedom from the British. Groups of up to 50 people each wear audio transmitted wrap-around headsets. Although anyone can see the giant projected images, only those wearing the high tech headsets hear the stories. Ask for the youth show (a fictional family, the Warren children, serve as headset hosts).

MUSEUM OF PHILADELPHIA, ATWATER KENT

Philadelphia - *15 South 7th Street, 19106. Phone: (215) 922-3031. Web: www.philadelphiahistory.org Hours: Daily 10:00am-4:00pm (except Tuesday). Admission: $5.00 adult, $3.00 senior and youth (13-17).* Whatever history you don't catch visiting buildings in the area, you'll get a touch of here. Included are: the wampum belt received by William Penn from the Lenni Lenape at Shakamaxon in 1682, the first German Bible in North America printed by Christopher Saur in 1743, personal items from Benjamin Franklin, and Phillies' Mike Schmidt's game-worn jersey. You'll also see Norman Rockwell's America showcasing all 322 magazine covers created by the country's most admired 20th-century illustrator for The Saturday Evening Post. Family Programs - toys of the past, hat making, children of the past.

NATIONAL CONSTITUTION CENTER

Philadelphia - *(Independence National Park, between Arch & Race, 5th & 6th Streets), 19106. Phone: (215) 923-0004. Web: www.constitutioncenter.org* The first-ever national museum honoring and explaining the U.S. Constitution...designed to increase awareness and understanding of the US Constitution, the Constitution's history, and the Constitution's relevance to our daily lives so that all of us -- "We the People" -- will better understand and exercise our rights and our responsibilities. It begins with an introduction to the extraordinary beginnings of our nation and Constitution. Wandering a "street scene" in 1787 Philadelphia, you can eavesdrop on fellow citizens and discover the forces that inspired the creation of the document. "Signers Hall," is where visitors are invited to play the role of Signer amidst life-size statues of the Founding Fathers. You then enter a theater-in-the-round, where you view The Founding Story, a multi-media production which orients you to the major themes of the Center and the basic historical context of the Constitution. The "National Tree" will interpret the theme by using video stories of Americans throughout history. The exhibit will illustrate how the diversity of American citizens has changed with the changes in the Constitution.

THADDEUS KOSCIUSZKO NATIONAL MEMORIAL

Philadelphia - *301 Pine Street (I-676 or I-95 Independence Hall exit), 19106. Phone: (215) 597-9618. Web: www.nps.gov/thko Hours: Daily 10:00am-5:00pm (June-October), Wednesday-Sunday 10:00am-5:00pm (rest of year). Admission: FREE.* Exhibits & audiovisual displays (English & Polish language) describing the help Thaddeus gave to the American Revolution. Learn why he was loved and then kicked out of his native Poland, why he carried a crutch and how his skills helped Americans strategically beat the British. He was a genius engineer!

TODD HOUSE

Philadelphia - *4th & Walnut Streets, 19106. Phone: (215) 597-8974. Web: www.ushistory.org/tour/tour_todd.htm Hours: Daily 9:00am-5:00pm. Admission: $3.00 adult.* This was the home of Dolly Todd before her marriage to James Madison (Dolly Madison pastries will get the kids on the same page). Representing a middle-class Quaker home, she became quite a First Lady when she moved from this house and married James Madison, fourth President of the United States.

U.S. MINT

Philadelphia - *5th & Arch Streets, 19106. Phone: (215) 408-0112. Web: www.usmint.gov/mint_tours/ Tours: Tours for groups of six or fewer citizens at a time may be arranged through Congressional sponsorship. Admission: FREE. Contact information can be found for your Senator at **http://www,senate.gov/senators/senator_by_ state.cfm** or for your Representative at **http://www.house.gov/ house/MemberWWW_by_State.htm**. Please note that two weeks advance notice is required for scheduling and security purposes.* While in the historic district of Philadelphia, be sure to take your family to the world's largest coinage operation (seen through a glass enclosed gallery). They make a million dollars worth of coins per day! (29 million coins!). See them start with blanks that are cleaned and then stamped, sorted, and bagged. To see coins in large bins or spilling out of machines is mesmerizing! Even little kids eyes sparkle. A "Stamp Your Own Medal" machine (press a big red button to operate) is located in the Gift shop. Great souvenir idea!

BALCH INSTITUTE OF ETHNIC STUDIES

Philadelphia - *1300 Locust Street, 19107. Phone: (215) 925-8090. Web: www.balchinstitute.org Hours: Tuesday-Saturday 10:00am-4:00pm.* Here, kids can use a computer to explore ethnic group sites around Philadelphia. Punch in your cultural heritage and receive a printout of sites related to that ethnic group. Begin at the museum here full of memorabilia then go out and discover your roots. Ethnic museums we're aware of:

□   NATIONAL MUSEUM OF JEWISH HISTORY - 44 North
    Fourth Street. (215) 923-3811.
□   CHINATOWN - Arch & Vine Streets. (215) 922-2156. Address
    Listing shows: 1011 Race Street
□   ITALIAN MARKET - 9th Street. (215) 922-5557.
□   AFRICAN-AMERICAN MUSEUM - 701 Arch St. (215) 574-0380
□   AMERICAN SWEDISH HISTORICAL MUSEUM - 1900
    Pattison Avenue in Roosevelt Park, (215) 389-1776.
□   POLISH-AMERICAN CULTURAL CENTER MUSEUM - 308
    Walnut Street. Near National Historic Park. (215) 922-1700.

PHILADELPHIA CITY HALL OBSERVATION DECK

Philadelphia - *Broad & Market Streets, 19107. Phone: (215) 686-2840. Hours: Monday-Friday 9:30am-4:15pm. Admission: Donation. Tours: Monday-Friday 12:30pm.* Every city has one building that stands as one of the tallest in town and usually it has a lot of history behind it. Most noted is the courtroom (available to view on the tour only) where a motion picture film was made and the 548 foot tall tower that has a statue of William Penn on top. At the base of the statue is the observation deck. This building is so breathtakingly beautiful and stands in the center of downtown...believe us, you can't miss it!

PHILADELPHIA MUSEUM OF ART

26th Street and Ben Franklin Parkway, **Philadelphia** 19130

❑　Phone: (215) 763-8100　**Web: www.philamuseum.org**
❑　Hours: Tuesday-Sunday, 10:00am-5:00pm. Wednesday & Friday evenings until 8:45 pm.
❑　Admission: $10.00 adult, $7.00 senior (62+), $7.00 child (13-18). Sundays - pay what you wish.

The 3rd largest museum in the country. 2000 years of fine and applied arts (crafts, interiors, architecture) with 200 galleries. Museum restaurant. Your kids *(or parents!)* will love running up the numerous steps to the top like Rocky (from the movie by the same name). Pretend you hear the crowd cheer as you step onto the brass glazed imprints of Rocky's shoes! Family Art Activities.

FAIRMOUNT PARK

Philadelphia - *Benjamin Franklin Parkway (info at Visitor's Center at Memorial Hall), 19131. Phone: (215) 685-0000.* **Web: www.phila.gov/fairpark/contactUs1.htm** *Tours: Trolley tours (215) 925-TOUR. Stops at all points of interest within the park. Small fee. Thursday-Sunday.* Along both sides of Schuylkill River, one of the world's largest city park's features include:

❑　ANDORRA NATURAL AREA - (215) 685-9285. Bartram's Historic Garden - (215) 729-5281. 18th Century home of colonial botanist, John Bartram.
❑　SMITH PLAYGROUND & PLAYHOUSE - (215) 765-4325. Emphasis on playhouse (3 story) for preschoolers with trains, foam blocks and comfortable reading rooms. Pick up a Cozy Car and drive along the play roads with stop signs and traffic lights. This 100 year old playground has a Giant Slide that four generations have slid down.
❑　JAPANESE HOUSE & GARDEN - Horticultural Center. (215) 878-5097. Small admission for tours.
❑　FOX CHASE FARM - tours.
❑　WISSAHICKON CREEK GORGE - hiking trails.

INSECTARIUM

Philadelphia - *8046 Frankford Avenue (I-95N to Cottman Ave. exit), 19136. Phone: (215) 338-3000. Web: www.insectarium.com Hours: Monday-Saturday 10:00am-4:00pm. Admission: $5.00 (ages 2+).* A collection of live insects (in naturalized settings), mounted specimens and learning displays help you to become "bug friendly". Check out the cockroach kitchen, glow-in-the-dark scorpion, live termite tunnel, or the 101 butterflies! Outside, there's a learning garden where you go on bug hunts.

MUMMERS MUSEUM

Philadelphia - *1100 South 2nd Street & Washington Avenue, 19147. Web: www.riverfrontmummers.com/museum.html Phone: (215) 336 - 3050. Hours: Tuesday - Saturday 9:30am-5:00pm, Sunday Noon-5:00pm. Closed Sundays in July and August and all Holidays. Admission: $2.00-$2.50.* What is a mummer? Audio and interactive displays, musical instruments, costumes, and artifacts from the traditional New Year's Day parade. See videos of past parades or watch how those colorful sparkly costumes are made.

FIRST UNION CENTER / SPECTRUM TOURS

Philadelphia - *3601 South Broad Street (South Broad Street & Patterson Avenue), 19148. Phone: (215) 389-9543. Web: www.comcast-spectacor.com/geninfo/tours.asp Tours: Groups of 15+ (may be added to another group if less than 15 in party). Weekdays (provided no events are scheduled). By reservation. $5.00-$6.00 per person.* Guided tours of the home of the Philadelphia 76ers and Flyers. See fields, locker rooms, and learn great inside scoops on the history of favorite players & teams.

KIXX SOCCER

Philadelphia - *3601 South Broad Street (Core States Spectrum - First Union Center), 19148. Phone: (888) 888-KIXX. Web: www.kixxonline.com (May-September) Admission: $10.00-$20.00.* MISL - Major Indoor Soccer League. Look for their mascot, SocceRoo.

PHILADELPHIA 76ers BASKETBALL

Philadelphia - *3601 South Broad Street (Office) (Core States Complex - First Union Center), 19148. Phone: (215) 339-7676.* **Web: www.nba.com/sixers** *Admission: $15.00-$60.00.* National Basketball Association. Family Pack Nights.

PHILADELPHIA EAGLES FOOTBALL

Philadelphia - *3501 South Broad Street (Lincoln Field), 19148.* **Web: www.philadelphiaeagles.com/** *Phone: (215) 463-5500. Admission: Average $45.00.* NFL Professional football team (August-December). Meet and greet players at the annual Eagles Carnival in August.

PHILADELPHIA FLYERS HOCKEY

Philadelphia - *3601 South Broad Street #1A (office) (First Union Center - home game arena), 19148. Phone: (215) 465-4500.* **Web: www.philadelphiaflyers.com** *Admission: $22.00-$68.00.* National Hockey League (October-March).

PHILADELPHIA PHANTOMS HOCKEY

Philadelphia - *3601 S. Broad Street (First Union Center), 19148. Phone: (215) 465-4522.* **Web: www.phantomshockey.com** Phantomaniacs Kids' Club. Phlex, the mascot plays host to many events with your favorite cartoon characters.

PHILADELPHIA PHILLIES BASEBALL

Philadelphia - *3551 South Broad Street or 330 S. 7th St. (Veteran Stadium, until 2004 then Phillies Ballpark), 19148. Phone: (215) 436-1000.* **Web: www.phillies.com** *Admission: $6.00-$28.00.* National League East Division. Look for Phillie Phanatic, the mascot stirring things up (watch out for his hot dog launcher).

FORT MIFFLIN

Fort Mifflin Road (I-95 to Island Avenue Exit - follow signs),
Philadelphia 19153

❑   Phone: (215) 685-4167 **Web: www.fortmifflin.org**
❑   Hours: Daily 10:00am-4:00pm. Closed major early winter holidays.

For updates visit our website: www.kidslovepublications.com

❑   Admission: $6.00 adult, $3.00 senior (65+) and child (6-13).
     Military FREE.

❑   Miscellaneous: Sundays suggested as there are military drills and
     craftspeople demonstrating their skills. Check out their
     educational Treasure Hunts for group tours.

"What Really Happened at Fort Mifflin?"... you'll find out that a lot
happened here. Starting in 1772, it was built by the British to
protect the colonies. Ironically, in 1777, it was used by Americans
trying to protect the Philadelphia and Delaware River from the
British (7 long, grueling weeks of siege). It also protected the city
of Philadelphia during the War of 1812 and was active as a
Confederate and Union prison camp during the Civil War. Until
1954, it was still used to store ammunition for the United States
military. A great place to check out and study several wars all in
one spot.

HEINZ NATIONAL WILDLIFE REFUGE

Philadelphia - *Lindbergh Blvd. & 86th Street, 19153. Phone:
(215) 365-3118.* **Web: http://heinz.fws.gov/** *Hours: Dawn to
Dusk.* Visitor contact station. Hiking trails to explore butterflies,
muskrats, frogs, flying geese, and loads of wildflowers.
Observation tower. The Cusano Environmental Education Center
is open daily from 8:30am-4:00pm, free of charge.

MORRIS ARBORETUM

Philadelphia (Chestnut Hill) - *100 Northwestern Avenue
(University of Pennsylvania), 19118. Phone: (215) 247-5777.*
Web: www.business-services.upenn.edu/arboretum/ *Hours:
Daily 10:00am-4:00pm (year round). Open until 5pm on Saturday
and Sunday (April - October). Admission: $8.00 adult, $6.00
senior (65+) and student, $3.00 child (3-12).* Romantic 92 acre
Victorian garden with many of Philly's rarest and largest trees, a
sculpture garden, a rose garden and the Fernery. Garden Railway
Display changes each season.

SESAME PLACE

100 Sesame Road (I-95 to US 1 north to Oxford Valley exit. Next to
     Oxford Valley Mall), **Philadelphia (Langhorne) 19047**

❑   Phone: (215) 752-7070 **Web: www.sesameplace.com**
❑   Hours: Daily 9:00am-8:00pm (mid May - Labor Day Weekend),
       Weekends (September & October) - Call for current schedule.
❑   Admission: ~$37.00 general admission. Parking $8.00.
❑   Miscellaneous: Late afternoon and family discounts. Bathing
       suits required for water attractions. We'd recommend staying all
       day to get your money's worth.

While your kids continue to peek over their shoulders for a glimpse of
a Sesame Street character like Big Bird (great photograph
opportunities), they'll be pulling your hand in every direction so they
won't miss anything. Catch a show like "Rock Around the Block",
then jump on Ernie's Bed Bounce (that even sounds like fun to adults,
doesn't it?) or scale "Cookie Mountain". Mechanical rides include: A
roller coaster called "Vapor Trail", or, a new 40-foot high balloon
tower ride carries you up in one of eight balloon baskets - providing a
bird's eye view of the park, and, also a character themed tea cup ride
turns you "round and round" - as fast or as slow as you want to go.
There's also 14 refreshing water attractions. As you float, zoom or
chute through Big Bird, Ernie's and Slimey's Rides, you'll be splashed
or trickled by a giant rubber ducky. Toddlers can be water trickled in
Teany Tiny Tidal Waves. Bet your kids just can't wait to walk down a
full-sized replica of Sesame Street and take pictures to show their
friends back home!

RALPH STOVER STATE PARK

Pipersville - *6011 State Park Road (State Park Road and Stump
Road), 18947.* **www.dcnr.state.pa.us/stateparks/parks/ralph.htm**
Phone: (610) 982-5560. 45 acres along the Tohickon Creek.
Warm-water fish species found in Tohickon Creek include
smallmouth bass, sunfish, carp and catfish. They stock trout, a
cold-water fish. There is one mile of easy walking trails that pass
through many habitats and near the millrace. The 'High Rocks'
section of the park features an outstanding view of a horseshoe
bend in Tohickon Creek and the surrounding forest.

NOCKAMIXON STATE PARK

Quakertown - *1542 Mountain View Drive (PA Route 563, Northeast Extension of the PA Turnpike, Exit 32), 18951. **Web: www.dcnr.state.pa.us/stateparks/parks/nock.htm*** *Phone: (215) 529-7300 or (215) 529-7308 (marina).* The name Nockamixon is synonymous with boating. Four public launching areas are provided on the lake and boats may be rented from a park concession. Visitors enjoy watching sailboats from a bench at the marina, and the equestrian, bicycle and hiking trails. Pool, Visitors Center, Horseback Riding, Modern Cabins, Fishing, and Winter Sports.

FULTON (ROBERT) BIRTHPLACE

Box 33 (Rte. 30 west to Rte. 372 west to US222 South of Quarryville), **Quarryville** 17566

❑   Phone: (717) 548-2679

    Web: www.fieldtrip.com/pa/75482679.htm

❑   Hours: Saturday 11:00am-4:00pm, Sunday 1:00-5:00 pm
    (Summer).

❑   Admission: $1.00 adult, children FREE (12 and under).

Robert Fulton, the inventor, the artist, and the engineer was born here in 1765. On display are many of his drawings, miniature portraits, and models (located throughout the living room). Being most famous for his steamboat, "Claremont" (the first steamboat), you'll see a strong connection between his artistic ability and his engineering ideas. Because his drawings were so well done, supporters could easily visualize his inventive ideas.

BERKS COUNTY MUSEUM

Reading - *940 Centre Avenue (Rte. 61 near Spring Street), 19601. **Web: www.berksweb.com/histsoc/museum.html*** *Phone: (610) 375-4375. Hours: Tuesday - Saturday 9:00am-4:00pm (Closed holiday weekends). Admission: $1.00-$2.50 (age 5+).* Industry, Transportation, Pennsylvania German Arts, Country liberty bell, Diffenbach organ, Conestoga wagon. Hands-on children's museum.

READING SYMPHONY ORCHESTRA

Reading - *136 N. 6th Street (Sovereign Performing Arts Center), 19601.* **Web: www.readingsymphony.com** *Phone: (610) 373-7557.* Some concerts feature Berk's children's chorus. RSOvertures offers pre-concert conversations about the music heard from the Music Director, soloists and special guests.

MID ATLANTIC AIR MUSEUM

Reading - *11 Museum Drive - SR183 (Reading Regional Airport), 19605. Phone: (610) 372-7333.* **Web: www.maam.org** *Hours: Daily 9:30am-4:00pm. Closed major holidays. Admission: $6.00 adult, $2.00 child (6-12). Miscellaneous: Aviation gift shop.* Airplane rides weekends in summer for additional fee. Restored, ready to fly, classic civilian and military aircraft. Of special interest are the classic commercial airliners, and the first night fighter ever built, history of aircraft manufacturers, and aviation movies and toys.

READING PHILLIES BASEBALL

Reading - *1900 S. Centre Avenue (FirstEnergy Stadium), 19605.* **Web: www.readingphillies.com.** *Phone: (610) 370-BALL or (610) 375-8469. Admission: $3.00-$7.00.* Minor League AA Class affiliate of the Philadelphia Phillies.

NOLDE FOREST STATE PARK

Reading - *2910 New Holland Road, 19608. Phone: (610) 775-1411.* **Web: www.dcnr.state.pa.us/stateparks/parks/nolde.htm** *Year-Round Education & Interpretation Center.* Nolde Forest encompasses more than 665 acres of deciduous woodlands and coniferous plantations. A network of trails makes the center's streams, ponds and diverse habitats accessible to both students and casual visitors. Teaching stations offer places for students to work and benches for those who wish to sit. There is a short, accessible trail by the mansion.

READING PUBLIC MUSEUM

Reading - *500 Museum Road (follow 222 South/422 East to West Reading/Penn Avenue exit), 19611. Phone: (610) 371-5850.* **Web: www.readingpublicmuseum.org** *Hours: Tuesday - Saturday 11:00am - 5:00pm, Sunday Noon - 5:00pm. Also Wednesday eve. Closed Christmas. Admission: $5.00 adult, $3.00 child (4-17).* Regional and international art, sculpture gardens, planetarium, and greenhouse. Public Star Shows on Sundays, Public Laser Shows on Saturdays (separate fee).

MARY MERRITT DOLL MUSEUM

Reading (Douglassville) - *843 Ben Franklin Highway - US422, 19518.* **Web: www.merritts.com/dollmuseum** *Phone: (610) 385-3809. Hours: Monday - Saturday 10:00am- 4:30pm, Sunday 1:00-5:00pm. Closed Tuesdays.* See 1500+ dolls ranging from the 7th Century Egypt to 20th century USA. 40+ miniature period rooms including a full-size replica of a Philadelphia 1850's toy shop. Special interests in Shirley Temple dolls, Paper mache dolls, circus, safari dolls, and mechanical dolls...they're all here. A two room Museum of Childhood is also on the premises. Small admission ages 5+.

READING RAGE SOCCER

Reading (Fleetwood) - *409 North Richmond Street (Ray Buss Field), 19522.* **Web: www.readingrage.com** *Phone: (610) 375-4405. Small Admission.* USL Pro League for Columbus Crew MLS team (late April-early August).

ROADSIDE AMERICA

Roadside Drive (I-78 / US22, exit 8 or exit 23)

Shartlesville 19554

❑   Phone: (610) 488-6241 **Web: www.roadsideamericainc.com**
❑   Hours: Weekdays 9:00am-6:30pm, Weekends until 7:00pm
(July-Labor Day). Monday-Friday 10:00am-5:00pm, Saturday &
Sunday 10:00am-6:00pm (September-June).
❑   Admission: $4.50 adult, $4.00 senior (65+), $2.00 child (6-11).

Roadside America (cont.)

Our kids lost their breath as they entered the enormous and wonderful train village! It's the largest known indoor miniature train village! As a young boy, Lawrence Gieringer saw buildings far away and felt they appeared tiny and toy-sized. As his carpentry skills grew, he began whittling blocks of wood into different scaled-down models of industries and buildings he saw all around him - all of them important to the development of the area. You'll see scenes of a coal breaker, a Pennsylvania Dutch farm, downtown small town USA, gristmills, and churches. Kids are enchanted by the moving trains (over bridges, through tunnels), trolleys, bubbling fountains, or aircraft swooping and diving through the air (there's even a hot air balloon). Parents relive childhood dreams playing with toy animals, people, machinery, etc. as they examine all the details. Kids' favorites are the 50+ pushbuttons that make trains or figures move - it gives them the chance to feel like they're helping to operate the huge display. Don't leave until you've seen the Night Pageant! Every half hour they turn day into night and back!

SPRING MOUNTAIN SKI AREA

Spring Mount - *Spring Mount Road, 19478. Phone: (610) 287-7300. Snow Report: (610) 287-7900.* Longest Run: 2220 ft.; 7 Slopes & Trails.

ED'S BUGGY RIDES

Strasburg - *SR 896 (across from Sight & Sound Theatre), 17572. Phone: (717) 687-0360. Admission: $8.00 adult, Children half-price.* 3 mile tour through Amish farmlands in an Amish buggy. Experience the beautiful Pennsylvania Dutch Country landscape, while watching the everyday routine of the Amish through hilly back roads in an authentic Amish buggy. Daily, year-round.

AMISH VILLAGE

Strasburg - *Route 896 - PO Box 115 (1 mile south of US30 & 2 miles north of Strasburg), 17579. Phone: (717) 687 - 8511. www.800padutch.com/avillage.html Hours: Daily 9:00am-5:00pm (Spring/Summer/Fall) Admission: $6.50 adult, $2.50 child (6-12).*

Tours: 20-25 minutes. Miscellaneous: Amish Village store.
Educational tour of an 1840 Old Order Amish home, authentically
furnished. The site includes a blacksmith, one room schoolhouse,
operating smokehouse, water wheel, farm animals, spring house
and windmill.

CHOO CHOO BARN, TRAINTOWN USA

Route 741 East, Box 130

Strasburg 17579

- ❏ Phone: (717) 687-7911 **Web: www.choochoobarn.com**
- ❏ Hours: Daily 10:00am-5:00pm (late March-weekend after New
  Years). Closed major winter holidays and Easter.
- ❏ Admission: $5.00 adult, $3.00 child (5-12)

A 1700 square foot mini display of Pennsylvania Dutch County
with area landmarks, 20 operating trains plus over 150 animated
and automated vehicles and figurines. The kids shriek with delight
at everything there is to see - esp. when it changes from daylight to
nighttime. Look for the skiers zooming down the slopes and the
dump truck that really moves. The working fire display shows a
house burning and then the fire truck comes to put it out, complete
with a fireman who climbs the ladder and makes a hole in the roof
to put out the fire. Most displays can be seen from "kids-eye" level
with only occasional "lifts" to get the "big picture". You have to
pass the well-stocked gift shop in and out of the exhibit so plan
some extra time for shopping.

FULTON STEAMBOAT INN

Strasburg - *PO Box 333 (US30 & SR896), 17579. Phone: (717)
299-9999 or (800) 922-2229. Web: www.fultonsteamboatinn.com*
After you spend the night sleeping on a steamboat, enjoy a meal in
a room full of steamboat antiques. The outside of this Inn looks
just like a steamboat complete with wheels and smoke stacks. As
you hear occasional seagulls sounds, select from Steamboat or
Mid-Ship Specialties for breakfast, lunch or dinner. Lodging with
indoor pool & jacuzzi, video gameroom and "ship-shaped"
playground. Family cabins with bunk beds.

NATIONAL TOY TRAIN MUSEUM

300 Paradise Lane (off SR 741 East & US 30)

Strasburg 17579

- ❑ Phone: (717) 687-8976
  Web: www.traincollectors.org/toytrain.html
- ❑ Hours: Daily, 10:00am-5:00pm (May-October), Weekends in
  April, November, and mid-December
- ❑ Admission: $3.00 adult, $2.75 senior (65+), $1.50 child (5-12),
  $9.00 family.

Five operating push button layouts in panoramic viewing. Meet toy
trains from the 1800's to the present in use as part of the layout. One
of the displays features large-gauge trains used for outdoors. The
Train Collectors Association operates it (they are often featured on
national TV). A continuously running video show in the Museum's
Theater area features cartoons and comedy films about toy trains.

RAILROAD MUSEUM OF PENNSYLVANIA

P. O. BOX 15 (300 Gap Road - SR741 East)

Strasburg 17579

- ❑ Phone: (717) 687-8628. **Web: www.rrmuseumpa.org**
- ❑ Hours: Monday-Saturday 9:00am-5:00pm, Sunday Noon-
  5:00pm. Closed Monday & Winter Holidays (November-early
  April)
- ❑ Admission: $7.00 adult, $6.00 senior (60+), $5.00 child (6-17).
- ❑ Miscellaneous: Whistle Stop Shop. Outdoor yard restoration
  available in good weather. Hands-On-Center. Orientation video.
  2nd floor observation deck.

Traces the development of railroads and rail transportation in
Pennsylvania from restored locomotives to modern streamliners.
Meet "Diesel", GG 1 Electric, Logging, Freight and Passenger
(actually get to look in or walk in) trains! More access than most

train museums. In the center of the museum is the railroad workshop where you can actually walk under a train! Great place to bring grandmas and grandpas to pass along stories to younger generations.

AAA BUGGY RIDES

Strasburg – *Phone: (717) 687-9962. Call to make a reservation. Admission charged per rider.* Available to tour three miles of scenic country roads past railroads in carriages built and driven by Amish families.

SIGHT & SOUND THEATRES / LIVING WATERS THEATRE

Strasburg - *Route 896 (off Rte. 30), 17579. Phone: (717) 687-7800.* **Web: www.bibleonstage.com** *Admission: Tickets range from $15.00-$35.00.* Special effects theatre with live Easter and Christmas performances. Shows the rest of the year focus on familiar bible characters like Noah or Daniel. Through inspirational productions, they seek to encourage others to be dedicated and wise stewards of our God-given talents and resources.

STRASBURG RAILROAD
SR741 East - P. O. Box 96, **Strasburg** 17579

- ❏ Phone: (717) 687-7522 **Web: www.strasburgrailroad.com**
- ❏ Hours: Daily 10:00am-7:00pm (July & August), 11:00am-3:00pm (April, June, September). Mostly long weekends (weather permitting) Noon-3:00pm (Rest of the year).
- ❏ Admission: $9.25-$15.25 adult, $4.75-$10.75 child (3-11), $1.00-$6.00 toddler.
- ❏ Tours: 45 minutes, departs on the hour. See schedule on website.
- ❏ Miscellaneous: Several gift shops with train souvenirs, books and loads of Thomas stuff! Restaurants with casual dining, picnic lunches and sweet treats on premises.

Strasburg Railroad (cont.)

Offering the most authentic train ride experience of the period, the Strasburg Railroad takes visitors back to a simpler time. This is the oldest short-line railroad. The restored Victorian open-air and coach cars offer wide views of the landscape (some cars even offer snacks and the "Lee Brenner" dining car offers meals). Visitors travel through farm fields still plowed by horses and mules. Amish buggies wait patiently at railroad crossings. Train travelers can even stop at an old-fashioned picnic grove and enjoy a snack while the trains rumble by. Each train has a narrator who tells the railroad's history spiced with a few tall tales. Be sure to check on seasonal events that your "little engineers" will love like "A Day Out With Thomas the Train!" (One ride on a life-size Thomas plus storytelling, Sir Topham Hatt, Play Tables, Thomas Coloring and Videos, and Live Musical Entertainment for the wristband price of $14.00 per person/ages 2+ - June, mid-September, early December). This is the place where Thomas spends the most time visiting.

BRANDYWINE POLO CLUB

Toughkenamon - *Polo Road (Call for field location), 19374. Phone: (610) 268-8692. Hours: Sunday afternoons at 3:00pm (May-October).* Pack your basket of tea sandwiches, and sparkling water, along with a blanket and lawn chairs. Be prepared to participate in the "divot stomp".

DELAWARE CANAL STATE PARK

Upper Black Eddy - *11 Lodi Hill Road (Rte. 611 and Rte. 32), 18972. Web: www.dcnr.state.pa.us/stateparks/parks/d-canal.htm Phone: (610) 982-5560.* A walk along the 60-mile towpath of the Delaware Canal is a stroll into American History. The Delaware Canal is the only remaining continuously intact canal of the great towpath canal building era of the early and mid-19th century. Mule drawn canal boat rides and the Lock Tender's House Visitor Center are at New Hope. Also, Horseback Riding, Mountain Biking, Fishing, Trails, Cross-Country Skiing.

VALLEY FORGE NATIONAL
HISTORICAL PARK

SR23 & N. Gulph Road - PO Box 953 (I-76 to exit 24 - SR202 south
to SR422 west to SR23 west)

Valley Forge 19482

- ❏ Phone: (610) 783-1077. **Web: www.nps.gov/vafo/index.htm**
- ❏ Hours: Daily 9:00am-5:00pm (except Christmas).
- ❏ Admission: $3.00 per person - only if you tour Washington's Headquarters.
- ❏ Tours: By bus (hop on & off at leisure) or self-guided driving with audio tape.
- ❏ Miscellaneous: Expanse of outdoor park areas available. Hiking and bike trails. Stop at the Visitor's Center first.

Explore the site of the Winter of 1777-78 encampment that was a difficult time for battling elements and disease. Some of the sites that you won't want to miss are:

- ❏ <u>ARTILLERY PARK</u> - long rows of cannons and forts.
- ❏ <u>WASHINGTON'S HEADQUARTERS</u> - Isaac Potts' House - looks exactly as it did when General George Washington and his wife, Martha were in residence. (Initially he shared the rough conditions with the soldiers in the field tents).
- ❏ <u>VISITOR'S CENTER</u> - Introduction film and exhibits. See a tent headquarters actually used by General Washington.
- ❏ <u>GRAND PARADE</u> - learn about the other hero (Von Steuben) who turned tattered, confused young men into soldiers.
- ❏ <u>WORLD OF SCOUTING MUSEUM</u> - A log cabin full of uniforms, handbooks, and badges. Daily, 11:00 am - 4:00 pm (Summer), Weekends (rest of the year).

Summer weekends are the best time to visit because the Muhlenberg Brigade is recreated in living history encampments - bringing the drudges of winter camp to life. Remember, these "huts" replaced tents but only offered a little more warmth. Brave a visit Winter weekends to see scout troops living under similar conditions as the soldiers did or inside Washington's Headquarters.

WASHINGTON CROSSING HISTORIC PARK

SR32 and SR532 (off I-95, exit 31)

Washington's Crossing 18977

- ❑ Phone: (215) 493-4076
- ❑ Hours: Monday-Saturday 9:00am-5:00pm, Sunday Noon-5:00pm.
- ❑ Admission: $3.00-$4.00 (age 6+) for walking tour. Park charges $1.00 per vehicle at entrance.
- ❑ Miscellaneous: Every Christmas (@ 1:00pm) the park re-enacts Washington's crossing and special events also occur on his birthday. Also on grounds is the Bowman's Hill and Wildflower Preserve.

It's December 25, 1776. Washington planned his attack on the British, first crossing the Delaware River by boat. In the Durham Boat House, you can see the boats that were actually used. A larger than life copy (20 ft. X 12 ft.) of the painting "Washington's Crossing" creates the best image of this historic Christmas Day for freedom. A total of 13 historic buildings are on site and your tour ticket includes Bowman's Hill Tower observation point, Thompson-Neely House (where Washington ate and slept), The Ferry Inn (where Washington dined before crossing the icy Delaware) and the Memorial Building where the giant painting stands. All of this, plus a short historical film is shown of the event. It'll give you goosebumps!

AMERICAN HELICOPTER MUSEUM

1220 American Blvd. (Brandywine Airport - Next to QVC Studios)

West Chester 19380

- ❑ Phone: (610) 436-9600. **Web: www.helicoptermuseum.org**
- ❑ Hours: Wednesday-Saturday 10:00am-5:00pm, Sunday Noon-5:00pm.
- ❑ Admission: $6.00 adult, $5.00 senior (65+), $4.00 child (3-18) or student.
- ❑ Miscellaneous: Older kids will want more information about the engineering of the rotocraft. Films and mechanics are available to fill in all of the details. Helicopter Rides (every 4th Saturday) - ask for adventure here! Fly-bys…wow!

This very kid-friendly museum exhibits the adventure and history of "rotary wing flight" at the country's only helicopter museum. Visitors come back here frequently because the kids can actually go on many units and work the rotors and play pretend. Helicopters from the earliest to the most modern are here, inside and outside (Coast Guard, Navy, Army, M.A.S.H.), plus interactive exhibits. Climb aboard and play with the controls inside the giant helicopters being restored or the red, smiley faced one). It's lots of fun!

CHESTER COUNTY HISTORY CENTER

West Chester - *225 North High Street (Brandywine Valley), 19380. Phone: (610) 692-4800. **Web: www.chestercohistorical.org** Hours: Monday-Saturday 9:30am-4:30pm. Admission: $5.00 adult, $4.00 senior, $2.50 child (under 17).* Early American furniture, clothing, dolls, and ceramics. History Lab - hands on family activities.

QVC STUDIO TOUR

Studio Park (I-76 or I-95, exit US202 to Boot Road - East to Wilson Drive), **West Chester** 19380

- ❏   Phone: (800) 600-9900 **Web: www.qvctours.com**
- ❏   Admission: $7.50 adult, $5.00 child (age 6+).
- ❏   Tours: Daily between 10:00 am - 4:00 pm. Leaves every hour on the hour. Groups of 10 or more must make prior reservations.
- ❏   Miscellaneous: Must be at least 6 years old.

Imagine a shopping medium that reaches over 16 million homes instantly and can process more than 30 calls per second! Founded in 1986, this cable shopping service stands for "Quality, Value, Convenience" and has become the largest of its kind. Your tour begins as you are greeted by photographs of famous celebrities that have visited QVC to merchandise their products. You will see 34 sets and 8 studios (there is even an 8000 square foot 2-story house in the studio complete with a garage). All of the cameras are remotely controlled from one central source during taping and the complete facility uses over 1 million watts of power (or enough to power 3000 average households!) You might even have a chance to see "Murphy the Dog" the QVC mascot - he is a golden retriever that is featured on the show and we are told he gets as much e-mail as any of the other hosts! See live broadcasts being done (without cue cards - everything is ad lib!). See the prop production and design facilities - the texture display is awesome! You can even be a part of a live studio audience with advance notice.

PETER WENTZ FARMSTEAD

Worcester - *Shearer Road (SR73 and SR363), 19490. Phone: (610) 584-5104. Hours: Tuesday - Saturday 10:00am-4:00pm, Sunday 1:00-4:00pm. Admission: FREE. Tours: Every 30 minutes by costumed guides.* A restored, colorfully decorated, 18th century Pennsylvania German working farm and mansion. Did you know that George Washington used this home as his headquarters (from time to time) during the Revolutionary War? Best to attend Saturdays when staff demonstrates colonial crafts, (candles, weaving, paper cut art - called "scherenschnitte") or tending to the animals. Special events and exhibits representing Pennsylvania German culture and early American farm life take place throughout the year.

BERK'S COUNTY HERITAGE CENTER

Wyomissing - *Red Bridge Road (off Route 183), 19610.* **Web: www.berksparkandrec.org/heritage/index.html** *Phone: (610) 374-8839. Hours: Tuesday-Saturday, Holidays 10:00am-4:00pm, Sunday Noon-5:00pm (May - October). Admission: $3.00-$5.00 (age 7+) per museum. Discount combo prices.* The Gruber Wagon Works survives as one of the most complete examples of an integrated rural manufactory of its kind in the nation. Wagon wheels were constructed in the bench shop, and wooden parts of the wagon were made from patterns in the wood shop. Wheels were "tired" and wagons were "ironed" and assembled in the blacksmith shop. The distinctive striping and scrollwork were applied by hand in the paint shop. C. Howard Hiester Canal Center: Canals saw their rise and fall in the 19th century. They offered means of bulk transportation and travel in the era prior to railroads when the only alternative to walking was the horse and wagon. Red Bridge (longest covered bridge in the state).

Chapter 9
South West Area

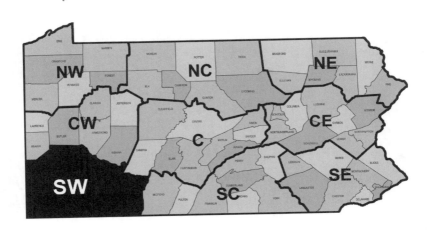

Our Favorites...

George Westinghouse Museum

Idlewild Park

Just Ducky Tours

L.E. Smith Glass Company

National Aviary

Pennsylvania Trolley Museum

Pittsburgh Children's Museum

Pittsburgh Inclines

Pittsburgh Regional History Center

Westerwald Pottery Tour

Get ready for a "Quack Attack"

MEADOWCROFT MUSEUM OF RURAL LIFE

401 Meadowcroft Road (I-79 - Exit 11 Bridgeville to SR50 West)

Avella 15312

❑   Phone: (724) 587-3412 **Web: www.meadowcroftmuseum.org**

❑   Hours: Wednesday-Saturday Noon-5:00pm, Sunday 1:00-5:00pm
     (Memorial Day-Labor Day). Weekends only (May, September,
     October). Open some weekends in November and December for
     special events.

❑   Admission: $7.00 adult, $6.00 senior (60+), $5.00 (6-16).

❑   Miscellaneous: Visitors Center and Café. Best during festivals
     for" hands on history" personalized sessions.

Re-live rugged rural life from 200 years ago as you walk the dirt
and stone roads of this reconstructed village. By touring a settler
log house, schoolhouse, country store, barn and blacksmith shop -
you'll be introduced to inhabitants like the Native Americans,
frontier   settlers,   farmers,   lumbermen,   coal   miners,   and
conservationists who have worked the land.   Get involved by
taking a real school lesson (with slate and chalk) in a 1 room
schoolhouse.   Shear sheep and then spin and weave wool, or,
actually practice using a Native American "atlatl" (spear throwing).
The grounds of this living history museum are on an archeological
prehistoric dig site. See a display of artifacts they've collected.

WILLOWBROOK SKI AREA

Belle Vernon - *RD #2, 15012. Phone: (724) 872-7272 or (724)
929-2294.* With one slope for beginners and another for
intermediates, the resort is perfect for learning new skills or
brushing up on old ones. Longest Run: 1500 ft.; 2 Slopes & Trails

NEMACOLIN CASTLE

Brownsville - *Front Street - US 40 east, 15417. Phone: (724) 785-
6882. Web: www.nemacolincastle.org Hours: Tuesday-Sunday
11:00am-5:00pm (Summer). Weekends only (Mid-March - May,
September - Mid-October). Admission: $6.00 adult, $3.00 child
(12 and under). Tours: 45 minutes.* Previously known as
Nemacolin Towers, the tudor style building dates back to the
1790's. The castle was built by Jacob Bowman who was appointed

by George Washington as Brownsville's first postmaster. The Bowman family were businessmen and bank founders. It looks like a castle because of the turret towers and battlements. Tour 20 rooms of formal Victorian plus the oldest part that was the original trading post Bowman set up.

LITTLE LAKE THEATRE COMPANY

Canonsburg - *500 Lakeside Drive, South, 15317. Phone: (724) 745-6300. Web: www.littlelaketheatre.org* Plays for the entire family for 50 years. Looking Glass Theatres, Fall Family Matinees.

SEVEN SPRINGS MOUNTAIN RESORT

Champion - *RR#1 Box 110 (I-76 exit 9 or 10, follow Rte. 31 or 711), 15622. Phone: (814) 352-7777, (800) 452-2223 (continental US). Snow Report: (800) 523-7777. Web: www.7springs.com* Longest Run: 1.2 miles; 30 Slopes & Trails. Pennsylvania's largest ski and year-round resort. Be sure to get all of the latest details by calling or visiting their website. The "resort cam" shows live pictures that are updated every 5 minutes. Tons of lodging & restaurants, indoor bowling, roller skating, swimming & mini-golf. Outdoor summer alpine slide, craft days, outdoor pool, horseback riding and tennis.

LIVING TREASURES ANIMAL PARK

Donegal - *SR 711 (south of rte. 31), 15628. Phone: (724) 593-8300. Web: www.ltanimalpark.com Hours: Daily 10:00am-8:00pm (Summer). Daily 10:00am-6:00pm (April, May, September, October). Admission: $6.50 adult, $6.00 senior, $4.50 child (3-11).* Watch kangaroos, tigers and wolves and ride the miniature horses. Kids love the petting area (babies, reindeer, camels) and feeding areas (bears, otters, monkeys, goats, sheep, & llamas).

ROUND HILL EXHIBIT FARM

Elizabeth - *651 Round Hill Road (SR51 & SR48 to Round Hill Road), 15037. Phone: (412) 384-4701. Hours: Daily 8:00am-DUSK. Admission: FREE.* A small scale working farm dating back to the late 1700's. A brick farmhouse with barns and fields

including dairy and beef cattle, pigs, chicken, sheep, horses, and a
duck pond. Be ready to watch the cows being milked daily at
8:30am and 4:30pm. You can tour the grounds, play with the
animals, plan a picnic, romp and play on the soccer fields, and
walk the trails.

FORT NECESSITY NATIONAL BATTLEFIELD

Farmington - *1 Washington Parkway - US40, 15437. Phone:
(724) 329-5805. Web: www.nps.gov/fone Hours: 8:00am-Sunset
(park), Visitor's Center 9:00am-5:00pm, Closed Christmas only.
Admission: $3.00 adult, Children FREE (16 and under).
Miscellaneous: Visitor's Center with slide show, exhibits, store.
Picnic areas.* Commemorates the 1754 battle - George
Washington's first battle of the French and Indian War. Beginning
at Jumonville Glen - the site where the first skirmish occurred with
the French. Washington feared they would return with backup
forces. So, he had this fort built quickly, out of "necessity". See the
reconstructed fort - 53 feet in diameter, the gate is only 3.5 feet wide.

LAUREL CAVERNS

Farmington - *200 Caverns Park Road (Chestnut Ridge in Laurel
Highlands, off US 40), 15437. Phone: (800) 515-4150 or (724)
438-3003. Web: www.laurelcaverns.com Hours: Daily 9:00am-
5:00pm (May-October). Weekends only (November, March, April).
Admission: $6.00-$9.00 (age 6+). Tours: 1 - 3 hours. Constant
temperature, 52 degrees Fahrenheit. Miscellaneous: Visitors
center, picnic areas, indoor mini-golf.* Pennsylvania's largest cave
2.3 miles. - well-lit tours of the "Grand Canyon" or Spelunking - 3
hour tour.

NEMACOLIN WOODLANDS RESORT SKI AREA

Farmington - *1001 LaFayette Drive, 15437. Phone: (800) 422-
2736. Snow Report: (724) 329-8555. Web: www.nemacolin.com*
Mystic Mountain Skiing Area. Longest Run: .5 miles; 7 Slopes &
Trails. A selection of resort lodging and activity packages are
available year round with 5 swimming pools, mini-golf, trails and
Equestrian Center, to name a few.

GREASE PAINT PLAYERS

Greensburg - *951 Old Salem Road (Civic Theatre), 15601. Web: www.act1.org/stage.htm* Phone: *(724) 836-PLAY.* Children's Theatre, produced during the summer at the Palace by the youth program, ACT I STAGE!.

WESTMORELAND MUSEUM OF AMERICAN ART

Greensburg - *221 North Main Street (downtown), 15601. Web: www.wmuseumaa.org Phone: (724) 837-1500. Hours: Wednesday-Sunday 11:00am-5:00pm. Thursday 11:00am-9:00pm. Admission: Suggested donation $3.00.* "Arty-Facts" educational programs for children. Kidspace interactive area. Regional industry, rural and cityscapes, toys of yesteryear, historical heroes.

BUSHY RUN BATTLEFIELD

Bushy Run Road (off US22 to Bus66 to SR993)

Harrison City 15636

❑   Phone: (724) 527-5584
    Web: www.bushyrunbattlefield.com/WelcomePage.html
❑   Hours: Wednesday-Saturday 9:00am-5:00pm, Sunday Noon-
    5:00pm. (April-October). Weekends only (November-March).
❑   Admission: $2.00-$3.00 (age 6+).
❑   Miscellaneous: Visitor Center

The battle that opened Western Pennsylvania to settlement - Pontiac's War in 1763. Native American forces lead by Chief Pontiac had occupied nearby forts. The British finally stopped advancements at Bushy Run - this reopened supply routes. Kids will either be scared or say "cool" when they see a life-size mannequin of an Indian Warrior dressed for battle with war paint from head to toe. In this same area, children can take turns dressing up like a British soldier (check out all the buttons!). Learn what "lock, stock, and barrel" means or discover all the different ways they used nature to provide basic needs (ex. Flour bags - fortification and wounds, or trees for gun stock, food, and dyes). View the electronic map of the battle - then walk outside to markers of the actual battlefield ground.

HIDDEN VALLEY SKI

Hidden Valley - *One Craighead Drive (PA Route 31), 15502. Phone: (814) 443-2600. Snow Report: (800) 443-7544.* **Web:** **www.hiddenvalleyresort.com** Longest Run: 1 mile; 17 Slopes & Trails. Sleigh rides, Children's Snow Play area, Snowtubing and snowboarding. Year-round sports and recreation at Hidden Valley Resort from golf, outdoor swimming, indoor swimming, and mountain biking in the spring, summer and fall. Lodging in condos w/kitchens.

DISALVO'S STATION RESTAURANT

Latrobe - *325 McKinley Avenue (Latrobe Train Station - downtown Amtrak station), 15650. Phone: (724) 539-0500.* **Web:** **www.westernpa.com/disalvos/home.htm** *Hours: Tuesday-Sunday, Lunch and Dinner. Early Bird specials 4:00-6:30pm ($6.95).* Reservations strongly suggested. Moderate to fine dining. An early 1900 train station that has been restored and decorated with railroad memorabilia. Ride from Pittsburgh on Amtrak to get here (adds to the railroad experience). When walking into the restaurant, you'll enter through a tunnel that trains pass over often. Feel and hear the rumble! Once through the tunnel, you may be seated in the atrium (formerly the train yard) with fountains, greenery and a full-size railroad dining car. Most families are seated in the original main concourse room with a continuously running model train above. A children's menu is offered.

PITTSBURGH STEELERS SUMMER TRAINING CAMP

Latrobe - *US30 at Fraser Purchase Road (St. Vincent College), 15650.* **Web:** **http://www.steelers.com/community/** *Phone: (724) 323-1200. Daily practice - get a schedule at the field. (Mid-July - August)* Since 1967, this has been the site of the NFL - Pittsburgh Steelers pre-season training camp. Young fans can root for their favorite team member in a much smaller and more intimate setting. Children can also learn that the glamour and the glory of the NFL only comes from hard, focused work each day on the practice field. If you're lucky, you might have a chance at get some autographs. Be sure to bring a pen and paper (or old program) for the players to sign!

COMPASS INN MUSEUM

PO Box 167 (US30 East, 3 miles east of Fort Ligonier)

Laughlintown 15655

- ❑ Phone: (724) 238-4983 **Web: www.compassinn.com**
- ❑ Hours: Tuesday-Saturday 11:00am-4:00pm, Sunday & Holidays Noon-4:00pm. (May-October)
- ❑ Admission: $5.00 adult, $2.00 child (6-17).
- ❑ Tours: Costumed tour guides take you on a 1 1/2 hour tour.

A great chance to see a restored 1799 stagecoach stop that was a typical roadside inn - complete with cramped sleeping quarters. In the reconstructed cookhouse, you'll learn what terms like "uppercrust" (the bottom of the bread was sooty from the stove - so the upper crust was much better) mean. The bottom of the bread was "caked" with soot. "Let them eat cake" had a meaning of "Let them eat dirt". Also view the contents of The Barn & Blacksmith Shop.

FORBES STATE FOREST

Laughlintown - *PO Box 519 (Del. Rt. 30E), 15655. Phone: (412) 238-9533.* **Web: www.dcnr.state.pa.us/forestry/stateforests/ forests/forbes/forbes.htm** *Fishing, Camping, Trails, Winter Sports.*

- ❑ <u>BLUE HOLE DIVISION</u> - a deep hole with water appearing blue, located on Blue Hole Creek and Cole Run Falls.
- ❑ <u>BRADDOCK DIVISION</u> - Pine Knob observation point overlooking Uniontown. Cabin Hollow Rocks is an interesting rock formation. Wharton Furnace, Old Water-Powered Grist Mill and Ponderfield Fire Tower.
- ❑ <u>LINN RUN DIVISION</u> - Grove Run Spring. Adams Falls is a miniature water fall. Rock formations and Bluestone Quarry (stone from this quarry was used to pave the streets of Pittsburgh).
- ❑ <u>KOOSER DIVISION</u> - Beck Springs, Old Sawmill Site, & Kooser Fire Tower, Old Logging Railroad Grades & Bridges.
- ❑ <u>NEGRO MOUNTAIN DIVISION</u> - many rock formations and Tarkiln is a kiln used to extract tar from the knots of pitch pine.

FORT LIGONIER

216 South Market Street (US30 & SR 711)

Ligonier 15658

- ❑   Phone: (724) 238-9701. **Web: www.fortligonier.org**
- ❑   Hours: Monday-Saturday 10:00am-4:30pm, Sunday Noon-
  4:30pm (May-October).
- ❑   Admission: $6.50 adult, $5.50 senior, $3.25 child (6-14).
- ❑   Miscellaneous: Fort Ligonier Days in October - reenactments in
  summer. Quaint town shops within walking distance - some are
  toy stores!

Built by the British during the French and Indian War (1758), it was
a vital link to the supply line to the West. You'll be able to view gun
batteries, the very visibly and painful sharp wooden pickets of re-
trenchment, the quarter master's store, a home, hospital (saws made
from bone), and the commissary. The Museum displaying models
and realistic dioramas, as well as a new audiovisual presentation,
serves as your gateway to the Fort complex.

IDLEWILD PARK & SOAK ZONE

Route 30 East, PO Box C (I-80 to I-76, exit 9, Donegal to 711, Left
at Route 30), **Ligonier 15658**

- ❑   Phone: (724) 238-3666 or
- ❑   (800) 4 FUNDAY **Web: www.idlewild.com**
- ❑   Hours: Opens at 10:00am (Memorial Day Weekend - Labor
  Day). Closed Mondays except Holidays.
- ❑   Admission: $15.00-$21.00 GENERAL (Children age 2 and under
  FREE).
- ❑   Miscellaneous: Goofy golf, rental boats and pony rides extra.

Ironically, this park was the favorite for both of us as kids *(even
though we never grew up together)* and each of us voted
StoryBook Forest as the best spot! I guess we were meant to be
together! Some featured spots include:

Idlewild Park & Soak Zone (cont.)

❏ <u>MISTER ROGER'S NEIGHBORHOOD OF MAKE BELIEVE</u> - ride as a real trolley introduces you to X the Owl , King Friday the XIII and other neighbors.

❏ <u>STORY BOOK FOREST</u> - The Three Little Pigs, Woman Who Lived in a Shoe, etc., (over 40 nursery rhymes and tales). Absolutely a memory in the making!

❏ <u>JUMPIN' JUNGLE</u> - crawl, climb, swing, and bounce.

❏ <u>HOOTIN' HOLLER'</u> - turn-of-century mining town with Cowboy Shows, Old West games & food, Confusion Hill and Loyalhanna Railroad.

❏ <u>SOAK ZONE</u> - water slides, pool, Little Squirts Kiddie area.

❏ <u>OLDE IDLEWILD</u> - roller coasters, merry-go-round, and Raccoon Lagoon kiddie rides (largest kiddie area in the US!)

FALLINGWATER

Route 381, PO Box R (I-76 exit 9, to SR31 East)

Mill Run 15464

❏ Phone: (724) 329-8501
   Web: www.faywest.com/fayette/fallingwater

❏ Hours: Tuesday-Sunday, 10:00am-4:00 pm. (April - Mid-November). Winter weekends only.

❏ Admission: $10.00-$15.00 per person.

❏ Tours: 45 minutes - 1 hour.

❏ Miscellaneous: For the safety and comfort of all visitors, children must be 6 years old to accompany adults on regular Fallingwater tours; 9 years old for the in-depth tour. Children 9 and under may remain at the supervised Child Care Center where they can enjoy indoor and outdoor games and toys related to architecture and nature. The fee is $2.00 per child per hour. Children's tours for ages 5 and up are available by advance reservation. Falling Water restaurant. Want to see more, visit nearby Kentucky Knob, in Ohiopyle.

One of the most famous houses in America - and a memorable experience that is sure to delight all ages. (See miscellaneous on previous page for age restrictions). The Edgar Kaufmann family used to vacation on this exact spot in the woods during the summer months and loved to picnic by this waterfall. They loved it so much that they commissioned Frank Lloyd Wright (the famous architect) to build a home that would allow them to live on this spot, but not take away from its natural beauty. Wright commented, "I wanted you to live with the waterfall, not just look at it." The home is built from several cantilevers (stacked like Legos) that hang over the waterfall (actually - the stream goes right through the inside of the house!). Boulders were used as flooring and windows and walls on the first floor. Closer cave-like spaces were used as bedrooms. This visit is sure to make a lasting impression!

L.E. SMITH GLASS COMPANY

1900 Liberty Street (I-70 to SR 119 south, then off SR31 - follow signs), **Mt. Pleasant** 15666

- ❑   Phone: (724) 547-3544 **Web: www.lesmithglass.com**
- ❑   Admission: FREE.
- ❑   Tours: Monday - Friday 9:30am-3:00pm, Gift shop until 5:00pm. Ages 6+ only.

The oldest industry in America - making glassware by hand, started in the early 1600's. This company makes glass pictures, goblets, plates, figurines, and even exclusives patterns for Martha Stewart. Your guide starts the tour explaining the glassmaking process from the beginning when glass powder (sand, cullet, color) are heated to 2000+ degrees F. in a furnace. Once melted, the molten glass is pulled on a stick and then molded or pressed, fire-glazed and then cooled in a Lehr which uniformly reduces the temperature to prevent shattering. They were making pedestal cake servers the day we were there. They still use many old-time tools and techniques - for example, to frost glass, they dip it in acid. Their warehouse discount prices are great! Fascinating, almost unbelievable, work conditions create an interest for kids.

OHIO PYLE STATE PARK

PO Box 105 Rt. 381 North, Off Rt. 40, **Ohiopyle** 15470

❑   Phone: (412) 329-8591
       Web: www.dcnr.state.pa.us/stateparks/parks/ohio.htm
❑   Miscellaneous: Suggested Whitewater Raft Companies in the
       area: Laurel Highlands River Tours, 800-4-RAFTIN. Mountain
       Streams and Trails Outfitters, 800-RAFT-NOW.
❑   Wilderness Voyageurs, 800-272-4141. White Water Adventurers,
       800-WWA-RAFT.

More than 14 miles of the Youghiogheny River Gorge churns
though the heart of Ohiopyle. The famous Lower Yough, below
the scenic Ohiopyle Falls, provides some of the best whitewater
boating in the Eastern US. You can also hike or bike the 28-mile
Youghiogheny River Trail.   Ferncliff Peninsula Park - trails,
flowers, trees, birds and wildlife abound. Sit in the creek bed and
ride the water through two natural waterslides in Meadow Run.
Parking is available adjacent to the SR 381 bridge. Visitor Center,
Boat Rentals, Mountain Biking, Fishing, Trails, Winter Sports.

SAND CASTLE

1000 Sandcastle Drive (I-376 exit 5, west Route 837)

Pittsburgh 15120

❑   Phone: (412) 462-6666. **Web: www.sandcastlewaterpark.com**
❑   Hours: Daily (June-Labor Day); June 11:00am-6:00pm, July &
       August 11:00am-7:00pm.
❑   Admission: ~$22.00 general (age 4+), ~$17.00 senior (65+).
       Discounts after 3:00pm.

15 water slides including "Cliffhangers" pond slide and Two
shotgun slides (patron rides on her/his back to a surprise ending - it
drops in a free fall to the water below), giant Lazy River, Wet
Willie's waterplay, Japanese tidal wave, kiddie and adult pools,
Boardwalk and the world's largest hot tub. Riverplex
Amphitheater.

PITTSBURGH ZOO & PPG AQUARIUM

One Wild Place (In Highland Park, SR 28 North to exit 6,
follow signs), **Pittsburgh** 15206

❑ Phone: (412) 665-3640 or 1-800-4-PGH-ZOO
Web: www.pittsburghzoo.com

❑ Hours: Daily 10:00am-6:00pm (Summer), 9:00am-5:00pm
(Winter). Zoo is open year-round except Christmas.

❑ Admission: $8.00 adult, $7.00 senior (60+), $5.00 child (2-13).
Parking $3.00. Reduced fees in the winter.

❑ Miscellaneous: Train, boat or carousel rides $1.00. Food
available. Fun "incline" escalator takes you up the hill to the zoo.
Nearby is the Radisson Hotel/Monroeville (412-373-7300) that
has a combo indoor/outdoor pool.

Over 4000 creatures both great and small. Natural settings with
themes like: Tropical Forest, Asian Forest (Siberian Tigers),
African Savanna (elephants), and newer PPG Aquarium -
wonderful use of glass that allows you to feel you can almost
"touch" the fish. Tunnels, too!

❑ KIDS KINGDOM - Where kids can act like animals! This
interactive facility is complete with playground equipment that
replicates animal motions and behaviors so kids can play like the
animals play. It's also full of hands-on animal experiences, like
the walk-through Deer Yard, where kids can actually touch a
white-tailed deer or the walk-through Kangaroo Yard where
Australian gray kangaroos get so close, kids can reach out and
touch them! There's also a friendly Goat Yard, beaver and otter
exhibits and a fabulous sea lion pool featuring several of these
playful marine mammals. Swing-like spiders, Turtle Race,
Penguin Slide, or climb through Mole Tunnel (big hits with the
kiddies!).

FRICK ART & HISTORICAL CENTER

Pittsburgh - *7227 Reynolds Street (I-376, Exit # 9), 15208. Phone: (412) 371-0600. Web: http://frickart.org/home/ Hours: Tuesday-Saturday 10:00am-5:00pm, Sunday Noon-6:00pm. Reservations suggested holiday weekends. Admission: FREE. Clayton is $8.00-$10.00. Reduced for Family Days tours.* Henry Clay Frick's (industrialist & art collector) mansion with original possessions, gardens, art museum and children's playhouse (now the Visitor's Center). Check out the floorboards that were once the bowling alley (playhouse). Kids will love the pretend food displayed in the dining rooms and Helen's bedroom. Family Days (ages 6-12) teaches about late 1800s life in Pittsburgh with a hands-on activity (dress up or craft) after the shortened tour with teen docents.

DUQUESNE INCLINE

1220 Grandview Ave (West Carson Street, or the Station Square access road which parallels the Monongahela and Ohio rivers)

Pittsburgh 15211

❑   Phone: (412) 381-1665. **Web: http://trfn.clpgh.org/incline**
❑   Hours: Monday-Saturday 5:30am-12:45am. Sundays and Major Holidays 7:00am-12:45am.
❑   Admission: $1.00-$2.00 (age 6+) - Fares are each way. Seniors are FREE.

One of the few remaining cable cars still in use. Look for the red lights heading up the hill and the wood carved, paneled and trimmed cars. The cars climb and descend 400 ft at a 30 degree angle. Up at the top of the station are mementos and exhibits and the best view of the city.

CARNEGIE SCIENCE CENTER

One Allegheny Avenue (near Stadium - off I-279 or I-376)

Pittsburgh 15212

❑   Phone: (412) 237-3400 **Web: www.csc.clpgh.org**
❑   Hours: Sunday-Thursday 10:00am-5:00pm, Friday & Saturday 10:00am-7:00pm. SportsWorks same except Monday-Thursday 10:00am-3:00pm.

- ❑ Admission: $14.00 adult, $10.00 senior (62+), $10.00 child (3-18). Omnimax & Laser Fantasy Show extra.
- ❑ Miscellaneous: Discovery Store. Restaurant café.

Over 250 hands-on exhibits! Here's a menu of what you can expect at this fun-filled science center:

- ❑ <u>EXPLORATION STATION & JUNIOR STATION</u> - Habitats, structures & building, magnets and electric.
- ❑ <u>OMNIMAX THEATER</u> - Movies that literally make you a PART of the action.
- ❑ <u>INTERACTIVE PLANETARIUM</u> - Keeps you on "an edge". Also features laser light shows.
- ❑ <u>WW II SUBMARINE</u> - Climb aboard the authentic USS Reguin. See demonstrations on dives, power generators, even touch a real torpedo!
- ❑ <u>SCIQUEST LIVE SCIENCE DEMONSTRATIONS</u> or <u>KITCHEN CHEMISTRY</u> - Push a button to create a 4 ft. tornado or learn cooking chemistry (in a themed classroom setting). Lots of waves and air here!
- ❑ <u>SEASCAPE</u> - A large coral reef aquarium and water play table.
- ❑ <u>SPORTWORKS</u> - Best Virtual Sports Facility we've seen for kids! Experience virtual reality basketball and pitching cage. Cruise down Olympic bobsleds, hang glide the Grand Canyon or mini-golf Math. 60 + interactives - all included in admission price. This place is family-interactive and lets each family member "show off" their skills. Plan to spend half your time in here!
- ❑ <u>MINIATURE RAILROAD & VILLAGE</u> - 2300 square feet of a re-created village connecting the history and culture of southwestern PA between late 1800s and the 1930s.

NATIONAL AVIARY

Allegheny Commons West (off I-279 North Shore exit - follow signs)

Pittsburgh 15212

- ❑   Phone: (412) 323-7235. **Web: www.aviary.org**
- ❑   Hours: Daily 9:00am-5:00pm (everyday but Christmas).
- ❑   Admission: $5.00 adult, $4.00 senior (60+), $3.50 child (2-12).
- ❑   Miscellaneous: Get up-close-and-personal with African Penguin "Stanley" or resident owls daily right before or after lunchtime.

See 220 species of birds live in natural habitats like rainforests, deserts, and marshes. The tropical areas have rare, exotic birds in free-flight atriums. Favorites to look for are the live Toucan (so animated, it appears mechanical!), a real cuckoo bird (that sings a loud, sweet sound), and the funny billed marsh birds (boat and spoon shaped, for example). The Tropical Rainstorm at 12:30pm daily in the Wetlands of the Americas 200,000 cubic foot walk-through exhibit is so-o-o cool! Don't you just love the birds flying overhead...especially entertaining during feeding times (early afternoons).

PHOTO ANTIQUITIES

Pittsburgh - *531 East Ohio Street, 15212. Phone: (412) 231-7881.* **Web: www.photoantiquities.com** *Hours: Monday - Saturday 10:00am - 4:00pm. Admission: $3.00 - $6.50 (age 5+).* Photo Antiquities Museum of Photographic History offers a history lesson on photography. The Museum, designed in the Victorian style with period music playing in the background, lends to the feeling of being in the 19th century. Photo and paper processes, antique cameras, vintage historical print exhibits.

PITTSBURGH CHILDREN'S MUSEUM

10 Children's Way - Allegheny Square (off I-279, follow signs - just blocks from the stadium), **Pittsburgh** 15212

- ❑   Phone: (412) 322-5058 **Web: www.pittsburghkids.org**
- ❑   Hours: Monday-Saturday 10:00am-5:00pm, Sunday Noon-5:00pm. (Closed Monday during the school year).

❑ Admission: $5.00 adult, $4.50 senior (55+), $4.50 child (2-18).

❑ Miscellaneous: Open until 8:00 pm on Fridays. Pecaboo Café. Workshops on Saturdays and some Friday evenings. Oh Baby! Area for infants/toddlers. Changing Lower Level Gallery. Surprises in Store Gift Shop.

A manageable 3 story hands-on museum with the mission to enrich and engage kids. Here are the favorites:

❑ PUPPETS - Jim Henson's creature puppets or Mr. Roger's Neighborhood puppet shows.

❑ THE THEATRE / STUFFEE – Inside-out stuffed huge doll that is designed to teach anatomy and health.

❑ THE WORKSHOP - Create artwork from recycled materials.

❑ THE STUDIO - exposure to paint, clay and make- your- own silkscreen. Intro (on kid's level) to Andy Warhol.

❑ KIDS CLIMBER - see through tunnel sculpture that you can climb through.

❑ FLYING MACHINES – Lift yourself or your kids on to these machines using applied physics.

PITTSBURGH PIRATES BASEBALL

Pittsburgh - *115 Federal Street (PNC Park), 15212. Phone: (412) 321-BUCS or or (800) BUY-BUCS. Web: www.pirateball.com Admission: $6.00-$9.00.* National League Professional Baseball (April-September).

PITTSBURGH STEELERS FOOTBALL / HEINZ FIELD TOURS

400 Stadium Circle (Heinz Field), **Pittsburgh** 15212

❑ Phone: (412) 323-1200 **Web: www.steelers.com**

❑ Admission: Usually seasons are sold out. Call or visit website for details.

❑ Tours: Monday-Friday (April-October). For more information on Heinz Field Tours please e-mail **tours@fans.steelers.com** or call the Heinz Field Tour Hotline (412) 697-7150.

Pittsburgh Steelers Football / Heinz Field Tours (cont.)

❑ Miscellaneous: Click on "Essentials"- Stadium Tours for Heinz Field Tours information.

NFL Professional football team. Home games played at the new Heinz Field. Heinz Field's horseshoe shape allows for a beautiful view of the city's unique skyline and the fountain at the Point while watching a University of Pitt (Saturday) or Steelers (Sunday/Monday) home game. Tours of Heinz Field consist of the Coca-Cola Great Hall, club, suite and service levels, press box, warning track, south plaza and much more.

CARNEGIE MUSEUM OF ART

Pittsburgh - *4400 Forbes Avenue (connected to Natural History Museum), 15213. Phone: (412) 622-3131.* **Web: www.cmoa.org** *Hours: Tuesday-Saturday 10:00am-5:00pm, Sunday Noon-5:00pm. Admission: $5.00-$8.00 (age 3+). Miscellaneous: ARTventures: family art activities, Saturday & Sunday afternoons, Ages 4 and up with an adult. Café open for lunch.* Paintings, sculpture, film and video projections reflect values and ideas from cultures long ago and today. Hall of Sculpture. Hall of Architecture.

PHIPPS CONSERVATORY & BOTANICAL GARDENS

Pittsburgh - *One Schenley Park (I-376 East, take the Forbes Ave./Oakland exit 2a), 15213. Phone: (412) 622-6914.* **Web: www.phipps.conservatory.org** *Hours: Tuesday-Sunday 9:00am-5:00pm. Hours extended to 9:00pm on Friday. Admission: $3.00-$6.00 (age 2+).* A historic landmark 13 room Victorian glass house featuring tropical and desert motifs plus one of the nation's finest Bonsai collections. Discovery Garden - outdoor hands-on learning for children (boxwood maze, sensory garden). Summer-Butterfly Forest.

PLAYHOUSE JR.

Pittsburgh - 222 Craft Avenue (Oakland), 15213. Phone: (412) 621-4445. **Web: www.ppc.edu/playhouse/index.shtml** Over 50 years of children's classics and new works like Snow White or Winnie-the-Pooh (November - May)

RODEF SHALOM BIBLICAL BOTANICAL GARDENS

Pittsburgh - *4905 Fifth Avenue, 15213. Phone: (412) 621-6566.*
Web: ***www.rodefshalom.org/biblicalgarden.htm#about*** *Hours:*
Sunday-Thursday 10:00am-2:00pm (also from 7:00-9:00pm on
Wednesday and from Noon-1:00pm Saturday). Admission: FREE.
Most complete garden of biblical plants. More than 100 tropical
and temperate species. All plants are labeled. A biblical verse
accompanies each plant. (June - mid-September)

SOLDIERS AND SAILORS MEMORIAL MUSEUM

Pittsburgh - *4141 Fifth Avenue, 15213. Phone: (412) 621 - 4254.*
*Web: **www.soldiersandsailorshall.org/index.html** Hours: Tuesday*
-Saturday 10:00am-4:00pm.   Admission: Small fee.   Veterans
Memorial building houses beginning with the Civil War and
ending with Persian Gulf activities. Also African-American and
Revolutionary War films.

ALLEGHENY OBSERVATORY

Pittsburgh - *Riverview Park (US19 in Riverview Park off*
*Perrysville Avenue), 15214. **Web: www.pitt.edu/~aobsvtry/** Phone:*
(412) 321-2400.   Hours: Thursday - Friday (by appointment -
evenings - April - October). Thursday night tours are held from
May 1st through the third week of August and the Friday night
tours are held from April 1st through November 1st. Admission:
FREE. Tours: All tours begin at 8:00pm and last until
approximately 10:00pm.   One of the foremost observatories in the
world.   A short slide or film presentation is shown followed by a
walking tour of the building finally ending up at the 13" Fitz-Clark
refractor.   If it's a clear night you would be shown whatever
celestial objects are within range of the telescope that night. Dress
for the temperature outside.

GATEWAY CLIPPER FLEET

9 Station Square Dock - Downtown (I-376 exit Smithfield Street)

Pittsburgh 15219

- ❑ Phone: (412) 355-7980 **Web: www.gatewayclipper.com**
- ❑ Admission: $7.00-$9.00 adult, $5.00-$6.00 child
- ❑ Tours: Sightseeing / Theme cruises usually depart between 11:00am-4:00pm (except Sunset at 7:00pm).
- ❑ Miscellaneous: On board gift shops and snacks available.

A "Pittsburgh River Tradition" has sightseeing cruises sailing the three rivers. They are the largest and most successful sightseeing vessels in the America. There are several different boats in their fleet (all climate controlled) and many targeted toward ages 12 and under. These include Sunday Fun Cruises (w/ DJ Dance), Good Ship Lollipop Cruise (meet Lolly the Clown), Lock N Dam Adventure Cruises and 2 hour Sunset Cruises. Other mascots who frequent kids' cruises are Deckster Duck, and River Rover.

JUST DUCKY TOURS

Station Square - Downtown (I-376 exit Smithfield Street)

Pittsburgh 15219

- ❑ Phone: (412) 402-DUCK. **Web: www.justduckytours.com**
- ❑ Hours: Daily (mid-April - October). November weekends.
- ❑ Admission: $16.00 adult, $15.00 senior/student, $12.00 child (3-12) $2.00 toddler (2 & under)
- ❑ Tours: Departures 10:30am, 12:00, 1:30pm, 3:00pm. Add 4:30pm (weekends) & 6:00pm (summer). Approximately 1 hour.

Venture aboard the funny, fully restored WW II Land and Water Vehicles! On land it uses wheels and conventional steering. On water it uses a propeller and a rudder. By land - narrated tours include Pennsylvania and Lake Erie Railroad, Penn Station, South End and many historical downtown buildings. Learn Pittsburghese and about many movies made here. By water - see the Allegheny River and Golden Triangle or the Monongahela. Kids may get the chance to be captain of the boat for awhile (they get a sticker to prove it!). You'll quack, sing and laugh a ton. Have fun!

MONONGAHELA INCLINE

Pittsburgh - *Carson Street at Station Square, 15219. Phone: (412) 442-2000. Hours: Monday-Saturday 5:30am-12:45am, Sunday & Holidays 7:00am-12:45am. Admission: Small fare each way.* The first US incline…boasting a 35 degree climbing angle and 358 foot elevation, this incline transports tourists and commuters daily from downtown to Mt. Washington. A special note to point out to the kids is that this engineering feat was designed in 1870 - before electric streetcars and the automobile! The trick is that one car climbs while the other descends - look for the green and yellow lights highlighting the track.

PITTSBURGH PENGUINS HOCKEY

Pittsburgh - *66 Mario Lemieux Place (Mellon Arena), 15219. Phone: (412) 642-PENS.* **Web: www.pittsburghpenguins.com** *Admission: $20.00-$75.00. Look for Family Programs where kids get admission for around $10.00 with paid adult.* National Hockey League (October-early April).

FORT PITT MUSEUM & POINT STATE PARK

101 Commonwealth Place (off I-376, I-279, SR8, or SR51 on the forks of downtown, Ohio River), **Pittsburgh** 15222

- ❑ Phone: (412) 281-9284
  Web: www.fortpittmuseum.com/WelcomePage.html
- ❑ Hours: Wednesday-Saturday 10:00am-5:00pm, Sunday Noon-4:30pm.
- ❑ Admission: $1.00-$2.50 (age 6+).
- ❑ Miscellaneous: Blockhouse welcome center and gift shop (free to visit). Living history re-enactments (Summer-Sunday afternoons).

This was the site of the largest British post in North America until they were forced to leave during the American Revolution. The fort played a pivotal role in the French and Indian War. Exhibits re-create the story of war, trade, and the founding of Pittsburgh. Listen to a taped explanation of the fort while viewing a scale model of Fort Pitt. There's also an 18th century trading post. Located at the tip of Pittsburgh's Golden Triangle, Point State Park has a fabulous water fountain, paved promenades along the riverfront

& overlooks with dramatic views of the city, busy waterways, impressive hillside scenery (**www.dcnr.state.pa.us/stateparks/parks/point.htm** or 412-471-0235).

HEINZ PITTSBURGH REGIONAL HISTORY CENTER

1212 Smallman Street (in the Strip District, off I-579 and I-376)

Pittsburgh 15222

- ❑ Phone: (412) 454-6000. **Web: www.pghhistory.org**
- ❑ Hours: Daily 10:00am-5:00pm. Closed Easter, Thanksgiving, Christmas, New Years.
- ❑ Admission: $6.00 adult, $4.50 senior (62+), $3.00 child (6-18).
- ❑ Miscellaneous: Museum shop, café.

The initiative of this museum is to preserve Western Pennsylvania history through intriguing exhibits such as:

- ❑ POINTS IN TIME - Emphasis is placed on Steelworkers that are immigrants. Meet Mary, the mother of 5 children and married to a steelworker. Or, an African American journey to Freedom.
- ❑ GREAT HALL - 1949 restored trolley with audio and a Conestoga wagon. ISALY's Dairy (Klondikes!) and the Steelers, too. Greeted by a robot that speaks fluent Pittsburghese.
- ❑ DISCOVERY PLACE – Tells a story of 8 real kids from the area – a steel worker, a servant, and an over-privileged child. Children even as young as 12-14 were laborers – learn how some of them did their jobs (ex. packing pickles for Heinz or ironing clothes for pennies).

People with a heritage from Pittsburgh should be very proud and touched by this emotional history center!

SOCIETY FOR CONTEMPORARY CRAFTS

Pittsburgh - *2100 Smallman Street (Strip District), 15222. Phone: (412) 261-7003. **Web: www.contemporarycraft.org** Hours: Tuesday-Saturday 9:00am-5:00pm.* Visitors discover latest trends in the gallery, the store and the children's studio. Weekends for Families include demos, performances & workshops related to current exhibits.

BEECHWOOD FARM NATURE PRESERVE

Pittsburgh - *614 Dorseyville Road (SR8 & SR28), 15238. Phone: (412) 963-6100. Web: www.aswp.org Hours: Tuesday - Saturday, 9:00am - 5:00pm. Sunday, 1:00-5:00pm. Admission: FREE.* Headquarters of the Audubon Society of Western Pennsylvania. 90 acres of fields, woodlands, ponds, and trails. The Bird observation room, Discovery Room & Outdoor Discovery field programs are favorites for kids.

PITTSBURGH'S PENNSYLVANIA MOTOR SPEEDWAY

Pittsburgh (Carnegie) - *(US 22 / 30, Noblestown Exit), 15106. Phone: (724) 853 - RACE. Web: www.ppms.com Hours: Saturdays at 7:00pm (April - mid-September).* Late Models, Limited Late Models, Pure Stocks, E-Mods, Amateur Stocks, DIRT DIVAS, and Demos on Dirt's Monster Half Mile.

BOYCE PARK SKI AREA

Pittsburgh (Monroeville) - *675 Old Frankstown Road (near U.S. 22 and right off of I-76), 15639. Phone: (724) 733-4656. Snow Report: (724) 733-4665 Web: http://pittsburgh.about.com/ library/blboyce.htm* This ski area may be tiny and run by a county park, but lift tickets are inexpensive ($9.00 weekdays and $13.00 weekends). The park offers nine runs including moguls, halfpipe, Nastar timing runs with gates, jumps and night skiing. Lodge with a roaring fireplace, hot food and drinks. There's also a fitness center, roller skating, swimming, outdoor hot tubs, snow tubing, sleigh rides and even bowling.

CARNEGIE MUSEUM OF NATURAL HISTORY

4400 Forbes Ave (I-579 to Oakland/Monroeville exit to Blvd. of the Allies or I-376E to Forbes Ave exit 2a), **Pittsburgh (Oakland)** 15213

❑   Phone: (412) 622-3131
       Web: www.carnegiemuseums.org/cmnh/
❑   Hours: Tuesday-Saturday 10:00am-5:00pm, Sunday Noon-5:00pm.
❑   Admission: $8.00 adult, $5.00 senior, $5.00 child (3-18).

Carnegie Museum of Natural History (cont.)

❑   Miscellaneous: Store, café. Earth Theater - 210 degree wrap
    around screen featuring tornadoes or meteors or dinos (extra
    small admission). Family Programs on weekends.

See a world famous dinosaur collection with a T-Rex and 9 other
species plus a PaleoLab and Bonehunters Quarry (Dino Hall).
Additional sites include Egyptian mummies and a crawl-thru
Egyptian tomb; a Discovery Room (hands-on); Hall of Geology or
Botany (the Stratavator is a fun, educational ride); American
Indians and the Natural World examines the belief systems,
philosophies, and practical knowledge that guide Indian people;
Hall of Minerals and Gems (fluorescent minerals, crystals); and
Polar World Dioramas illustrate the Arctic environment and the
traditional Inuit way of life. Scenes depict kayak hunting, ice
fishing, and a life-size recreation of an Inuit snowhouse.

NATIONALITY CLASSROOMS

1209 Cathedral of Learning (I-376 west to exit 7A, University of
Pittsburgh), **Pittsburgh (Oakland)** 15260

❑   Phone: (412) 624-6000. **Web: www.pitt.edu/~natrooms/**
❑   Hours: Monday-Saturday 9:30am-3:00pm, Sunday 11:00am-
    3:00pm.
❑   Admission: $3.00 adult, $2.00 senior (60+), $0.50 child (8-18).
❑   Tours: 90 minute hour guided or tape recorded tours. Please
    request a tour that is adapted to younger audiences.
❑   Miscellaneous: While on campus, the musically inclined may
    want to visit the Stephen Foster Memorial Museum (ex. Foster's
    piano, musical instruments and compositions. (412) 624-4100 or
    www.pitt.edu/~amerimus/museum.htm.

"Tour the World in 90 Minutes!" - Visit 24 classrooms depicting
heritages of different ethnic communities. See authentic examples
of cultural architecture and décor from Africa, Asia, Middle East,
and Eastern and Western Europe including: Gothic Commons.
Ukrainian Room – wood carvings on beams and doors, hand
painted pottery and tile. German - stained glass fairy tales. African
- Sankofa birds.

For updates visit our website: www.kidslovepublications.com

KENNYWOOD PARK

4800 Kennywood Blvd. (I-376, Exit 9)

Pittsburgh (West Mifflin) 15122

- ❏   Phone: (412) 461-0500 **Web: www.kennywood.com**
- ❏   Hours: Monday-Sunday 11:00am-after dark (Mid-May - Labor Day). Open some weekends in early May & early September.
- ❏   Admission: $7.00-$8.00 general (age 3+). Individual ride tickets are less than $1.00 each. All day passes available (~$30.00).

A traditional amusement park -- National historic landmark. Home of the world's fastest coaster, 5 roller coasters (including one in the dark!), 3 water rides, 14 Kiddieland rides, live shows, arcades, mini-golf, paddle boats, and Lost Kennywood Lagoon area.

FRIENDSHIP HILL NATIONAL HISTORIC SITE

Point Marion - *223 New Geneva Road (US 119 to PA 166), 15474. Phone: (724) 725-9190.* **Web: www.nps.gov/frhi** *Hours: Daily 8:30am-5:00pm. Closed Christmas day only. Admission: FREE.* Visit the home of Albert Gallatin (a famous local financier, scholar and diplomat of the early republic). "A country, like a household, should live within its means and avoid debt", says Albert Gallatin. He was elected to the US Senate, played a role in the Whiskey Rebellion and served in Congress. Ranger guided tours (summer) and Audio tours (rest of year).

LINN RUN STATE PARK

Rector - *Linn Run Road (US 30east & PA Rte. 81south), 15677.* **Web:** **www.dcnr.state.pa.us/stateparks/parks/linn.htm** *Phone: (412) 238-6623.* The varied topography and mixed hardwood and evergreen forest make this park a scenic place for picnicking, hiking and cabin rentals. Grove and Rock runs join to make Linn Run, an excellent trout stream which has a waterfall, Adams Falls. Boat Rentals, Mountain Biking, Sledding, Campsites and Rustic Cabins.

LAUREL RIDGE STATE PARK

Rockwood - *1117 Jim Mountain Road, 15557. Phone: (724) 455-3744. Web: www.dcnr.state.pa.us/stateparks/parks/l-rid.htm* Laurel Ridge State Park stretches along the Laurel Mountain from the Yougiogheny River at Ohiopyle to the Conemaugh Gorge near Johnstown. Most visitors come to hike the 70 miles of trails. Snowmobiling and cross-country skiing on trails in winter.

WESTERWALD POTTERY

40 Pottery Ln (US 40 - 7.5 miles east of I-79), **Scenery Hill** 15360

- ❑   Phone: (724) 945-6000
- ❑   Hours: Monday-Friday 8:00am-5:00pm.
- ❑   Admission: FREE.
- ❑   Tours: By appointment.
- ❑   Miscellaneous: Gift shop. Llama herd on site. Discounted pieces outside.

Potters making their signature country-style decorative wares are simply amazing to watch! Watch a pre-measured lump of clay get hand thrown on a wheel and shaped before your eyes. They make pots, plates, mugs, and cute (and useful) apple bakers. The Westerwald signature is on every piece and they specialize in personalized giftware. You'll even get to see the drying (hardening kilns bricked up for 3 days) and the artists who glaze and paint each piece by hand. The blue and gray stoneware is a reproduction quality of those made in Germany's Westerwald region (thus the company name) as early as the 16th century. Look for a specialized name piece as a souvenir.

WEST OVERTON MUSEUM

Scottdale - *Overholt Drive (West Overton Village - SR819), 15683. Web: http://fay-west.com/westoverton/ Phone: (724) 887-7910. Hours: Tuesday-Saturday 10:00am-4:00pm, Sunday 1:00-5:00pm (Mid-May - Mid-October). Admission: Small.* A 19th Century industrial village with a museum (30 minute film "Pillars of Fire" about coke - for steel making operations), Homestead, Birthplace of H.C. Frick (millionaire by age 30 with steel coke business), barns, and a gristmill.

KOOSER STATE PARK

Somerset - *943 Glades Pike (PA Route 31), 15501. Phone: (814) 445-8673 or (888) PA-Parks. Web: www.dcnr.state.pa.us/ stateparks/parks/kooser.htm*   Kooser State Park is bounded by Forbes State Forest on two sides and is an ideal spot to start an overnight backpacking trip on the 70-mile Laurel Highlands Hiking Trail. The early settlers told of an American Indian battle that was fought nearby and a number of war arrows and spearheads have been found in the area. Beach, Campsites, Rustic Cabins, and Fishing.

LAUREL HILL STATE PARK

Somerset - *1454 Laurel Hill Park Road (Pennsylvania Turnpike Exit 110 (Somerset), drive west on PA Rte. 31), 15501. Phone: (814) 445-7725. Web: www.dcnr.state.pa.us/stateparks/parks/l-hill.htm*   The 63-acre Laurel Hill Lake is a focal point of the park. A beautiful stand of old growth hemlocks lies along the Hemlock Trail. Remains of a logging railroad, like a wooden cross-tie or a rusty rail spike, can be seen along the Tramroad Trail. Beach, Year-round Education & Interpretation Center, Boat Rentals, Campsites, Fishing, and Trails.

SOMERSET HISTORICAL CENTER

10649 Somerset Pike (SR601 and SR985)

Somerset 15501

❑   Phone: (814) 445-6077
     Web: www.somersetcounty.com/historicalcenter
❑   Hours: Tuesday-Saturday 9:00am-5:00pm, Sunday Noon-5:00pm
     (May-October). Open summer holidays, too.
❑   Admission: $2.00-$4.00 (age 5+).
❑   Miscellaneous: 12 minute film about the history of the mountain
     barrier area.

This center interprets daily rural life in southwestern Pennsylvania from 1750 - 1950. Isolated because of the Allegheny Mountains, they had to produce necessities from home - maple sugar, ginseng, and furs were traded - food was produced on the farm. With the Industrial Revolution came advances in farming (hand labor to machines and commercial crops). The site includes a log house, a smokehouse, a log barn, a covered bridge, a maple sugar camp, a general store, and various machines (corn husker & shredder, reaper, buggy). Pioneer and agricultural demonstrations daily. Current staff efforts are focused on preservation of history from the September 11, 2001 crash of Flight 93 in Somerset County, Pennsylvania (artifacts and eye-witness accounts are being collected and some may occasionally be on display before a permanent memorial on-site in Shanksville is built).

TOUR-ED MINE AND MUSEUM

748 Bull Creek Road (SR28 north, exit 14 - Allegheny Valley Expressway), **Tarentum** 15084

- ❑   Phone: (724) 224-4720. **Web: www.tour-edmine.com**
- ❑   Hours: Wednesday-Monday, 1:00 - 4:00 pm. (Memorial Day-Labor Day). Weekends in September & October.
- ❑   Admission: $4.00-$7.00.
- ❑   Tours: Given by guides who are real miners - approximately 2 hours. Last tour leaves at 3:20pm.
- ❑   Miscellaneous: Cool temperatures below - about 50 degrees F. - A jacket or sweater is suggested. Gift shop.

Wearing required hardhats and ducking down a little, you'll board a modernized mining car as you travel 1/2 mile underground into an actual coal mine. Original mines began in 1800 when labor was all done by hand. See demonstrations of this plus setting up a new mine area (installing the roof supports to prevent cave-ins), and the most modern mining - a continuous miner (robotic). Above ground, you can take a stroll to the past again as you view company stores, housing, strip mines, and a sawmill.

SEARIGHTS TOLL HOUSE MUSEUM

Uniontown - *US40 west, 15401. Phone: (724) 439-4422. Hours: Tuesday-Saturday 10:00am-4:00pm, Sunday 2:00-6:00pm (Mid-May - Mid-October). Admission: Very small.* In 1806, the National Road began construction connecting the East and West. Searights Tollhouse received its name from its location near the village of

Searights, named for its most prominent citizen, William Searight. Searight owned a prosperous tavern on the National Road, the ruins of which may still be seen today. The National Road tollhouse is kept as it once was, with a toll keeper's office, kitchen, and living room.

PENNSYLVANIA TROLLEY MUSEUM

One Museum Road (I-79 to Meadowlands, exit 8)

Washington 15301

- ❏ Phone: (877) PA-TROLLEY **Web: www.pa-trolley.org**
- ❏ Hours: Daily 11:00am-5:00pm (Memorial Day-Labor Day), Weekends & Holidays (April, May, September, December).
- ❏ Admission: $6.00 adult, $5.00 senior(65+), $3.50 child(2-15).
- ❏ Miscellaneous: Museum store. In cooler weather, heated trolleys are running. Trolley theatre videos. Air conditioned museum.

Because the kids will be heavy with anticipation once they see the rail yard full of trolleys - plan on taking a ride right away! The trolleys are run on four miles of Pennsylvania rail and each ride takes approximately 30 minutes. Along the rail, you'll learn the history of the vehicle that you are riding on and why it's so special. As you complete your guided or self-guided tour, you'll get to meet CAR #832 - "The Streetcar Named Desire" used in the stage play by Tennessee Williams. Be sure to peek in the car shop where volunteers are restoring cars for future use.

WASHINGTON COUNTY MUSEUM

Washington - *49 East Maiden Street (Route 40 - downtown), 15301. Web: www.wchspa.org/html/house.htm   Phone: (724) 225-6740. Hours: Tuesday - Friday 11:00am-4:00pm, Saturday Noon-4:00pm (March-December). Admission: $2.00-$4.00.* The LeMoyne House was owned by a leader in unpopular activities such as anti-slavery and herbal health remedies, Dr. F. Julius LeMoyne. See the beds under which runaway slaves hid and the beehive in the herb garden on the roof.

GREENE COUNTY MUSEUM

Waynesburg - *PO Box 127 (I-79, exit 3 to SR21), 15370. Phone: (724) 627-3204.* **Web: www.greenepa.net/~museum** *Hours: Wednesday-Friday 10:00am-4:00pm, Saturday & Sunday Noon-4:00pm (May - August). Thursday - Sunday Noon - 4:00pm (September, October). Admission: $2.00-$4.00. Miscellaneous: The Historical Society also maintains the Young Foundry and Machine Shop - Century old, belt driven machine shop and foundry with 25 fully operational machines.* Colonial to Victorian... displays of local artifacts dating from the early native Monongahela culture to the early 20th Century. One of the rooms is devoted to an exhibit of early watches and clocks. The early watch and clockmaker was a talented craftsman, capable of very precise work. He was also the village jeweler. "Monongahela Culture" is the name for prehistoric Indians from the area. Look at the way they constructed their houses, the types of pottery they made and used, the stone materials they used for their tools, weapons, and cultivation of crops. Also on display are quilts, period clothing, early glassware & pottery, and an extraordinary birdhouse that stands over six feet tall and contains 104 rooms. A fun and informative worksheet is available for an interactive view of the exhibit. A fun project for families.

GEORGE WESTINGHOUSE MUSEUM

Castle Main - 325 Commerce Street (US30 to SR148 - Fifth Avenue - Left on Herman Avenue, Left on Commerce)

Wilmerding 15148

❑   Phone: (412) 823-0500 **Web: www.georgewestinghouse.com**
❑   Hours: Monday-Friday 10:00am-4:00pm, Saturday 11:00am-3:00pm. Closed holidays.
❑   Admission: Donation.

A tribute to George Westinghouse - the inventor and entrepreneur - plus key people who worked for his companies. The small museum is broken down into four rooms - The Family Room (personal & home belongings), the Inventions and Room of Achievement (highlights of 361 patents, the first radio broadcast in the country -

KDKA in Pittsburgh!, time capsules) and the Appliance Room. Highlights for kids are the Spencer switch display where two metals put together in a disc, react differently to temperature. As they heat, they jump away from the hot plate, and as they cool, they freely jump back. The principle was used for discs to regulate an iron's temperature. The kids are greeted by "Saranade" - the first electronic doll, in the Appliance Room, along with other "Every House Needs Westinghouse" inventions. These include washer, dryers, irons, waffle grills, radios, and home entertainment centers.

RYERSON STATION STATE PARK

Wind Ridge - *361 Bristoria Road (both sides of Bristoria Road, just off of PA Route 21), 15380. Phone: (724) 428-4254 or (888) PA-Parks.   Web: www.dcnr.state.pa.us/stateparks/parks/ryerson.htm* Pool, Visitor Center, Boat Rentals, Sledding, Campsites, Fishing, and Winter Sports. The trails invite you to explore the park on foot during spring, summer, fall and on cross-country skis in winter. The trails traverse many habitats, like forests, wet valley bottoms, evergreen plantations and fields. There are several opportunities to observe the beauty of Duke Lake.

Seasonal & Special Events

Christmastime in Pittsburgh with Great-Grandma

JANUARY

FESTIVAL OF ICE

CE – White Haven. Mountain Laurel Resort, PA534 (off I-80, Exit 41). (800) 458-5921. Join the crowd to watch champion ice carvers compete to create the most magnificent sculpture. Winter activities are offered and food and drinks are available. Admission is free for spectators. (mid-January weekend)

WINTERFEST

CE - Shawnee on Delaware. Shawnee Mountain Ski Area. (570) 421-7231. Fun activities open to all skiers, snowboarders, and tubers! Product sampling, give-aways, contests, prizes, equipment demonstrations, entertainment, ski party and more. Admission. (first Saturday in January & March & third Saturday in February)

ENDLESS MOUNTAINS WINTERFEST/
SLED DOG RACES

NE - Estella. Camp Brule. (570) 836-5431. Sled dog teams compete for cash prizes. Mid-distance and sprint races. Food, displays. Admission. (Last weekend in January or first weekend in February)

WINTER FUN DAYS

NW - Warren. County Park. (814) 726-1222. Ice skating, auction, snowmobile races, Horse-drawn trolley rides, snow sculptures, food, entertainment, door prizes, games. FREE. (Last two weeks in January)

PENNSYLVANIA FARM SHOW

SC – Harrisburg, Farm Show Complex. (717) 787-5373. The largest indoor agricultural event in America. The Farm Show Complex houses 16 acres under roof, spread throughout 7 buildings. America's Top Rodeo/Livestock Events. FREE. (second week of January)

CHINESE NEW YEAR CELEBRATION

SE – Philadelphia. University of Penn Museum of Archeology & Anthropology. (215) 898-4890. Children's workshops, storytelling, arts & crafts, martial arts demos, dance and grand finale – the Lion Dance. Museum Admission. (last Saturday in January)

FIRE & ICE FESTIVAL

SW – Somerset. Uptown. www.somersetborough.com. (814) 443-1748 or Ice sculptures, carving, food and winter events. (mid-January weekend)

BATTLE OF THE BULGE RE-ENACTMENT

SW – Waynesburg. Lebanon City. (724) 627-8545. World's largest WW II re-enactment with battle demos, equipment displays and many veteran reunions. (last Sunday in January)

FEBRUARY

GROUNDHOG DAY

CW - Punxsutawney. (800) 752-PHIL. Join thousands of Phil's faithful followers for his annual prediction. Fun for everyone. Hours vary. www.groundhog.org. (morning of February 2)

WINTER SLEIGH RALLY

NE - Forksville. Montanvale Farm. (570) 946-4160. Antique sleighs compete in various classes. Horse-drawn bobsled rides. Food. Weather permitting: snow is needed. Admission. (Sunday of Presidents Day Weekend in February)

WINTER FUN DAYS

NW – Jamestown. Pymatuning State Park. (724) 932-3142. Guided trail rides, chain saw carving, snowmobile games, sledding, skating and hayrides. (first weekend in February)

GREATER PHILADELPHIA SCOTTISH AND IRISH MUSIC FESTIVAL AND FAIR

SE - King of Prussia. Valley Forge Convention Center. (610) 825-7268. Scottish and Irish musical entertainment with Highland and step dancing, bands, singers, storytellers, exhibits, craft vendors

February (cont.)

Scottish and Irish foods and fraternal organizations. Admission. (mid-February weekend)

WINTERFEST

SW - Champion. Seven Springs Mountain Resort. (800) 452-2223. Includes ski races, craft show, children's activities, celebrity olympics, torchlight parade and other fun and games. No Admission. (first week in February)

MARCH / APRIL

MAPLE SUGARING

Actual tapping of trees. Syrup making. Demonstrations of coopering and sugaring off in a realistic sugar camp. Pancakes and syrup served.

- ❑ **C – State College** (Charter Oak). Shavers Creek Environmental Center, Stone Valley Rec Area. (814) 863-2000.
- ❑ **CE - Swiftwater**. Delaware State Forest, Messing Nature Center. (570) 895-9000. (March)
- ❑ **CW – Slippery Rock**. Jennings Environmental Education Center. (724) 794-6011. (Mid-March)
- ❑ **NE - Troy**. Endless Mountains. Mt. Pisgah State Park. (570) 297-2791. (Last weekend in April)
- ❑ **NW – Edinboro**. Hurry Hill Maple Syrup Farm. (814) 734-1350. Tours by appointment.
- ❑ **NW – Erie**. Asbury Woods Nature Center. (814) 835-5356 or **www.ashburywoods.org**. (end of March weekend)
- ❑ **NW – Spartansburg**. Firth Maple Products. (814) 654-7265 or **www.firthmapleproducts.com**.
- ❑ **SC – Harrisburg**. Fort Hunter Mansion & Park. (717) 599-5751. FREE. (early March)
- ❑ **SE – Downingtown**. Springton Manor Farm. (610) 942-2450.
- ❑ **SE – Media**. Tyler Arboretum. (610) 566-5431 or **www.tylerarboretum.org**. (mid-February)
- ❑ **SE – Philadelphia**. Andorra Natural Area in Fairmount Park. (215) 685-9285. (Late February – Early March)

❑   **SW – Meyersdale**. US 219 Meyers Ave. Historic Bldgs. (814) 634-0213 or **www.pamaplefestival.com**. War encampment, too. (second & third weekend in March)

ST. PATRICK'S DAY

❑   **NE – Scranton** (Moosic). Lackawanna County Stadium or Downtown Scranton. (800) 22-WELCOME.
❑   **NW – Meadville**. Downtown. (814) 333-1258.
❑   **SW – Pittsburgh**. Downtown. (412) 621-0600.

EASTER EGG HUNTS

❑   **NW - Erie**. Erie Zoo. (814) 864-4091.
❑   **SC - York**. (717) 840-7440.
❑   **SE – Philadelphia**. Elmwood Park Zoo. (610) 277-DUCK.

EASTER BUNNY TRAIN OR BOAT RIDES

Candy treats with the Easter Bunny riding along. Admission. (Easter Weekend)

❑   **CE - Jim Thorpe**. (570) 325-4606 or **www.railtours-inc.com**. Departures all day. Egg hunt at the end of ride.
❑   **NE - Honesdale** Train Station. Stourbridge Line. (570) 253-1960. 1 1/2 hours. Mr. Mouse, too! Entertainment.
❑   **NW – Titusville**. OC & T Railroad. Perry Street Station. (814) 676-1733. Departure 2:00pm. (Weekend before Easter)
❑   **SC - Middletown**. Race Street Station. (717) 944-4435. Live music. (Easter weekend and weekend before)
❑   **SC - York**. Stewartstown Railroad. (717) 993-2936. Admission. (Easter weekend and weekend before)
❑   **SE – Strasburg** Railroad. (717) 687-7522 or **www.strasburgrailroad.com**
❑   **SW – Pittsburgh**. Gateway Clipper. (412) 355-7980 or **www.gatewayclipper.com**. Easter crafts, DJ Dance Party.
❑   **SW – Washington**. PA Trolley Museum. (877) PA-TROLLEY.

March / April (cont.)

CHARTER DAY - MARCH

Commemorates the original charter given to William Penn for the land that is today the Commonwealth of Pennsylvania. FREE admission to all Pennsylvania State Museums.

- ❑ **NW – Erie**. Maritime Museum. (814) 452-BRIG.
- ❑ **NW - Titusville**. Drake Well Museum. (814) 827-2797. (Afternoon)
- ❑ **SE – Chadds Ford**. (610) 459-3342. Tours of historic homes and living history demos.
- ❑ **SE - Horsham**. Graeme Park. (215) 646-1595. (Afternoon)
- ❑ **SE – Lancaster**. Landis Valley Museum. (717) 569-0401.
- ❑ **SE – Strasburg**. Railroad Museum of PA. (717) 687-8628.

REVOLUTIONARY ROCKFORD

SE - Lancaster. Historic Rockford Plantation. (717) 392-7223. Gigantic Revolutionary War Encampment featuring over 1000 costumed re-enactors. Enjoy 18th century music and demonstrations at the historic home of Edward Hand, George Washington's Adjutant. Admission. (early April weekend)

MAY

MOTHER'S DAY SPECIALS

- ❑ **C – Rockhill Furnace**. Rockhill Trolley Museum. **www.rockhilltrolley.org**. Moms FREE with another paid fare.
- ❑ **CE - Jim Thorpe** River Adventures. (800) 424-RAFT.
- ❑ **CE - Pocono** Whitewater. (800) WHITEWATER
- ❑ **SC - Middletown**. Race St. Station. "Take Mother To Dinner Train". The M & H Railroad offers a two-hour dinner train ride in vintage coaches along the Swatara Creek. Narration and live music. Pre-paid reservations required. (717) 944-4435.
- ❑ **SW - Avella**. Meadowcroft Museum of Rural Life. (724) 587-3412. ½ off admission for Mom.

❑ **SW – Pittsburgh.** Gateway Clipper. (412) 355-7980. FREE Family Photo for Moms. Meal included in cruise price.

❑ **SW – Washington.** PA Trolley Museum. (724) 228-9256.

CIVIL WAR ENCAMPMENT

C - Boalsburg. Pennsylvania Military Museum Parade Grounds. (814) 466-6263. Northern and Southern military units encamped throughout the area. Daily living history demonstrations. Live fire artillery demonstrations. Day-long festivities in nearby Boalsburg. Did you know that this is the birthplace of Memorial Day? Parking fee only. (Memorial Day Weekend)

MIFFLINBURG BUGGY DAYS

C - Mifflinburg - SR45 - Downtown. (570) 966-1355. Explore the actual home, carriage house, and workshop of the Heiss Coach Works, the only operation rescued from almost 50 different buggy works in the area (early 1900's). It looks as it did before the Heiss family left. Working demonstrations and buggy rides. (Memorial Day Weekend)

GREEK FESTIVAL

CE – Stroudsburg, Holy Cross Greek Orthodox Church, 135 Stokes Ave. (570) 421-5734. Listen to the Greek music, watch the dancing exhibitions or enjoy the exhibits and church tours, but we challenge you to leave without buying some outstanding homemade Greek cuisine. FREE. (mid-May)

AMBRIDGE NATIONALITY DAYS

CW - Ambridge. Merchant Street from 4th to 8th Street. (724) 266-3040 or **www.nationalitydays.org**. A celebration of ethnic pride offering tasty foods from all over the world plus entertainment, crafts, and special children's attractions. (Mid-month, Thursday-Sunday in May)

UNIVERSAL SOLDIER AND PIONEER DAYS

CW - Hanover Township. Raccoon State Park. (724) 899-2200. A living history encampment presenting pioneer craft and musical entertainment. Demonstrations and drills by Revolutionary, Civil, World I and II, and modern military. FREE (third weekend of May)

May (cont.)

FISHING DERBY

CW – Sigel. Clear Creek State Park Beach. (814) 752-2368. Annual kids' fishing derby for ages 15 and under. FREE. (first weekend of May)

BLOSSBURG COAL FESTIVAL

NC - Blossburg. Island Park. **www.blossburg.org/coalfest/** or (717) 638-2527. Crafts, coal museum, carnival, car show, general store. Parade Saturday morning. No Admission. (Wednesday-Saturday, Mid-month- May)

HIGHLAND GAMES & SCOTTISH FESTIVAL

NW – Edinboro University. (814) 732-2745. Highland dance, pipe band competition, music, sheep-herding, medieval camp, kids games & crafts. (mid-May weekend)

APPLE BLOSSOM FESTIVAL

SC – Arendtsville, Adams County. South Mountain Fairgrounds. (717) 677-7444 or (717) 374-6274. Live entertainment, orchard tours, scenic train rides, delicious apple foods, plus! (first weekend of May)

MAY DAY FAIRIE FESTIVAL

SC - Glen Rock. Spoutwood Farm. **www.fairiefestival.net**. (717) 235-6610 or Fairie tale-telling, fairie market place. Come in costume or make fairy crafts, May pole dancing & music. (first weekend in May)

NATIONAL ROAD FESTIVAL

SC - 26 Municipalities. **www.washpatourism.org/nrfestival.html**. or (800) 925-7669. 90 miles of fun, food, entertainment, crafts, wagon train re-enactments, historic tourism. Family reunions on the road commissioned by Jefferson that opened travel to the West. (Mid-month in May)

NATIVE AMERICAN POW-WOW

SC - Wrightsville. Sam Lewis State Park. (717) 653-6915. Crafts, story-telling, dancing, songs, and food. No Admission. (second weekend of May)

MERCER MUSEUM FOLKFEST

SE - Doylestown. Mercer Museum. (215) 345-0210 or **www.buckscountyhistorical.org/folkfest/index.html**. Traditional artisans make the skills and trades of early America come to life during this nationally acclaimed festival. Entertainment, militia encampment, and full picnic fare. Admission. (Mothers Day weekend - May)

RHUBARB FESTIVAL

SE – Intercourse. (800) 732-3538. Kitchen Kettle Village. Annual festival that teaches us that rhubarb (a red-stalked vegetable) is no longer just for pies. You won't believe the colorful menus of rhubarb-inspired foods, baked goods and beverages, and the Rhubarb Jams made special at festival time. Kids can play games (even build mini-racecars – The Rhubarb Race Car Derby). Food and games. FREE. (third Friday/Saturday in May)

INTERNATIONAL CHILDREN'S FESTIVAL

SW - Pittsburgh. Allegheny Center, North Shore. (412) 321-5520. Indoor main stage performances by world class professional theater companies along with outdoor stages, strolling performers, workshops, and recreational, educational, and cultural activities. Admission. (second week of May)

ST. NICHOLAS GREEK ORTHODOX CATHEDRAL GREEK FOOD FESTIVAL

SW - Pittsburgh (Oakland). St. Nicholas Cathedral Community Center, 419 S. Dithridge St. (412) 682-3866. People from all over enjoy authentic Greek cuisine. (first full week of May)

MAY/JUNE

STRAWBERRY FESTIVALS

Sample strawberry treats like fresh strawberry shortcakes and strawberry ice cream or sundaes. From great beverages and tempting sweets to colorful side dishes and barbecued meats grilled with berry sauces. Entertainment, demonstrations, contests and prizes. Kids' activities.

- ☐ **SC - Loganville**. Brown's Orchards. (717) 428-2036. Amish hayrides. FREE. (first weekend of June)
- ☐ **SC - McConnellsburg**. McConnell Park. (717) 485-4064.
- ☐ **SE – Intercourse**. Kitchen Kettle. www.kitchenkettle.com
- ☐ **SE – Lahaska**. Peddlers Village (Rte. 202 & Rte. 263). (215) 794-4000 or **www.peddlersvillage.com**. (first weekend in May)
- ☐ **SW - Finleyville**. Trax Farms. (724) 835-3246. Watch them make strawberry jam. Pick your own. (second weekend of June)

JUNE / JULY / AUGUST / SEPTEMBER (SUMMER)

INDIAN POW WOWS

Native American singing and dancing. Arts and crafts. Native food storytelling and much more!

- ☐ **CE – Lehighton**. Lenape Tears Pow Wow. McCall's Farm, Rte. 443. (610) 681-3709 or (570) 929-3102. (last weekend in September & first weekend in October)
- ☐ **NC - Whitneyville**. Tioga County Fairgrounds. (570) 265-5040. Admission. (end of July)
- ☐ **NE - Forksville**. Sullivan County Fairgrounds. Rte. 154. Eastern Delaware Nations' Pow Wow. (570) 924-9082. (second weekend of June)
- ☐ **NE – Hawley**. Triple W Riding Stables. (570) 226-2620. Horseback Western riding and live country music too. (mid-June & early September)

For updates visit our website: www.kidslovepublications.com

- ❑   **NW – Erie**. Rte. 430 & Williams exit. (814) 459-8509.
  Woodland Indian Veterans Memorial Festival. (early June
  weekend)
- ❑   **SE - Media**. Ridley Creek State Park. (610) 566-1725. Native
  Americans of the Delaware Valley present a Pow Wow at
  Colonial Pennsylvania Plantation. Admission. (second weekend
  in September)

JUNE

FATHER'S DAY SPECIALS

- ❑   **C – Rockhill Furnace**. Rockhill Trolley Museum.
  www.rockhilltrolley.org. Dads FREE with another paid fare.
- ❑   **NE - Scranton**. Steamtown National Historic Site. (717) 340-
  5200. (3rd Sunday of June)
- ❑   **SE - Kutztown**. Train Station. (610) 683-9202. Noon - 2:00pm.
  Admission.
- ❑   **SW - Avella**. Meadowcroft Museum of Rural Life. (724) 587-
  3412. Dads ½ off.
- ❑   **SW – Washington**. PA Trolley Museum. (724) 228-9256.

RAYSTOWN REGATTA

C - Huntingdon - Seven Points Recreation Area. 16652. (800) 269-
4684 or   (888) RAYS-TOWN. **www.raystown.org**. Boat racing,
concerts, kids' activities, area Pow Wows, & fireworks. (June weekend)

THUNDER IN THE ALLEY MOTORCYCLE RALLY

C - Johnstown - (Johnstown and Cambria County Area). (814)
255-6515. Hill climbs, dirt drags, dual sport ride, Heritage ride,
parade, Kids Art Festival @ Community Arts Center. (last full
weekend in June).

CANAL FESTIVAL

CE - Easton. Hugh Moore Park. (610) 559-6613. Annual canal
festival featuring canal boat rides, 19th century living history
encampments and reenactments, Locktender's House tours,
continuous music and entertainment, food. Parking $5.00. (last
Sunday of June)

June (cont.)

PATCH TOWN DAYS

CE - Hazelton. Eckley Miners Village. (570) 636-2070. Family-oriented living history festival featuring street fair, coal mining and dance troups, wagon rides, huge craft show with period demos, children's activities, and ethnic food. Admission. (third weekend of June)

ORIGINAL PENNSYLVANIA DUTCH FOLK FESTIVAL

CE - Pennsburg. Schuylkill County Fairgrounds. (215) 679-9610. An annual celebration of the Pennsylvania Dutch lifestyle with demonstrating craftsmen, entertainment, food, nature center, antique farm museum and much more. Admission. (last Saturday, June and first Saturday, July)

FOREST FEST

NC - Bradford & Kane. Allegheny National Forest. (814) 362-4613. Fishing tournament, guided nature walks, interactive programs, fish hatchery tours, open houses, a festival that highlights the operation and beauty of the forest. FREE. (third weekend of June)

AMERICAN FOLKWAYS FESTIVAL

NW - Clintonville. I - 80, Exit 415. (814) 385-6040. Pioneer theme show set in rustic woods. Demonstrations, music, food. FREE. (Last weekend in June & August)

STREET ROD NATIONALS - EAST

SC – York. Expo Center. (717) 848-4000. Over 4500 pre-1949 street rods, games, live entertainment, food. Admission. (first full weekend in June).

STAHL'S POTTERY FESTIVAL

SC - Zionsville. Stahl's Pottery, 6826 Corning Road. (610) 965-5019. Tour historic, early 20th century wood-fired kiln and pottery site. Potting techniques demonstrated. Over 15 contemporary potters display and sell their wares. Light lunch available. FREE. (third Saturday of June)

CHERRY FAIR

SE - Schaefferstown. Alexander Schaeffer Farm Museum. (717) 949-2244. Celebrating Cherry Season with food, games, traditional period craftsmen, musical entertainment, cherry quilt raffle, and homemade cherry pies, fritters, and ice cream. FREE. (last Saturday of June)

JULY

JULY 4TH CELEBRATIONS

Parades, music, food, fireworks & contests.

- ❏ **C - Martinsburg**. Morrison's Cove Memorial Park. (814) 793-2176. Rides, too! (Weeklong)
- ❏ **CW - New Wilmington**. Westminster College. Lawn of Brittain Lake. (412) 946-7354. (July 3rd)
- ❏ **NC - Galeton**. (814)435-2321. Firemen's competition. (July 3rd and 4th)
- ❏ **NE – Milford**. **www.pikechamber.com**.
- ❏ **NW – Edinboro**. Lakeside Association. (814) 734-3184.
- ❏ **NW – Erie**. Mercyhurst College. (814) 824-2000.
- ❏ **NW - Sharon**. Three by the River. (412) 981-3123. Small Ships Revue (anything that floats) regatta. (July 3rd)
- ❏ **SC - York**. Fairgrounds. (800) 372-7374.
- ❏ **SE - Doylestown**. Fonthill Museum. (215) 348-9461. Pony rides, contests. Admission.
- ❏ **SE – Kutztown**. Fairgrounds & Railroad Station. (610) 683-1597 or **www.kutztownfestival.com**. Pennsylvania Dutch culture and food. Folk artists, children's activities, farmyard zoo. Meet Uncle Sam with patriotic sing-a-longs on the railroad . Admission. (week of July 4th)
- ❏ **SE – Lititz**. Spring Park. **www.lititzspringspark.org**. Oldest continuous community-wide celebration in the U.S., since 1818.
- ❏ **SE – Philadelphia**. Welcome America Festival. **www.americasbirthday.com**. Top name musical groups and dramatic readings by famous actors. FREE.
- ❏ **SW - Avella**. Meadowcroft Museum of Rural Life. (724) 587-3412. Historical patriotic activities. Admission.

July 4th Celebrations (cont.)

❑   **SW - Latrobe**. Downtown. (724) 537-8417.
❑   **SW – Pittsburgh**. Point State Park. (412) 255-8983.

REVOLUTIONARY WAR DAYS

C - Altoona. Fort Roberdeau Historic Site. (814) 946-0048. Experience danger on the 1778 frontier when British Rangers and Iroquois attack patriots and ruin bullet-making at General Roberdeau's lead mine fort. Admission. (second weekend in July)

CENTRAL PENNSYLVANIA FESTIVAL OF THE ARTS

C - State College - (Downtown & PSU Campus). (814) 237-3682 or **www.arts-festival.com**. The first day is usually Children and Youth Day featuring art creations of local kids ages 8-18. Art and mask parade with costumed characters, storytelling, marionettes, and concerts. (second Full Week of July, Monday - Friday)

BLUEBERRY FESTIVAL

CE - Bethlehem. Burnside Plantation, Schoenersville Road, (610) 882-0450. Enjoy blueberry delights galore on a 250 year old restored Moravian farm. Crafts, demonstrations, children's activities, and special tours are featured. Admission. (third weekend of July)

SCHUYLKILL COUNTY FAIR

CE – Pottsville Fairgrounds (PA 183 & PA 895). (570) 622-3742 or **www.schuylkillfair.com**. Normal fair food, livestock and entertainment plus county Ag Museum with large collection of old & antique farm equipment and household appliances. (late July, early August for one week)

INTERNATIONAL BASEBALL INVITATIONAL

CW - Freeport. (724) 353-9426 **www.fortheloveofthegame.org**. They come from around the world (15 to 19 year-olds, that is) to compete. Also, Pittsburgh Pirates Alumni participate in an "Old Timers" game mid-week. Fireworks. FREE. (late July weekend)

FIREWORKS CAPITAL OF AMERICA FIREWORKS FESTIVAL

CW – New Castle. Downtown area. (724) 654-8408. Children's activities, street dancing, musical entertainment, "Ducky Derby", Ice Cream Social, plus a Fireworks Spectacular. No Admission. (second Saturday of July)

BARK PEELER'S CONVENTION

NC - Galeton. Pennsylvania Lumber Museum. (814) 435-2652 or **www.lumbermuseum.org/bark.htm**. Annual woods festival. Events include crafts, music, saw milling, woodhick demonstrations. Contests: birling, fiddling, tobacco spitting, frog jumping. Admission (weekend after July 4th)

ARMED FORCES SHOW

NE–Scranton/Wilkes-Barre. Wilkes-Barre/Scranton International Airport. (877) 2-FLYAVP. Best Air Show in the East. World-class aerobatics. Top Gun fighter demonstrations. Parachuting, Vintage Warbirds and classics. Over 100 aircraft and exhibits on display. Admission. (second weekend of July)

AIR SHOW

NW - Erie. (814) 833-4258. (mid July weekend)

GREEK FESTIVAL

NW - Erie. Assumption Greek Orthodox Church, 4376 West Lake Road. (814) 838-8808. Greek food and pastries, Greek music and dancing. FREE parking and church tours. (weekend after July 4th)

PIONEER AND ARTS FESTIVAL

NW - Jamestown. Pymatuning State Park. (724) 932-3141. Displays, demonstrations, arts and crafts, Indian dancers, frontier activities, encampment, historical program, tour of the Gatehouse, food and live entertainment. No Admission. (last weekend in July)

BATTLE OF GETTYSBURG

SC – Gettysburg Battlefield. (717) 338-1525. Reenactments, events at Yingling Farm (site of film) include camps, gallant stands and charges. (long week of July 4th)

July (cont.)

CIVIL WAR ENCAMPMENT

SE - Berks County. Berks County Heritage Center. (610) 374-8839. The year is 1863, and Pennsylvania Federal Regiment try to enlist new recruits and demonstrate military life. Free. (second weekend in July)

SCOTTISH HERITAGE FESTIVAL

SE - Horsham. Graeme Park. (215) 343-0965. Explore the Scottish Heritage of the Keith and Graeme families through music, dance, exhibits, food and more. See Scottish games and crafts. Admission. (third Sunday of July)

VINTAGE GRAND PRIX

SW – Pittsburgh. Schenley Park(412) 471-7847. Racing and car shows. Run by volunteers with proceeds benefiting mentally retarded and autistic children and adults. (third weekend in July)

AUGUST

ALL-AMERICAN AMATEUR BASEBALL ASSOCIATION TOURNAMENT (AAABA)

C - Johnstown - Point Stadium. **www.johnstownpa.com/aaaba**. or (814) 536-7993. Major League Scouts are in attendance to watch sixteen teams of 18-20 year-olds compete for the championship. Also, visit the AAABA Hall of Fame featuring tournament legends who made it to the "big leagues". (first weekend in August)

AG PROGRESS DAYS

C - Rock Springs. Larson Ag Research Center - SR45, (814) 865-2081 or (800) PSU-1010 or **http://apd.cas.psu.edu**. Ag museum (open mid-April to Mid-October). One of the largest agricultural shows in the country features a petting zoo, live animal expos, games and food, and farming technology demos. Kids Climb a 25 foot tree, fishing center, corn maze and ImAGination Station with other fun things for kids. FREE (Tuesday – Thursday, mid-August)

MUSIK FEST

CE - Bethlehem. More than 650 FREE performances indoor and outdoors. All styles of music, children's activities, fireworks, international foods. (second weekend of August)

CIVIL WAR ENCAMPMENT

CE – Hazleton. Eckley Miners Village. (570) 636-2070. Living history event. Civil War re-enactors display authentic camp life, cavalry drill demonstrations, and cannon firings. Period music, wagon rides, house tours, town ballgame, and period church service. Admission. (third weekend in August)

POCONO STATE CRAFT FESTIVAL

CE – Shawnee on Delaware. Sun Mountain Recreation area, Hollow Road. (570) 476-4460. Craft demonstrations, musical entertainment and an interactive children's play area are among the activities held under tents at this lakeside center. Admission (12+). (late August)

FIREFIGHTERS COMPETITION

CE – Tannersville. Camelbeach at Camelback. (570) 629-1661. Local fire departments compete in the keg on a wire (two teams armed with firehoses use a spray of water to push the keg over the opponents' marker), bucket brigade (firefighters heave buckets of water onto a roof, and the runoff flows into a single bucket), decathlon (a multiple-skills event including hose connections, wood splitting, ladder climbing, bucket brigade and transporting a contestant on a backboard) and drafting contest (hooking up a hose and spraying a cone off a barrel). Fire-safety demonstration, fire apparatus exhibits and equipment vendors also are featured. FREE. (late August)

CROOK FARM COUNTY FAIR

NC – Bradford. (814) 362-6730. 1800s restored buildings including a farmhouse, one-room schoolhouse, blacksmith's shop, carpenter's shack, a barn and candle-making shop. Carnival, entertainment, tours, old-fashioned cooking and craft demonstrations. Admission. (mid-August weekend)

August (cont.)

CHERRY SPRINGS WOODSMAN SHOW

NC - Galeton. Cherry Springs State Park. (814) 435-2907. Lumberjack competition and horse pulling contest. Entertainment, displays, food. No Admission. (first weekend of August)

MT. JEWETT SWEDISH FESTIVAL

NC - Mt. Jewett. (814) 778-5441. A community-wide festival celebrating Swedish heritage. Highlights include a parade, fireworks, Swedish smorgasbord. Entertainment for all ages. (third weekend of August)

WAYNE COUNTY FAIR

NE – Honesdale. Rte. 191. (570) 253-3240. County Farm Museum. (first full week in August)

OIL FESTIVAL

NW - Titusville. Throughout town. (814) 897-2797. Heritage festival celebrating the history of oil. Festival includes sporting events, concerts, parades, children's events, historic tours, and a stagecoach robbery. FREE. (early August)

PERRY COUNTY FAIR

SC – Newport. Fairgrounds. (717) 567-2490. Old-fashioned, one of the largest fairs in SC PA. (one week, mid-August)

HANS HERR HERITAGE DAY

SE - Lancaster - US222 to 1849 Hans Herr Drive, 17584. (717) 464-4438 or **www.hansherr.org/heritageday.htm**. House Tours. (April - early December). Tour the oldest Mennonite meeting house in America. Site includes stone house, farm, orchard, and picnic areas plus a Visitor's Center. During this farm festival see demonstrations of 18th and 20th Century farm activity. Wagon rides, food. Admission (first Saturday in August)

PENNSYLVANIA RENAISSANCE FAIRE

SE - Manheim. Mount Hope Estate, 83 Mansion House Road. (717) 665-7021 or **www.parenfaire.com**. Hundreds of costumed merrymakers create a fantasy of bygone days and knights. Admission. (weekends, mid-August thru mid-October)

ANNIVERSARY OF THE BATTLE OF BUSHY RUN

SW - Harrison City. Bushy Run Battlefield. (412) 527-5584. Live re-enactment of the Battle of Bushy Run, 1763. Period British and Native American campsites, and a variety of other programs. Admission. (first weekend in August)

GREATER PITTSBURGH RENAISSANCE FESTIVAL

SW – Mt. Pleasant. Renaissance Festival village. (724) 872-1670 or **www.pgh-renfest.com**. l6th century European village atmosphere with combat jousting, crafts, theater, food, and Lords/Ladies. Eat with your hands! Admission. Free parking. (mid-August weekends thru mid-September weekends)

PITTSBURGH THREE RIVERS REGATTA

SW – Pittsburgh. Point State Park. (412) 338-8765. Downtown rivers and shores host the world's largest inland regatta. Air shows, powerboat races, hot air balloon races, fireworks and water-skiing demos. FREE. (first week in August)

PONY LEAGUE WORLD SERIES BASEBALL

SW – Washington. Lew Hays Pony Field. 15301. (800) 531-4114 or (724) 222-9315. **www.ponyworldseries.com**. The world's best 13 and 14 year-old Pony League players meet. (third week of August)

SEPTEMBER

WOODHICK WEEKEND

C - Penfield. Parker Dam State Park. (814) 765-0630. A hands-on competition in old logging events to see who is the best woodhick of the year. X-cut sawing, log rolling, shoe pitching, seed spitting, and more. FREE. (Sunday of Labor Day Weekend)

September (cont.)

CELTIC CLASSIC HIGHLAND GAMES & FESTIVAL

CE - Bethlehem. Historic Downtown Area. (610) 868-9599 or **www.celticfest.org**. Exciting and educational weekend celebrating the cultures of Ireland, Scotland, and Wales. Music, dance, bag piping, athletic competition, children's activities, and authentic vendors. FREE. (last weekend of September)

SCOTTISH & IRISH FESTIVAL

CE - Shawnee on Delaware. Shawnee Mountain Ski Area. (570) 421-7231. Non-stop Irish and Scottish music, Scottish and Irish dance exhibitions, bagpipe bands and Highland athletic demonstrations, Scottish & Irish vendors, food, Shawnee Mountain chair lift rides, and more! Admission. (Mid-September)

SHAWNEE ON DELAWARE RODEO

CE - Shawnee on Delaware. Shawnee Mountain Ski Area. (717) 421-7231. Hours: Noon - 5:00 pm. Bull riding, bareback, saddle, barrel, steer wrestling, clowns and entertainment. PRCA sanctioned. Admission. (last weekend in September)

KINZUA BRIDGE "FESTIVAL OF THE ARTS"

NC - Mt. Jewett. Kinzua Bridge State Park. (814) 887-3235. Features local arts & crafts, vendors, & food concessions. Native American village & crafts, live family-oriented entertainment, children's games, antique cars. No Admission. (third weekend of September)

LA FESTA ITALIANA

NE - Scranton. Courthouse Square. (570) 346-6384. Italian style festival features delicious ethnic food, crafts and live entertainment to suit young and old. Great fun for the whole family. FREE. (Labor Day weekend)

CIVIL WAR REMEMBERED

SC – Middletown. M&H Railroad. (717) 944-4435. **www.middletownboro.com/calendar/civilwar.asp**. Reenactment with skirmishes along the tracks and during the ride. Trains leave two times each day. Admission. (last weekend in September)

POLISH AMERICAN FESTIVAL

SE - Doylestown. National Shrine of Our Lady of Czestochowa. Ferry Road. **www.polishshrine.com.** Polish folk song dance ensembles, polka bands, entertainment shows, Polish and American foods, and amusements. Admission. (1st two weekends of September)

MUSHROOM FESTIVAL

SE - Kennett Square - US-1 (Downtown area). (800) 932-6963. **www.mushroomfest.com.** Parade, entertainment, cooking contest, tours of Mushroom Museum at Phillips Place with film, slides, and mushroom growing exhibits. Varieties of every mushroom for sale. (third weekend in September)

SCARECROW COMPETITION & DISPLAY

SE - Lahaska. Peddler's Village. (215) 794-4000, Unusual and delightful bird-chasing creations compete for over $1400 in prizes. Vote for your favorite traditional, contemporary, whirl-a-gig and amateur. Displayed throughout the village. Pumpkin painting, square dancing. Make one workshop. (Mid-September to Mid-October)

HIGHLAND GAMES

SW - Ligonier. Idlewild Park. **www.ligoniergames.org** or (412) 851-9900. Scottish Fair. Massed bagpipe bands on parade, Highland dancing, athletics, Scottish breed dog exhibit, genealogy services. children's games. Admission. (second weekend of September)

MT. PLEASANT GLASS & ETHNIC FESTIVAL

SW - Mt. Pleasant. Washington Street & Veterans Park. (724) 547-7738. Over 100 arts, crafts and ethnic food booths. Two stages of national and regional entertainment. Parade, contests, rides and glass blowing demonstrations. FREE. (last weekend of September)

September (cont.)

PITTSBURGH IRISH FESTIVAL

SW - Pittsburgh. Amphitheater, Station Square. (412) 422-5642. Entertainment, food, marketplace, cultural and educational children's activities, bingo, Irish dogs, customs. Admission. (second weekend of September)

COVERED BRIDGE FESTIVAL

SW - Washington. (800) 531-4114. Enjoy the rich heritage of Washington and Green Counties' 9 different covered bridges during this festival. Old time fiddlers, country style foods, petting zoo, wagon rides. No Admission. (third weekend of September)

SEPTEMBER / OCTOBER

FALL PLAYLANDS

Petting zoo, refreshments, pumpkin patch, corn maze, pony or wagon rides.

- ❑ **CE – Allentown**. Game Preserve. **www.gamepreserve.org**. Hay play area. Admission.
- ❑ **CE - Breinigsville**. Grim's Corny Maze. (610) 395-5655 or **www.grimsgreenhouse.com**. 4 acre maze. Straw maze and corn box. Free. (Weekends, last week of August - last week of October)
- ❑ **CE - Catawissa**. Pumpkin Fall Festival. Rohrbach's Farm Market. (570) 356-7654 or **www.rohrbackfarm.com**. Flashlight nights too. (Corn Maze begins Labor Day weekend. Pumpkin Patch weekends in October)
- ❑ **CW – Butler**. Schramm's Farm Market, 291 Crisswell Road. (724) 282-3714.
- ❑ **CW – Valencia**. Harvest Valley Farms, 125 Ida Lane (off Rte. 8). (724) 443-5869 or **www.harvestvalleyfarms.com**. Entertainment on weekends. (weekends, end of September thru October)
- ❑ **NE - Uniondale**. Fall Festival. Elk Mountain Ski Resort. (717) 679-4400. Scenic chair lift rides, entertainment. (second weekend in October)

- **NW - Cambridge Springs**. Pumpkinville. Finney's Farm. Rte. 99 South. (814) 398-4590. Pumpkin characters out in the field.
- **NW – McKean**. Thunder Valley Stables. Scarecrow contest. (814) 476-1632.
- **SC – Gettysburg**. The Maize, Rte. 30 & Rte. 94. (717) 624-9435 or **www.cornfieldmaze.com**. Ten acre labyrinth maze of corn.
- **SC - New Park**. Maize Quest. Maple Lawn Farm. (717) 382-4846. 10 acres of corn maze with fountains and bridges. Admission.
- **SE - Monocacy**. UFO Corn Maze. SR 724. (610) UFO MAZE. Enter the largest UFO ever spotted, explore Area 51, see crop circles. Then, can U Find Out? Admission. (Friday-Sunday and weekdays starting mid-October)
- **SE - Ronks**. Amazing Maize Maze. Cherry Crest Farm. (717) 687-6843 or **www.cherrycrestfarm.com**. Different design each year. (i.e. Noah's Ark). Also 4 smaller mazes and hay jump on property. Admission.
- **SW - Champion**. Autumnfest. Seven Spring Mountains Resort. (800) 452-2223. Scenic chair lift rides, Alpine slide, open-spit cooked foods. (last weekend in September, all October weekends)
- **SW - Clinton**. Hozak Farms. (724) 899-2400. Admission. (October weekends)
- **SW – Clinton**. Janoski's Farm, 1714 Rte. 30. (724) 899-3438. Pumpkinland. (October weekends)
- **SW – McMurray**. Simmons Farms, 170 Simmons Road. (724) 941-1490. (daily)
- **SW – Monongahela**. Triple B Farms, 823 Berry Lane. (724) 258-3557 or **www.triplebfarms.com**. Maize Quest.
- **SW – Ohio Township**. Reilly's Farm, 1120 Roosevelt Road. (412) 364-8662. Craft activities. (weekends in October)

September / October (cont.)

FALL HARVEST FESTIVALS

Tractor pulls, antique steam engines, parades, food (made with steam), threshing, baling, cider and apple butter making, hayrides, children's activities, petting zoo & fall crafts.

- ❑ **C - Centre Hall**. Nittany Antique Steam Engine Days. Penn's Cave Grounds. (814) 364-1664. Admission. (first week of September)
- ❑ **CE - Stroudsburg**. Harvest Festival. Quiet Valley Living Historical Farm. (570) 992-6161. Admission. (second weekend in October)
- ❑ **CW – New Wilmington**. Apple Castle (Rte. 18). (724) 652-3221. Bag your own apples, focus on apples. (second Saturday in October)
- ❑ **CW - Portersville**. Fall Fling. NW PA Steam Engine & Old Equipment Show Grounds. (724) 452-9545. Admission. (first weekend in October)
- ❑ **NE - Forksville**. Endless Mountains Flaming Foliage Show. Sullivan County Fairgrounds. (570) 247-7625. (first or second weekend in October)
- ❑ **NE - Hawley**. Harvest Hoedown. Keystone Street & Main. (570) 226-3191. FREE. (first Saturday in October)
- ❑ **SC - Harrisburg** - Fort Hunter Day. (717) 599-5751. (third Sunday in September)
- ❑ **SC - McConnellsburg**. Fall Folk Festival. Fulton County Fairgrounds. (717) 485-4064. Admission. (third weekend in October)
- ❑ **SC – Williams Grove**. Williams Grove Historical Steam Engine Association Show. (717) 766-4001. (week of Labor Day)
- ❑ **SE - Harleysville**. Apple Butter Frolic. Indian Creek Haven Farm. (215) 256-3020. Admission. (first Saturday in October)
- ❑ **SE - Lancaster**. Harvest Days. Landis Valley Museum. (717) 569-0401. Admission. (second weekend in October)

- **SE - Schaefferstown**. Harvest Fair. Alexander Schaeffer Farm Museum. (717) 949-2244. Admission. (2nd weekend in September)
- **SW - Avella**. Rural Heritage Days. Meadowcroft Museum of Rural Life. (724) 587-3412. Admission. (third weekend in October)
- **SW - Somerset**. Farmers Jubilee. New Centerville area. (814) 926-3142. Admission. (weekend after Labor Day)

OCTOBER

PUMPKIN FESTIVALS

Pumpkin painting and carving, pie-eating contests. Pumpkin patch (wagon rides out there). Refreshments.

- **CE – Forest Inn**. Country Junction (US 209). (610) 377-5050. Petting zoo. (October weekends)
- **CE – Kunkletown**. Old Homestead Tree Farm (US 209). (610) 381-2582. (October weekends)
- **CW - Volant**. Main Street. (724) 533-2252. (second Saturday)
- **NW - Conneaut Lake** Park. (800) 332-2338. (second weekend)
- **SE - Chadds Ford**. (610) 388-7376. (last weekend)
- **SE - Doylestown**. Fonthill Park. (215) 345-6644. Admission. (last weekend)
- **SE - Lancaster**. Landis Valley Museum. (717) 569-0401. (last weekend)
- **SE – Langhorne**. Cornell Pumpkin Festival. (215) 357-4005.

OCTOBERFESTS

German music, dance, foods & cultural exhibits. "Um-pah-pah" bands & cloggers.

- **CE – Pocono Lake**. The Edelweiss (PA 940). (570) 646-3938. (Labor Day weekend)
- **CE – Tannersville**. Camelback Ski Area. (570) 629-1661. Pumpkin painting and hayrides. FREE. (late October)

Octoberfests (cont.)

- ❑ **CW - Ambridge**. Old Economy Village. Erntefest. (724) 266-4500. Admission. (last Saturday in September or first Saturday in October)
- ❑ **CW – Enon Valley**. Rec Center (PA 108). (877) 767-5732.
- ❑ **NW – Erie**. St. Nick's Picnic Grove. (814) 891-7669 or **www.dank-erie.org**.
- ❑ **SC - Bedford**. Old Bedford Village. (800) 238-4347. Admission. (third weekend in September)
- ❑ **SE – Doylestown**. Township Central Park. (215) 348-9915 (first weekend in October)
- ❑ **SE – Lancaster**. Salunga Exit off Rte 283. (717) 898-8451. (late September/early October weekends)

RAILFEST

C – Altoona. (814) 946-0834 or (888) 4-Altoona or **www.railroadcity.com/railfest2003.htm**. Historic locomotives pull excursions and available for viewing. Admission. (first weekend in October)

APPLE HARVEST FESTIVAL

CE - Catawissa. Krum's Orchards. (570) 356-2339 or **www.krumorchards.com**. Hayrides, entertainment, apple cider, baked goods, farm tours, Apple Dumpling Special, caramel apples, scarecrow making, apple butter, barbecue, etc. (Saturdays in October)

COVERED BRIDGE AND ARTS FESTIVAL

CE - Elysburg & Forks. Knoebels Amusement & Twin Bridges Park. (570)784-8279 or **www.cmtpa.org/festival.html**. Crafters, demonstrations, entertainment, and food. For the children, face painting, clowns, and a selection of rides will be open in the park. End your day with a bus tour of several covered bridges including the nation's only twin covered bridges. FREE. (first weekend in October)

FALL FOLIAGE FESTIVAL

CE - Jim Thorpe. ASA Packer Park. (888) JIM - THORPE. Crafts, ethnic food, bands, and 3-hour train or whitewater excursions. Last Dam Release of season – rushing whitewater against background of peak fall colors. Tour the Old Jail and Home. (weekends in October)

SHAWNEE AUTUMN HOT AIR BALLOON FESTIVAL

CE - Shawnee on Delaware. Shawnee Inn & Golf Resort. (570) 421-1500. More than 25 hot air balloons aglow, daytime and night. Crafters, food, music, amusement rides, children's shows, animals, and pony/mule rides. Fall foliage in full bloom. Admission. (third weekend in October)

SHAWNEE LUMBERJACK FESTIVAL

CE - Shawnee on Delaware. Shawnee Mountain Ski Area. (570) 421-7231. As seen on Outdoor Life TV, Eastern Ironjack Competition. Birling, pole climbing, buck sawing, skunk races, pony rides, chair lift rides, chainsaw carving and more! Admission. (second weekend in October)

NATIONAL APPLE HARVEST FESTIVAL

SC - Arendtsville and Adams County. South Mountain Fairgrounds. (717) 677-9413. An Old time festival of apple products, live country music, hundreds of arts and crafters, antique autos and tractors, steam engines, orchard tours and food. Gettysburg Scenic Railway train ride thru apple countryside. Admission. (first and second weekend in October)

HERSHEYPARK IN THE DARK BALLOONFEST

SC - Hershey. (800) HERSHEY or **www.hersheypa.com**. See 50 colorful and unusually shaped hot air balloons at the annual Balloonfest. Includes several launches, balloon glows, rides, entertainment, crafts and food. Fall harvest foods, storytelling, Frightlights Laser Show, flashlight tours of nocturnal zoo animals & costumes everywhere. Parking fee. (last two weekends in October)

October (cont.)

OLD FASHIONED CIDER SQUEEZE

SC – Newport. Little Buffalo State Park. (717) 567-9255. Apple butter cooked in large copper kettles. At Shoaff's Mill, apples are ground and pressed. Corn is also ground and sold. Tasty foods. (third weekend in October)

1777 ENCAMPMENT RE-ENACTMENT

SE - Fort Washington.   (215) 646-1595.   Admission. (late October, early November)

HARVEST MOON TRAIN

SE – Kempton, WK&S Railroad. (610) 756-6469. Autumn moonlight train ride with musicians and light refreshments. Admission. (third weekend in October)

HAY CREEK APPLE FESTIVAL

SE - Morgantown. Historic Joanne Furnace.   (610) 286-0388. Homemade apple specialties. Scarecrows, pumpkin paintings, hay and pony rides. FREE. (second Saturday in October)

BATTLE OF GERMANTOWN RE-ENACTMENT

SE - Philadelphia - Germantown Avenue on Market Square, (215) 848-1777 or **www.cliveden.org.** This historic district is home to Cliveden (family homestead with original furnishings and bullet marks still visible) plus a museum with an overview of America's first German settlement. This land was the scene of a Revolutionary Battle of Germantown, the birthplace of writer Louisa May Alcott, and the site of the Underground Railroad. What some kids may feel are normally boring museums, become more interesting during a festival as history is relived. (first Saturday in October)

SNITZ FEST

SE – Lancaster (Willow Street).   Hans Herr House & Museum (717) 464-4438. Fall celebration of the harvest, especially the apple harvest. See cider being pressed, apple "schnitzing", taste historic apple varieties. Games for children. Admission. (first Saturday in October)

FORT LIGONIER DAYS

SW – Ligonier, Midtown. (724) 238-4200. Commemorates the key battle of the French and Indian War. (second weekend of October)

PUMPKIN PATCH TROLLEY

SW - Washington. PA Trolley Museum. (724) 228-9256. Ride orange-colored trolleys and the kids get to pick a pumpkin, too! (second or third weekend in October)

NOVEMBER

HERSHEYPARK CHRISTMAS CANDYLANE

SC - Hershey. Hersheypark. **www.hersheypa.com** or (717) 534-3090. More than 1,000,000 lights, unique shops, holiday entertainment, great food and rides. Look for Santa and his live reindeer! Admission for rides, park entrance free. Lodging packages. Breakfast with Santa. (mid-November - New Year's weekend)

ANNIVERSARY OF LINCOLN'S GETTYSBURG ADDRESS

SC - Gettysburg. Daytime, Gettysburg National Cemetery. (717) 334-1124. The annual observance of President Abraham Lincoln's famous address with brief memorial services and noted speakers. (one day in the third week, as announced, in November)

PEDDLER'S VILLAGE ANNUAL APPLE FESTIVAL

SE - Lahaska. Peddler's Village. (215) 794-4000. Live music, marionettes, pie-eating contests. Apples served up in fritters, pastries, butter, dipped in chocolate and caramel, or enjoyed plain. (first weekend in November)

WINTER WONDERLAND

SE – Lancaster. Dutch Wonderland. (866) Fun-At-DW or **www.dutchwonderland.com**. Selected rides and attractions open. Santa. Decorate cookies. Storytelling by the Princess of DW. FREE (rides & crafts, pay as you go). (late November-December)

November (cont.)

TAFFY PARTIES

SW - Avella. Meadowcroft Museum. (724) 587-3412. Taffy pulling party in log house, holiday programs in one-room schoolhouse. Make an ornament. (mid-November and early December weekend)

PITTSBURGH MODEL RAILROAD MUSEUM

SW - Gibsonia - 5507 Lakeside Drive (I-79N exit Wexford to Rte. 910east & Hardt Road). (724) 444-6944 **www.wpmrm.org**. Holiday Miniature railroad displays the transportation systems in Pittsburgh during the 1950's. Accent on coal, steel, and steam production in use. Admission. (Friday evenings & weekends, mid-November - early January)

LIGHT UP NIGHTS & PITTSBURGH SPARKLES

SW - Pittsburgh. Downtown area. (412) 566-4190 or **www.downtownpittsburgh.com**. Celebrate the holiday season in downtown Pittsburgh! Over 1,000 displays, performances, activities & events - many free! Boat rides (**www.gatewayclipper.com**). Wintergarden Santa Display & outdoor Ice Rink at PPG Center. Nativity Scene at US Steel. Includes Parade, fireworks and carriage rides. Go to the website for details! (third week November - first week of January)

NOVEMBER / DECEMBER

FESTIVAL OF LIGHTS

Glistening lights. Visit with Santa. Hot chocolate. Freshly baked cookies. Toy/gift shops. Weekend entertainment. Admission. (Evenings - late November through New Year's Day unless noted otherwise)

- ❑ **C - Altoona**. Lights on the Lake. Lakemont Park. I-99 Frankstown Rd. Exit. **www.lakemontparkfun.com** or (814) 949-7275. Model train display.
- ❑ **CE - Allentown**. Lights in the Parkway. (610) 437-7616.
- ❑ **CW – New Castle**. Cascade of Lights. **www.newcastlepa.org**.

- ❑ **NE – Scranton**. Montage Mountain. Road. Holiday Lights Spectacular. (570) 344-3990.
- ❑ **NW - Erie**. Zoolumination. Erie Zoo. (814) 864-4091. Walk-thru. (mid - to - late December only)
- ❑ **SC - York**. Christmas Magic. Rocky Ridge County Park. (717) 840-7440. Walk-thru.
- ❑ **SE - Bernville**. Koziar's Christmas Village. Off SR 183. (610) 488-1110. Top 10 PA Travel Attractions. Walk-thru.
- ❑ **SE – Philadelphia** (Norristown). Elmwood Park Zoo. (610) 277-BUCK or **www.elmwoodparkzoo.com**.
- ❑ **SW - Greensburg**. Overly's Country Christmas. Westmoreland Fairgrounds. (800) 9-Overly or **www.overlys.com**. Mini railroad display. Talking & dancing trees. Train ride. (mid-November thru early January)
- ❑ **SW - Indiana**. "It's A Wonderful Life". Blue Spruce Park. (724) 463-7505. Jimmy Stewart's home town. See "Blue the Spruce Ness Monster". Sleigh and pony rides. Drive-thru.
- ❑ **SW - Pittsburgh**. Winter Zoofari. (412) 365-2532. Walk-thru. Adults $2.00 off admission, children FREE. (begins mid-December)

TRAIN RIDES WITH SANTA

Sing songs and eat treats as you ride the train with Santa aboard. Admission. (Thanksgiving - December weekends)

- ❑ **C – Bellefonte** Historical Railroad. (810) 355-0311. Holiday excursions thru Victorian Christmas. (first weekend in December)
- ❑ **C – Rockhill Furnace**. Rockhill Trolley Museum. **www.rockhilltrolley.org**. Polar Express & Santa. (Thanksgiving weekend and first weekend in December)
- ❑ **CE - Jim Thorpe**. (570) 325-4371. Heated cars. Model train display and horse-drawn trolley ride, too. (first two weekends)
- ❑ **NE - Honesdale**. Stourbridge Line Rail. (800) 433-9008. Mrs. Claus and Rudolph, too! Stop at Winterfest in Hawley. (first two weekends in December)

Train Rides With Santa'– November/December (cont.)

- ❑ **NE - Scranton**. Steamtown National Historic Site. (888) 693-9391. Face painting, live music. Polar Express. (first & third weekends in December)
- ❑ **NW - Titusville**. OC & T Railroad. Perry Street Station. (814) 676-1733. (second weekend in December)
- ❑ **SC – Gettysburg** Scenic Railway. (717) 334-6932 or **www.gettysburgrail.com**.
- ❑ **SC - Middletown**. Race Street Station. (717)944-4435. Santa Express or The Polar Express. (Saturdays in December)
- ❑ **SC – York**. Stewartstown Railroad. (717) 993-2936.
- ❑ **SE – Kempton**. WK&S Railroad. (610) 756-6469. Frosty and elves too. (first weekend in December)
- ❑ **SE – New Hope** & Ivyland Railroad. (215) 862-2322 or **www.newhoperailroad.com**. North Pole Express.
- ❑ **SE – Strasburg** Railroad. (717) 687-7522 or **www.railroad.com**. (two weekends before Christmas)
- ❑ **SE - West Chester**. Brandywine Service Railroad. (610) 430-2233. (Thanksgiving - Christmas)
- ❑ **SW - Washington**. PA Trolley Museum. (724) 228-9256. Toy train lay-out.

DECEMBER

"THE NUTCRACKER" AND CHRISTMAS MUSICALS

- ❑ **C – State College**. Ballet Theatre of Central PA. (814) 234-4961.
- ❑ **CE – Avoca**. NE PA Philharmonic. Kirby Center & Scranton Cultural Center. Home for the Holidays. (570) 457-8301.
- ❑ **CW – New Castle**. Parou Ballet Company. (412) 652-1762.
- ❑ **NW – Erie**. Ballet Theater Company. Warner Theatre. (814) 871-4356 or **www.lakeerieballet.com**. (weekend before Christmas)
- ❑ **NW - Franklin**. A Christmas Carol and Handels Messiah. Barrow Theatre. (814) 437-3440.
- ❑ **SC - Chambersburg**. A Christmas Carol. Caledonia Theatre Company. Capitol Theatre. (717) 352-2164. (Month-long)

- ❑ **SC - Hershey**. Christmas in Chocolate Town. Dinner with chocolate desserts plus Holiday Musical Review. Hershey Lodge. (800) HERSHEY or **www.holidaysinhershey.com**.
- ❑ **SE - Lancaster**. American Music Theatre. (800) 648-4102.
- ❑ **SE – Lancaster**. Dutch Apple Theatre. Holly Jolly Holiday. (717) 898-1900 or **www.dutchapple.com**. (December, except Mondays)
- ❑ **SE - West Chester**. Brandywine Ballet Company. (610) 696-2711.
- ❑ **SE – Philadelphia** Orchestra. Handels Messiah & Winter Wonderland. **www.philorch.org**.
- ❑ **SE – Strasburg**. Sight & Sound Theatre. (717) 687-7800 or **www.bibleonstage.com**. (early November thru early January)
- ❑ **SW – Pittsburgh**. Pittsburgh Ballet Theatre, Benedum Center. The new Nutcracker. (412) 456-6666 or **www.pbf.org**. (evenings and some matinees in December)
- ❑ **SW - Pittsburgh**. Pittsburgh Pops and Mendelsohn Choir. Heinz Hall. (412) 392-4900.

CHRISTMAS OPEN HOUSES

Tours of decorated, historical buildings. Refreshments and musical entertainment. Admission.

- ❑ **C - Altoona**. Baker Mansion Museum. (814) 942-3916. Admission. (Thanksgiving weekend plus 1st two weekends in December)
- ❑ **C – Bellefonte**. Talleyrand Park. (814) 355-0311 or **www.bellefonte.org**. Gingerbread house contest, mini-trains, buggy rides & Victorian tea parties.
- ❑ **CE - Bethlehem**. (800) 360-8687. Admission. (Thanksgiving weekend thru weekend after New Year's)
- ❑ **CE - Hazelton**. Eckleys Miners Village. (570) 636-2070. Wagon rides, arts & crafts, and storytelling. (Thanksgiving weekend)
- ❑ **CE – Stroudsburg**. Quiet Valley Old Time Christmas Farm. (570) 992-6161. (first two weekends in October)
- ❑ **CW - Ambridge**. Old Economy Village. (724) 266-4500. Traditional craft activities. (1st weekend in December)

Christmas Open Houses – November/December (cont.)

- ❑ **CW - Butler**. Butler County Shaw House. (724) 283-8116.
- ❑ **CW - Clarion**. Sutton-Ditz House Museum. (814) 226-4450. (day after Thanksgiving)
- ❑ **CW – Harmony**. Museum Complex, Main & Mercer Sts. (888) 821-4822.
- ❑ **NE – Milford**. Grey Towers. (570) 296-9630. Home of Gifford Pinchot, the founder of USDA Forest Service.
- ❑ **SC - Bedford**. Old Bedford Village. (814) 623-1156. Reenactors. (first & second weekend in December)
- ❑ **SC - Gettysburg**. Downtown. (717) 334-6274. Admission. (first & second weekend in December)
- ❑ **SC - Harrisburg**. Fort Hunter Mansion. (717) 599-5751. Admission. (December 1st-23rd)
- ❑ **SE – Chadds Ford**. Brandywine River Museum (US 1 & SR 100). Model railroad, Victorian dollhouse and whimsical "critter" ornaments. (610) 388-2700. (Thanksgiving weekend thru weekend after New Years)
- ❑ **SE – Doylestown**. Fonthill Museum & Tile Works. (215) 348-9461. (first weekend in December)
- ❑ **SE – Elverson**. Hopewell Furnace Iron Plantation. (610) 582-8773. (first Saturday in December)
- ❑ **SE – Ephrata** Cloister. (717) 733-6600. (late December)
- ❑ **SE - Fort Washington/Fort Mifflin**. (610) 834-1550. (weekends in December)
- ❑ **SE – Hilltown**. Pearl S. Buck House. Green Hills Farm. (215) 249-0100. (Tuesday – Saturday)
- ❑ **SE – Lancaster**. Hans Herr House. (717) 469-4438.
- ❑ **SE - Lancaster**. Landis Valley Museum. (717) 569-0401. Lunch & dinner tours. (first & second Wednesday - Saturday in December)
- ❑ **SE - Lancaster**. Wheatland. (717) 382-8721. (first & last week in December)
- ❑ **SE - Morrisville**. Pennsbury Manor. (215) 946-0400. (second weekend in December)
- ❑ **SE - Kennett Square**. Longwood Gardens. (610) 398-1000. (Thanksgiving thru early January)

- ❏ **SE - Strasburg**. Railroad Museum of Pennsylvania. (717) 687-8628. (second Sunday in December)
- ❏ **SW - Brownsville**. Nemacolin Castle. Candlelight tours. (724) 785-6882. (Friday after Thanksgiving and December weekends)
- ❏ **SW – Finleyville**. Trax Farms. (412) 835-3246 or **www.traxfarms.com**. Lunch/breakfast with Santa. (weekends after Thanksgiving)
- ❏ **SW - Indiana**. Jimmy Stewart Museum. It's a Wonderful Life Festival. (800) 83-JIMMY. (Thanksgiving weekend thru December)
- ❏ **SW - Laughlintown**. Compass Inn Museum. (724) 238-4983 or **www.compassinn.com**. Admission. (1st Saturday in November thru 2nd Saturday in December - weekends only)
- ❏ **SW - Pittsburgh**. Cathedral of Learning Nationality Rooms. (412) 624-6000. Admission. (Month of December)
- ❏ **SW – Pittsburgh**. Hartwood Acres (north of downtown). (412) 767-9200. Estate tours. (mid-November thru December)
- ❏ **SW - Pittsburgh**. The Henry Clay Frick Estate. Pittsburgh (412) 371-0600. Reservations suggested. (3rd Thursday in November – early January, Tuesday – Sunday)
- ❏ **SW – Pittsburgh**. Phipps Conservatory. (412) 622-6914. Candlelight paths. (evenings mid-December thru December)
- ❏ **SW - Washington**. LeMoyne House. (412) 225-6740. (first & second weekend in December)

FESTIVAL OF TREES

Indoor display of 50+ artificial decorated trees. Gift shop. Snacks. Entertainment. Santa & Christmas/Winter characters. Arts & crafts.

- ❏ **C - State College**. Penn State Ag Arena. (800) 350-5084. (second week of December)
- ❏ **CW – Beaver Falls**. Beaver County, Brady's Run Park Lodge (Rte. 51). (724) 775-4510. Mini-railroad. Small admission.(Thanksgiving weekend and first weekend in December)
- ❏ **CW – Lucinda** (Rte. 66). (814) 226-7288.
- ❏ **NE - Scranton**. Electric City Trolley Station. (570) 963-6590. Admission. (mid-December through New Year's weekend)

DECEMBER

COCK 'N BULL RESTAURANT'S COLONIAL DINNER

SE - Lahaska. Peddler's Village. (215) 794-4000. Observe preparation of foods colonial-style over an open hearth. Enjoy a four-course meal from colonial era. Keepsake menu. Historical characters, live music. Perfect for families, schools and groups. Check out the Gingerbread House Display. (early December – Late March)

SANTAS CANDYLAND FEAST

SE – Philadelphia Zoo. (215) 243-5254 or **www.phillyzoo.org**. Food, arts & crafts, games, face painting, Santa & Mrs. Claus, sing-alongs, storytime and sweets. By reservation. (weekends in December before Christmas)

SANTA FAMILY FUN CRUISES

SW - Pittsburgh. Gateway Clipper Fleet. (412) 355-7980 or **www.gatewayclipper.com**. 2 hours of DJ Dance Party with costumed mascots, visit from Santa with treat, and make your own ornaments. Admission. (weekends in December)

NEW YEAR'S EVE - FIRST NIGHT

An alcohol-free, family-oriented celebration for New Year's Eve. Music, dance, theatre, comedy, poetry. Giant ice sculptures. Fireworks. Arts and crafts, storytellers and puppets. Admission.

- ❑ **C - State College.** Downtown and Penn State Campus. (800) 358-5466.
- ❑ **NW - Erie.** Downtown.
- ❑ **NW – Oil City.** (800) 483-6264.
- ❑ **SC - Harrisburg.** Downtown. (717) 255-3020.
- ❑ **SE – Newtown.** (215) 860-0819.
- ❑ **SW - Pittsburgh.** Downtown. (412) 392-4533.
- ❑ **SW – Pittsburgh.** Phipps Conservatory. (412) 622-6914. Garden circus from 6:00-9:00pm.

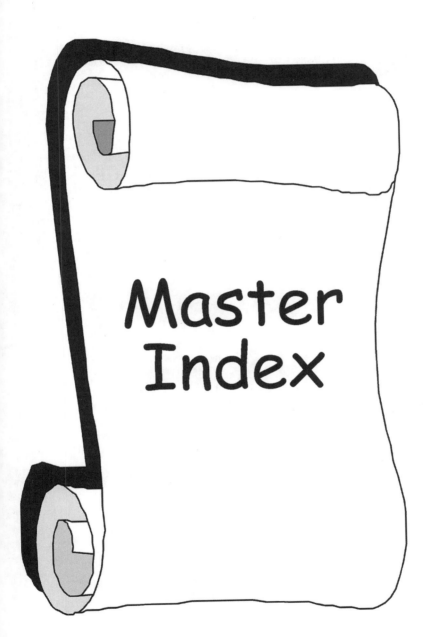

Master
Index

OUTDOORS *(cont.)*

PENNSYLVANIA HISTORY

GROUP DISCOUNTS &
FUNDRAISING OPPORTUNITIES!

We're excited to introduce our books to your group! These guides for parents, grandparents, teachers and visitors are great tools to help you discover hundreds of fun places to visit. Our titles are great resources for all the wonderful places to travel either locally or across the region.

We are two parents who have researched, written and published these books. We have spent thousands of hours collecting information and *personally traveled over 20,000 miles* visiting all of the most unique places listed in our guides. The books are kid-tested and the descriptions include great hints on what kids like best!

Please consider the following Group Purchase options: *For the latest information, visit our website:* **www.kidslovepublications.com**

❑ **Group Discount/Fundraising** – Purchase books at the discount price of $2.95 off the suggested retail price for members/friends. <u>Minimum order is ten books</u>. You may mix titles to reach the minimum order. Greater discounts (~35%) are available for fundraisers. <u>Minimum order is thirty books</u>. Call for details.

❑ **Available for Interview/Speaking** – The authors have a treasure bag full of souvenirs from favorite places. We'd love to share ideas on planning fun trips to take children while exploring your home state. The authors are available, by appointment, *(based on availability)* at (614) 792-6451. A modest honorarium or minimum group sale purchase will apply. Call or visit our website for details.

<u>**Call us soon at (614) 792-6451 to make arrangements**</u>!
Happy Exploring!

YOUR FAMILY MEMORIES!

Now that you've created memories with your family,

it's time to keepsake them by scrapbooking

in this unique, family-friendly way!

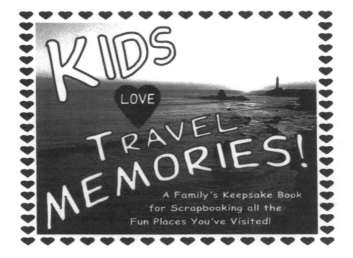

Check Out These Unique Features:

* **The Book That Shrinks As It Grows!** - Specially designed pages can be removed as you add pictures to your book. This keeps your unique travel journal from becoming too thick to use.

* **Write Your Own Book** - The travel journal is designed to get you started and help you remember those great family fun times!

* **Design Your Own Book** - Most illustrations and picture frames are designed to encourage kids to color them.

* **Unique Chapter Names** - help you <u>simply</u> categorize your family travel memories.

* **Acid Free Paper** - was used to print your book to keep your photos safe for a lifetime!

Writing Your Own Family Travel Book is This Easy...

Step 1 - Select, Cut and Paste Your Favorite Travel Photos

Step 2 - Color the Fun Theme Picture Frames

Step 3 - Write about Your Travel Stories in the Journal (We get you started...)

Step 4 - Specially Designed Pages are removed to reduce thickness as you add photos

Remove This Page
(to reduce binding thickness as you add personal photos)

The Perfect Companion to the Best-Selling "Kids Love" Travel Series!

Create Your Family Travel Book Today!

Visit your local retailer,

use the order form in the back of this book,

or our website: www.kidslovepublications.com

Attention Parents:

All titles are "Kid Tested". *The authors and kids personally visited all of the most unique places* and wrote the books with warmth and excitement from a parent's perspective. Find tried and true places that children will enjoy. No more boring trips! Listings provide: Names, addresses, telephone numbers, websites, admissions, directions, and descriptions. All books include a bonus chapter listing state-wide kid-friendly Seasonal & Special Events!

❑ **KIDS LOVE INDIANA** - Discover places where you can "co-star" in a cartoon or climb a giant sand dune. Over 500 listings in one book about Indiana travel. 8 geographical zones, 213 pages.

❑ **KIDS LOVE KENTUCKY** - Discover places from Boone to Burgoo, from Caves to Corvettes, and from Lincoln to the Lands of Horses. Over 500 listings in one book about Kentucky travel. 6 geographic zones. 224 pages.

❑ **KIDS LOVE MICHIGAN** - Discover places where you can "race" over giant sand dunes, climb aboard a lighthouse "ship", eat at the world's largest breakfast table, or watch yummy foods being made. Almost 600 listings in one book about Michigan travel. 8 geographical zones, 229 pages.

❑ **KIDS LOVE OHIO** - Discover places like hidden castles and whistle factories. Over 800 listings in one book about Ohio travel. 9 geographical zones, 260 pages.

❑ **KIDS LOVE PENNSYLVANIA** - Explore places where you can "discover" oil and coal, meet Ben Franklin, or watch your favorite toys and delicious, fresh snacks being made. Over 800 listings in one book about Pennsylvania travel. 9 geographical zones, 268 pages.

❑ **KIDS LOVE THE VIRGINIAS** – Discover where ponies swim and dolphins dance, dig into archaeology and living history, or be dazzled by record-breaking and natural bridges. Over 900 listings in one book about Virginia & West Virginia travel. 8 geographical zones, 262 pages.

❑ **KIDS LOVE TRAVEL MEMORIES!** – The Perfect Travel Journal & Scrapbook Companion. – See display page (or our website) to learn more about the features of this unique book.

ORDER FORM

KIDS LOVE PUBLICATIONS

1985 Dina Court
Powell, Ohio 43065
(614) 792-6451
Visit our website: **www.kidslovepublications.com**

#	Title		Price	Total
	Kids Love Indiana		$13.95	
	Kids Love Kentucky		$13.95	
	Kids Love Michigan		$13.95	
	Kids Love Ohio		$13.95	
	Kids Love Pennsylvania		$13.95	
	Kids Love the Virginias		$13.95	
	Kids Love Travel Memories!		$14.95	
COMBO PRICING* - *Indicate Titles Above*				
	Combo #2 - Any 2 Titles*		$23.95	
	Combo #3 - Any 3 Titles*		$33.95	
	Combo #4 - Any 4 Titles*		$42.95	

*Note: All combo pricing is for **different titles only**. For multiple copies (10+) of one title, please call or visit our website for volume pricing information.		**Subtotal**	
	(Ohio Residents Only)	5.75% Sales Tax	
	$2.00 first book $1.00 each additional	Shipping	
		TOTAL	

[] Master Card   [] Visa

Account Number _ _ _ _ - _ _ _ _ - _ _ _ _ - _ _ _ _
Exp Date: _ _ / _ _ (Month/Year)
Cardholder's Name _____
Signature *(required)* _____

(Please make check or money order payable to: KIDS LOVE PUBLICATIONS)

Name: _____
Address:_____
City:_____ State:_____
Zip:_____ Telephone:_____

All orders are shipped within 2 business days of receipt by US Mail. If you wish to have your books autographed, please include a legible note with the message you'd like written in your book. Your satisfaction is 100% guaranteed or simply return your order for a prompt refund. Thanks for your order. Happy Exploring!

"Where to go?, What to do?, and How much will it cost?", are all questions that they have heard throughout the years from friends and family. These questions became the inspiration that motivated them to research, write and publish the "Kids Love" travel series.

This adventure of writing and publishing family travel books has taken them on a journey of experiences that they never could have imagined. They have appeared as guests on hundreds of radio and television shows, had featured articles in statewide newspapers and magazines, spoken to thousands of people at schools and conventions, and write monthly columns in many publications talking about "family friendly" places to travel.

George Zavatsky and Michele (Darrall) Zavatsky were raised in the Midwest and have lived in many different cities. They currently reside in a suburb of Columbus, Ohio. They feel very blessed to be able to create their own career that allows them to research, write and publish a series of best-selling kids' travel books. Besides the wonderful adventure of marriage, they place great importance on being loving parents to Jenny & Daniel.